Vote

of Confidence

AASHTI BHARTIA is a story-teller who stumbled upon political writing. She was educated at Columbia University in History and Anthropology. Her thesis on chaotic deportations in post-9/11 America, *Reading Kafka in an Immigration Court: The Trial of Sulaiman Oladokun*, was published by the Duke University Press. She has previously written for the *Indian Express* and *Elle* magazine.

OTHER LOTUS TITLES

Ajit Bhattacharjea	*Sheikh Mohammad Abdullah: Tragic Hero of Kashmir*
Anil Dharker	*Icons: Men & Women Who Shaped Today's India*
Aitzaz Ahsan	*The Indus Saga: The Making of Pakistan*
Alam Srinivas & TR Vivek	*IPL: The Inside Story*
Amarinder Singh	*The Last Sunset: The Rise & Fall of the Lahore Durbar*
Amir Mir	*The True Face of Jehadis: Inside Pakistan's Terror Networks*
Ashok Mitra	*The Starkness of It*
CNN-IBN	*Real Heroes*
H.L.O. Garrett	*The Trial of Bahadur Shah Zafar*
Kiran Maitra	*Marxism in India: From Decline to Debacle*
L.S. Rathore	*The Regal Patriot: The Maharaja Ganga Singh of Bikaner*
M.B. Naqvi	*Pakistan at Knife's Edge*
M.J. Akbar	*Byline*
M.J. Akbar	*Blood Brothers: A Family Saga*
Maj. Gen. Ian Cardozo	*Param Vir: Our Heroes in Battle*
Maj. Gen. Ian Cardozo	*The Sinking of INS Khukri: What Happened in 1971*
Madhu Trehan	*Tehelka as Metaphor*
Nayantara Sahgal (ed.)	*Before Freedom: Nehru's Letters to His Sister*
Nilima Lambah	*A Life Across Three Continents*
Peter Church	*Added Value: The Life Stories of Indian Business Leaders*
Sharmishta Gooptu and Boria Majumdar (eds)	*Revisiting 1857: Myth, Memory, History*
Shashi Joshi	*The Last Durbar*
Shashi Tharoor & Shaharyar M. Khan	*Shadows Across the Playing Field*
Shrabani Basu	*Spy Princess: The Life of Noor Inayat Khan*
Shyam Bhatia	*Goodbye Shahzadi: A Political Biography*
Vir Sanghvi	*Men of Steel: Indian Business Leaders in Candid Conversations*

FORTHCOMING TITLES

Hussain Zaidi	*Dongri to Dubai: Six Decades of Mumbai Mafia*
Masood Hyder	*October Coup: A Memoir of the Struggle for Hyderabad*

of Confidence

PROFILES OF YOUNG POLITICIANS

Aashti Bhartia

Lotus
Roli

Photo Credits:

Ravi Batra: Pages 18, 34, 48, 62, 76, 90, 120, 134, 158, 170, 186, 198

The Hindu: Page 90

Getty Images: Page 144

Ashwinee Kumar Pati: Page 170

Janardhana Swamy: Page 104

Lotus Collection

First published in India in 2012

The Lotus Collection
An imprint of
Roli Books Pvt. Ltd
M-75, Greater Kailash II Market, New Delhi 110 048
Phone: ++91 (011) 40682000
Fax: ++91 (011) 2921 7185
E-mail: info@rolibooks.com
Website: www.rolibooks.com
Also at Bangalore, Chennai & Mumbai

Cover: Eisha Chopra
Layout: Sanjeev Mathpal
Production: Shaji Sahadevan

ISBN: 978-81-7436-879-9

Printed at Sanat Printers, Haryana

Contents

Introduction

I had written a long piece on Amar Singh in August 2009 and put it up on a blog. Amar Singh was very sick at that time. The General Elections had finished a few months earlier and the Samajwadi Party (SP) had fallen in Uttar Pradesh to twenty-three seats, from thirty-five in 2004. Amar Singh was brooding over the results. His hatred for Azam Khan and his fondness for Jaya Prada misguided him, he admitted. 'It became an ego fight.' Singh spent the election making sure Azam Khan, his own SP candidate, lost. He also lost sight of the larger election, Singh said in regret, and seven or eight other seats, which the Samajwadi Party could have won, suffered.

It was a rare admission for a politician to make. At the time, Singh's house looked empty but he hadn't been ousted from the SP as yet.

During the interview, Amar Singh said, the Congress had used him like a 'contraceptive' in the Nuclear Deal and flushed him out after a 'political ejaculation.' Later, in a reflective mood, he spoke of his feelings of inferiority while growing up and his relationship with his father. When Singh wanted to go to St. Xavier's College, his father mocked him. When he joined a political party, his father threw him out of the house.

Singh talked about how the idea of proving wrong his arch enemy – his father – drove him for years. He always needed a 'powerful enemy', 'a major crisis', and personal enmity to motivate him, Singh told me, voluntarily revealing his psychological underpinnings, his strongest driver and his greatest weakness.

Singh was so eager to talk that when his wife, Pankaja, interrupted to take him to the hospital, Singh told her to hold on; he wanted to finish the interview first. Later, she insisted and he told me to come with them. I sat beside him, my voice recorder still running in the car all the way to the hospital.

It was after reading this piece on Amar Singh, written after one interview, that Priya Kapoor, my publisher at Roli, called and asked me to write a book on younger politicians.

Profiles of Members of Parliament (MPs) under the age of forty – that was my broad brief. The 'Young MP' theme rang a bit clichéd at first. However, I was intrigued by the idea of poking around Ministries, figuring out what the young politicians are up to, and clearing the cobwebs of party politics. I realized also that despite all the glossy press on 'Young MPs', most people didn't know much about them. How did each of them go about elections, what were they doing in their ministries, what were they up to, in general, what did being an MP involve? I was curious to know.

The interview with Amar Singh had been easy and I foolishly assumed that all the profiles would be that simple. The thing about Singh is if you go to him for a story, he hands it to you on a platter – political scandal and dark psychological insight, all together.

The younger politicians are much harder to get talking. Many of the lesser known, first time MPs, were hesitant – they aren't used to telling stories about themselves and are uncertain what to reveal. The young two-term MPs, often second generation politicians, have been interviewed too many times and are weary of journalists. They drop rehearsed sound bytes.

Over time, as I met MPs, I learned how to steer conversations and get a sense of what interested them. I learned to pick arguments, to bring up touchy subjects again and again, to push them to speak their minds and to talk about things they cared about. As I met the MPs for the second time, traveled to their constituencies with them, dug around them, or talked to people close to them, each of their stories developed interesting contours.

There is no job description for an MP or a Minister; each of them go about their work as they choose. I came to realize how different each of their visions are, how different and particular their strengths and respective ways of thinking about their responsibility.

Even senior journalists I spoke to admitted not knowing much about the younger politicians. In articles, the second generation politicians in particular are often summed up in one sentence or spoken of sweepingly as if they're all the same.

However, each of them has specific strengths. I found Jyotiraditya Scindia a dedicated and capable manager, something India's Ministries desperately need. I came to find Sachin Pilot a thoughtful, level-headed speaker, clear and comfortable talking about caste politics and other prickly subjects. Pilot could, in future, make a good spokesperson and public face for the Congress.

Even if they have opinions on the better known faces, most journalist friends I spoke with didn't have much to say about the first time MPs, the ones without any family connections. No one knew of Meeanakshi Natarajan's amazing ground-level sloganeering in student politics. No one I met had heard of how Ghanshyam Anuragi became a local legend in central Uttar Pradesh, before he turned politician.

These are the young people India has elected to power. They will, in the years to come, be running the country.

Akhilesh Yadav's recent success in UP and the clamor for him to become Chief Minister proves that voters place a premium on youth – perhaps they're tired of the jaded faces they've been seeing, perhaps they feel young politicians, with their careers still ahead of them, would be more eager to prove themselves in office, or because they feel younger politicians would be more in tune with their needs. Whatever the reason, we're seeing a changing of guard.

To answer the question 'Why Young MPs?' in summary, I thought it would be good to know what each of their visions are, if any, their particular strength, their style, and their story. I thought it would be interesting to watch, in the years to come, how they execute that vision, how they build on those strengths, whether they lose track, and how they change when greater power comes to them.

***

In mid-2011, while I was writing this book, the Anna Hazare Anti-Corruption protests broke. Ironically, as the country's mood turned anti-politician, I found myself writing profiles of young politicians.

I am thankful to Anna Hazare, whatever the issues with the Lokpal Bill (Should the CBI be under it? Should the states?). The Bill is bringing government reform and systemic reform to the forefront of national debate. The first step had been the Right to Information Act, but after that, nothing. With scandal after scandal breaking, there was a profound sense of apathy building up in the country. But governance reform was not something we were in the habit of discussing.

The Anna Hazare movement, which started as anti-corruption, also took another swing and became broadly anti-politician. However, it's crazy to think that, all things remaining the same, if we were to do away with the current set of politicians, we would, from somewhere, get a better (incorruptible) set of leaders.

Most people are corruptible. Corruption is not just a political, or even a public sector problem. In the private sector too, in construction, in factories, at media houses, everywhere, corruption is rife; everybody's making a 'cut'. However, the scale of corruption in private companies is, perhaps, more controlled. Private companies need to report results and there are checks and consequences for corruption.

So it's not that corruption is only found amongst politicians; what's missing in political and public life is a sense of accountability, a feeling that there are consequences for corruption and ineffectiveness. As Ajay Kumar, the newly elected MP from Jamshedpur said about his work in the police in Bihar, 'you can't hope to raise people's morality, you can only monitor them' and make sure it's harder to do something wrong.

Politics is the only job I've seen so far where you're not answerable to anyone for five years. For a Member of Parliament from a constituency, voters decide and we can't have elections every year. But it's odd that even ministers (of Education, Health, Agriculture, Aviation, or Oil & Gas) who control a huge chunk of the country's resources, aren't hauled up on performance. Until a massive scandal erupts, or some major oversight is uncovered, everyone stays on.

Even the Lokpal Bill isn't enough, as Kumar mused, we need wider systemic reform. We need a set of performance indicators for each Ministry. We need Ministers to report regularly, publicly, on performance and important decisions. And we need the Prime Minister, or whoever's in charge, to change a Minister if his or her Ministry's performance falls.

Even for Members of Parliament, as Deepender Hooda suggested, we need to report better statistics – statistics on jobs created, school drop-out ratios, teacher absenteeism, agricultural productivity, infrastructure improvements (and more) for each constituency year on year. So voters can figure out: What did our MP do or not do? What areas did he or she focus on?

The Anna Hazare and anti-corruption movement also became anti-Congress.

On the Congress, I'll say, despite his defeats, I think Rahul Gandhi has had an interesting approach. He's focused on the Youth Congress, given opportunities to some very interesting people (Meenakshi Natarajan, Ashok Tanwar, Manick Tagore, and others). He's taken the onus of driving the Congress in UP. These are novel, fairly courageous steps – however they panned out.

What does stand out as odd about the Congress is that everyone else in the party stays so low-key, you're hard up to figure out who they really are and what they believe in. At the national level, in the Congress, it seems, a culture of projecting only the Gandhi family has seeped in.

Meenakshi Natarajan, who'd made a big stir in student politics, hasn't led any movements for the party. In 2011, she should have been on the streets, explaining the Congress stand on the Lokpal Bill, championing slogans. I wish Pilot, Scindia, Hooda, Tanwar, and others made more noise too. I wish they spoke out loudly on national issues, talked about what they're passionate about, argued their opinions.

The Congress doesn't project itself as a constellation of strong leaders – in the states or at the center.

If the 2012 state elections in UP and Punjab show one thing, they show that people want to elect local champions who can be held accountable, not far-away mega-stars. The Congress, it seems, needs to rethink its big-banner branding to project strong, local politicians in every state, each backed by the larger Congress brand.

More immediately, in the 2014 General Election, I think the Congress should move on from a soft, family brand and bring to the front its many capable faces. It should pitch Natarajan, Pilot, Scindia, Hooda, and Tanwar as a new committed, intelligent (not to mention youthful) team behind Rahul.

Perhaps, it should give each of them a mandate (education, health, or unemployment) and project a diversely informed team. Most importantly, it should give each of them the space to speak, to be known.

The Bharatiya Janata Party (BJP), a cacophony though it can be, at least gives the impression of having independent thinkers

– the BJP ally Nitish Kumar, the staunch Narendra Modi, the opinionated lawyer Arun Jaitley, the savvy Sushma Swaraj. They are always making themselves heard, constantly letting it be known who they are. Now, Anurag Thakur, Varun Gandhi, Janardhana Swamy – the younger BJP lot – are doing the same.

A culture of deference doesn't make for strong, credible leaders. Independent thinking, vocal, visible people do. Even if you disagree with them, at least you know what they stand for.

***

I chose some of the sixteen MPs profiled here because they're written about in the press all the time, but not much is known about them. I've written about some because they are young Ministers of State and I wanted to know about their work in the Ministries. I've written about others for the opposite reason – very little is known about their unusual journeys to Parliament.

The process was also somewhat random: I've written about whoever I read or heard something interesting about, whoever I managed to get an introduction to, whoever was able to give me enough time, or whoever picked up my phone calls when I called their number – which I'd gotten off the Lok Sabha website.

I ended up with nine MPs from the ruling party, the Congress, and seven from other parties: two from the Bhartiya Janata Party (BJP), two from the Biju Janata Dal (BJD), one from the Jharkhand Vikas Morcha (JVM), one from the Rashtriya Lok Dal (RLD), and one from the Samajwadi Party (SP). Three of the MPs I've written about fought from reserved (*dalit*) seats. I ended up including (unfortunately) only one woman. The piece on Akhilesh Yadav, who's now no longer an MP but Chief Minister of Uttar Pradesh, is a bonus addition to the collection. It chronicles his work in turning around a deflated party while he was still a relatively unknown MP.

I did interview some other MPs, including other young women MPs, but, in the end, couldn't include them here because they couldn't give me enough time, or because they didn't want to speak to me on certain subjects, which left the profiles incomplete.

Nine of the sixteen MPs I've written about are hereditary politicians; their fathers have been in important political positions. Patrick French wrote about the growing phenomena of family politics in India in his 2011 book, *India, A Portrait.* His chapter on hereditary politics made it to the cover of *Outlook* magazine. About fifty per cent of all Indian MPs under the age of fifty, French showed, are hereditary MPs and about sixty-six per cent of MPs younger than forty are hereditary MPs (or 'HMPs' as French calls them).

In my selection, too, fifty-six per cent are hereditary politicians, six of them from the Congress and another three from other parties. However, in writing about the hereditary politicians, I've tried to tell their story, discover what they're doing. I've written about their fathers' influences, but didn't judge them for who their fathers were.

I did also make sure I met MPs who didn't come from political families: I ran after Meenakshi Natarajan, the only non-hereditary MP among women MPs under forty in the Congress. I made sure I met Janardhana Swamy and Ashok Tanwar. I read about Ghanshyam Anuragi in a newspaper; he, luckily, picked up my phone the first time I called. Very last minute, I also decided to include Ajoy Kumar – though he's forty-nine and not as young as the others – because his story is so incredible.

Before I finish, I'd quickly like to thank everyone who helped me in this book: my publisher Priya Kapoor and editor Selina Sheth, for edging me on through the long haul. All the MPs who spoke with me, and gave me access to the people around them. The families and associates of the young MPs who agreed to meet with me. Arun Jaitley and Shobhana Bhartia for their support and for helping me get in touch with MPs I may not have met otherwise. Eisha Chopra for her meticulous design. I'd especially like to thank Vir Sanghvi for his encouragement and for sharing his own stories with me, Shekhar Gupta, and his buoyant edit team, for their time and advice, and Aditi Phadnis for her impromptu, thoroughly engrossing, lessons on political history, and finally, Tarun Tejpal for his attention.

In this past year, when democratic politics in India has gotten such a dressing down, I hope these stories present a glimmer of the possibilities Indian democracy offers – despite everything that's wrong with it.

The Man Who Became Chief Minister

The Samajwadi Party results in the 2012 UP assembly elections were a complete turnaround from 2009 when the party looked like it would slowly fade away. The 2012 results were not a windfall, however. They were the result of an incredibly well-honed campaign by a thirty-eight-year-old party president.

AKHILESH YADAV
Samajwadi Party
Born on 1 July 1973
27 years of age at first election
Formerly MP from Kannauj, Uttar Pradesh
Currently Chief Minister, Uttar Pradesh,
from 15 March 2012

There's a feeling of jubilation, and of suspense on Vikramaditya Marg in Lucknow, where the Samajwadi Party (SP) office and also Mulayam Singh Yadav's home are, a short distance from each other.

After a six month *yatra* through Uttar Pradesh, Mulayam Singh's son Akhilesh Yadav has, at the age of thirty-eight, become the youngest Chief Minister (CM) India has today.

Along Vikramaditya Marg, there are booths selling red SP flags and life-size cut-outs of Akhilesh. In the party office, there are endless clusters of people waiting to congratulate and to bring their problems to the new CM.

On television, there is already critical speculation about why Akhilesh has chosen his father's old associates as ministers; why a man with more than forty murder cases pending against him has been chosen as Prisons Minister. There are reports that SP workers are roughing up people; that the unemployment allowance the SP promised pre-election is now being shoddily implemented. One week in, the sweet celebration period hasn't yet ended, but an intense scrutiny of the new Chief Minister has begun.

However, this is not the story of what is to come. It's too early to tell how the Akhilesh Yadav government will pan out. This is the story of how the thirty-eight year-old became Chief Minister of the most populous and politically crucial state in India. After its sorry performance in the 2007 Uttar Pradesh (UP) state elections and the 2009 general elections, the Samajwadi Party seemed as if it would fall of the map. Everyone had written it off. The Hindi edition of *Tehelka* did a story after the 2009 elections, '*Ek thi Samajwadi Party* (once there was a Samajwadi Party).' But then, in the 2012 state assembly elections, the SP won 224 out of 403 seats, a neat majority. This is how they did it.

Akhilesh Yadav, Samajwadi Party's founder and national head Mulayam Singh's son, took out a six-month long '*Kranti Rath Yatra*' that travelled widely around UP. But, his was not the only *yatra* at large in the state. *Yatras*, a kind of crusade, a march or a tour, building up a specific issue or a set of issues before elections, have become common strategy in Indian politics. Every major party had a *yatra* out for the UP state elections.

L.K. Advani, that old *yatra* veteran, was on the road again with a '*Jan Chetna Yatra*'. His was pegged as an 'anti-corruption *yatra*', but it suffered from the overhang of Advani's earlier communal *Ram Janmabhoomi yatra* in 1990.

A sallow, 84-year-old Advani set out in a bus in October 2011 to talk about 'the ills that have weakened the nation.' From the day it started, his *yatra* was already a tired affair.

Rahul Gandhi, General Secretary of the Congress Party, had his own road show, a '*Jan Sampark Yatra*'. Over two months, he held rallies in 207 of the total 403 constituencies in Uttar Pradesh. Rahul Gandhi's popularity, his charisma, was expected to boost the Congress' fortunes in the assembly elections. The media followed hot on his trail. But Rahul sounded stilted and monotonous at his rallies. He trashed the Mayawati government and the Samajwadi manifesto – literally; in a strange mood, he tore up the SP manifesto with its list of promises and threw it off stage. But he didn't speak of a vision for UP, or make any promises of his own. The long-awaited Rahul show was lackluster in the end.

Jayant Chaudhury, Ajit Singh's son from the Rashtriya Lok Dal (RLD), had his own straggly *pad yatras* (walking *yatras*) in mid 2011. One set of the BJP also took out a '*Jan Swabhiman Yatra*'– with special events in Lucknow to woo Muslim voters.

However, it was Akhilesh's low-key *Kranti Rath Yatra* that was the most successful. It was also the longest, most persistent, of them all – it flagged off in early September 2011, covered about 250 constituencies, 9,000 miles and ten meetings a day over six months.

***

'*Dilli mein media ko lagta hai ki cheh mahiney mein UP mein koi chamatkar ho gaya* (in Delhi, the media thinks that there's been some magic in UP in the last six months),' Anand Bhadauria of the SP tells me in Lucknow. The Delhi media has made a brouhaha over Akhilesh's *yatra*, as if it were the only reason the SP won. 'But this was not a six-month miracle,' Bhadauria corrects, 'it's the result of five years of work.'

I am with Anand Bhadauria, National President of the *Lohia Vahini*, one of the Samajwadi youth organizations and Sunil

Yadav, or Sunil Sajan, National President of the Chhatra Sabha, the SP student wing, in the Chatra Sabha office in Lucknow a few days after Akhilesh has taken oath as CM.

Sunil and Anand are the two being written about everywhere in the media as 'core members' of 'Team Akhilesh.' They are both hardened student politicians: 'We always say that anyone who's been to Lucknow University and who has lived in the hostels there, he can't be made a fool of anywhere,' they tell me, offhandedly.

After the 2007 state elections, Mayawati had come to power with a clear majority in UP. She had, almost immediately, banned student unions in UP colleges and universities. She claimed it was to control rowdiness and let students focus on their studies. A few months later, in January 2008, the Samajwadi Party held major demonstrations against the ban on student unions and against proposed university fee hikes. The police had been sent out to charge at and push back the SP protestors.

On the first day of the protests, Sunil Yadav's head had been split. Sunil, then State President of the student wing, had been thrown into jail and denied hospital treatment. On hearing about the incident, Akhilesh, angry, without security, with just one other party member, went to sit in protest outside the office of the Lucknow superintendent of Police at about 12.30 a.m. They demanded Sunil be released and sent to hospital. 'Even a much smaller man wouldn't have dared to go without security at that time of the night,' Bhadauria muses, telling the story.

In the heat of the 2008 demonstrations, one SP student worker was killed and another set himself on fire in protest. Over two days, Akhilesh was arrested, put in prison and released three times.

The SP's agitation for reopening of students unions would continue for the next five years. In March 2012, as one of his first decisions as Chief Minister, Akhilesh finally overturned the decision. However, the 2008 protests have gone down in party history – they established Akhilesh Yadav's temerity as party leader, his willingness to lead from the front and to stand with his party workers through thunderous crackdowns.

Anand and Sunil share other stories of protests through the years and of umpteen cycle *yatras* in different districts.

In 2011, the SP had organized a peaceful procession against price rise and corruption in the ruling Bahujan Samaj Party (BSP) government. Akhilesh was arrested coming into the city from Delhi and taken to prison directly from Lucknow airport. During the protests, the District Inspector General (DIG) of Police threw Bhadauria to the ground and pinned his neck under his shoe – another moment that has become part of Samajwadi lore. Showing his spirit, Akhilesh refused to get out of jail till his comrades – Anand, Sunil, and others – were also released.

Akhilesh's *yatra* was meticulously planned and executed, but Sunil and Anand mull in the Chhatra Sabha office, it was just the last leg of a much longer overhaul in the Samajwadi Party. 'He was constantly doing things in UP, which wasn't visible to the media in Delhi,' they say, dismissing the faraway Delhi media who are rarely able to pick up trends on the ground till after the fact. 'Just because the media wasn't covering it doesn't mean nothing was happening.'

***

Faisal Fareed, the skinny, conspiratorial *Indian Express* Lucknow correspondent, drops in to meet Sunil and joins us. Faisal has been following the Samajwadi for years. He points at the SP's loss in Firozabad in a by-election in 2009 as the big turning point for the party.

In the 2007 state assembly elections, the SP had lost decisively to Mayawati. In the 2009 general election, the Samajwadi's total tally of seats again plummeted – to twenty-three Lok Sabha seats of the total eighty in Uttar Pradesh, thirteen less than they'd won in the last general elections. After that, four assembly constituencies came up for re-election; the SP lost each one.

In October 2009, Akhilesh's wife, Dimple Yadav, made her political debut and stood for the Firozabad by-election. (Akhilesh married Dimple, an army officer's daughter, after much opposition from his father. He was madly in love with her; he was twenty-five and she twenty-one. When she fought the Firozabad election, Dimple was thirty-two.) Dimple lost the Firozabad seat to, the Congress' actor-turned-politician, Raj Babbar. Firozabad was the seat Akhilesh had earlier won, and then given up for Kannauj. The family had never doubted that Dimple would win; Akhilesh had campaigned for Dimple throughout. Her defeat was gut-wrenching.

Rahul Gandhi had put all his weight behind the Firozabad election. The Congress had fielded a star candidate and Rahul himself had come to Firozabad to campaign for Raj Babbar. In Indian politics, where even opposition parties pay some obeisance to key candidates, it was seen as an act of effrontery. So in a press conference, the day after the election results, Akhilesh had said, in a moment of anger, 'It's me versus Rahul Gandhi now.' (It's a stand he's chosen never to take again, always speaking of Rahul Gandhi with equanimity in other interviews.)

After the Firozabad defeat, Akhilesh realized that the family name could not be taken for granted to deliver elections. It is, perhaps, an experience that every legacy politician should have.

Dimple Yadav's loss, Faisal mulls now over tea in the Chhatra Sabha office, finally hit home for Akhilesh that the Samajwadi Party was unraveling.

After the SP lost in 2007, Akhilesh had been involved in protests and agitations for the party. But after Dimple's defeat from Firozabad, Akhilesh took real control of the Samajwadi Party.

A few months down, in 2010, he was appointed State President of the SP. Mulayam Singh Yadav, a former district-level wrestler, had been heavily influenced in his early career by Socialist leaders Ram Manohar Lohia (after whom the SP youth organization Lohia Vahini is named) and Raj Narain. He had exited the Janata Dal (Socialist) and founded the Samajwadi Party in 1992. But, by 2009, Mulayam Singh too saw that the SP had lost its moorings. It was apparently the Communist Party (CPIM) politician Somnath Chatterjee who, having known Akhilesh, advised Mulayam to give him a free hand in the party. In the run up to the 2012 elections, he stepped back and made Akhilesh State President.

One of the first things Akhilesh did was to end Mulayam Singh Yadav's long-time confidante, the die-hard Amar Singh's tenure with the party (Amar Singh is said to have proposed Dimple Yadav fight from Firozabad because it would be an easy win for the SP).

With Amar Singh, went an entire brand of politics. Bollywood actors Jaya Prada, Jaya Bachchan, and Sanjay Dutt had flown down to campaign for Dimple's election. In the 2007 state elections too, Amitabh Bachchan had featured in the Samajwadi advertisement. The Bachchans had campaigned for the SP in 2009. There had been rumors that Bollywood megastar Aishwarya Rai Bachchan would next fight an election for the SP. The Samajwadi party had seemed to turn into a Disney-like parade.

After becoming State President, Akhilesh severed the Samajwadi from star-obsessed politics. Before the 2012 election, an SP member said, 'The party is strictly against Bollywood stars for campaigning.' In 2012, the Bachchans and Bollywood were nowhere on the campaign trail.

***

Akhilesh pulled the party's focus back to ground-level workers.

He dissolved many party office bearers (Party District Presidents, Block Presidents) who were wasting their seats. In these positions, and in the party's frontal organizations, he slowly installed new office bearers, people who were known to have worked diligently for the party.

In 2010 itself, Akhilesh began picking the right candidates for 2012: Which candidate would be best for each Vidhan Sabha seat? This selection was, perhaps, his biggest feat, and what he paid greatest attention to, in the run up to the 2012 assembly elections.

The process of picking election candidates is fuzzy in most parties – well-known people, some close associates, are handed out tickets in a somewhat random way, with limited knowledge. '*Us samay ticket batwara bahut accha nahin tha* (at that time, ticket distribution wasn't so great),' Bhadauria admits, looking back at the SP's distribution of tickets in 2007.

For the 2012 election, for the first time ever, aspiring candidates were made to apply through a formal college-like application process.

***

At the Samajwadi Party office on Vikramaditya Marg, I wait outside Akhilesh's personal secretary Gajendra Singh's office to see if I can manage some time with the Chief Minister.

Gajendra Singh isn't in office, but there are many others waiting. There are villagers from faraway places in weather-beaten *kurtas* waiting patiently. One man is waiting to speak to the Chief Minister about getting electricity in his village; another wizened old man wants a hospital in his area and to complain about the local *pradhan* who eats up development money.

A big, saddened man in a *kurta* and sneakers walks up and down. He had received a ticket this election, but, after a few months, his ticket was given to a candidate who defected from the BSP. He's waiting now to congratulate the new CM, he shares slowly.

Two restless Allahabad University students buzz here and there. They are trying manically to get through to Akhilesh's phone, or to his secretary's phone. '*Parishan ho rahe subhey sey* (we've been going crazy all day),' I hear one of them say.

One of them, Abhishek Yadav, in a blue *kurta* and jeans, tells me he applied for a ticket from Phulpur, Allahabad, this election.

Each applicant had to fill in a form and appear for an oral interview. Even old, veteran candidates, who were sure to get nominations, had to apply formally. The form asked, what have you done for the party? What movements have you organized? How many people have you recruited into party membership? Have you recruited at least fifty members?

Someone who has been waiting nearby, listening in to our conversation, adds that the application form also asked aspiring candidates about the caste ratios in their constituency – to gauge whether the aspiring candidate would stand a chance of winning if they weren't from the majority caste. Also, perhaps, to judge how well the to-be candidate knew their area.

There was an application fee of Rs 20,000, part of it for an annual subscription to the party magazine. (If candidates weren't able to pay or to collect donations for the application fees, Abhishek reasons with me, they'd have really no chance of being able to collect funds an election).

The last date for submission was 30 April 2010, two years before the actual election. More than 4,000 aspirants applied for the 403 Legislative Assembly seats, about 10 applicants average per seat.

Within just two months, by June 2010, each applicant was given an appointment at the party office in Lucknow for an oral interview. The interview panel consisted of Akhilesh, Shivpal Yadav (also Akhilesh's uncle), and party old-timers Rajen Choudhary, Bhagwati Singh, Omprakash Singh, and Ahmed Hassan.

Abhishek Yadav prepared at length for the interview. He made a power-point presentation that showed various newspaper clippings of the movements he'd organized – to lift the ban against student unions and against the privatization of education. When Rahul Gandhi came to speak at Allahabad

University in November 2011 Abhishek had led a protest against him (the Congress hadn't lifted the BSP ban on student unions even in central universities, of which Allahabad is one). Abhishek and his friend had waved a big black flag at Rahul's speech. Their pictures had splashed across UP media.

Even now, as we stand around, people come over and slap Abhishek on the back, '*Aap hai* Rahul Gandhi *ko kala jhanda dhikhaney wale*! (So you're the one who showed Rahul Gandhi a black flag!)'

Shivpal Chacha was very impressed with my presentation, Abhishek recollects.

However there was a hiccup. Abhishek turned 25, the minimum age to fight elections, on 26 January 2012. Elections were expected in January or February 2012, so announcing his nomination was too risky. For his age (and, perhaps for other reasons too) Abhishek wasn't given the ticket.

After the interviews in June 2010, deliberations on candidature for the 403 seats began. The SP's first list of 160 candidates – the expected, safe names, old winners, sons and daughters of SP politicians or important bureaucrats – was announced in April 2011, much before any other party. This way the SP candidates got a head start to build their names and begin work.

The SP's second, third, and fourth lists, which brought to a close the nomination of 300 candidates (of the total 403), were out by May 2011. The Congress, on the other hand, did not announce it's first list with just 73 candidates till as late as August 2011.

The SP nomination for Phulpur, Abhishek's home constituency, was announced in October 2011. Vijma Yadav, a four-time winner from the Samajwadi Party, got the election ticket. Later, in January 2012, a month before elections, the candidates of Phulpur and Pratappur were interchanged, Abhishek tells me. The candidate from Pratappur was Sayeed Ahamad, who had defected from the Bahujan Samaj Party. But Pratappur is majority Yadav voters, while Phulpur has a majority Muslim community. So, in the last instance, Ahamad, a Muslim, fought from Phulpur and Vijma Yadav fought from the Yadav-majority Pratappur.

'What in Mayawati's time, I suppose, they used to call "social engineering,"' Abhishek grins, narrating the story. Though there was an application process to make the party's decisions better informed, eventual nominations factored in every consideration – caste, community, old loyalties and obligations.

The Samajwadi Party won both seats from Phulpur and Pratappur.

Akhilesh and the party high command continued to keep a close watch on the candidates even after the tickets were given out. If candidates dilly-dallied in forming 'booth committees' – committees in charge of recruiting members to the party and encouraging people to vote – their nominations were summarily cancelled.

In November 2011, for instance, a whole host of candidates, from Rae Bareilly, Kanpur, Agra, Allahabad, were changed, and others were given warnings.

Sunil Yadav, the Chatra Sabha President, explains how they'd track a candidate's progress. Chatra Sabha members would scatter in different constituencies and anonymously ask people, at *chai* shops, in local restaurants or in the fields, what they thought of the local candidates. Who would win? What was the SP candidate like? They'd gather feedback on their own candidate's image – whether he was doing good work, whether he behaved well, whether he had a chance. Reports would funnel up to Akhilesh and Mulayam Singh Yadav.

Ground-level information, in the SP, tends not to get overlooked because reporting to Akhilesh and Mulayam Singh Yadav is easy and direct. Sunil tells me, '*Yaha toh ek Ward President bhi Neta koh phone karkey report dey sakta hai* (here, even a Ward-level President can call up a party leader and report what's going on).'

Till the end, Sunil Yadav and his merry band of students,

Anand Bhadauria and his youth volunteers, and all the arms and organizations within the party, watched each seat. When reports were consistently bad, candidates were changed.

For the Lambhua assembly seat, for instance, Abhishek marvels, candidates were changed nine times. The Samajwadi Party eventually won that seat too.

While surveying the constituencies, Sunil and the student and youth wings, would sniff for other information too. In many constituencies, twenty people had applied to fight the assembly elections, but the ticket had gone to one. They would find out if any of the other nineteen aspirants within the SP was sabotaging the election. If they found that someone was, they would make the disgruntled aspirant meet with Akhilesh or Mulayam Singh Yadav; they would understand his issues, manage his ego, soothe his nerves, and cajole him back into the fold of the party.

In every party, internal sabotage by competing aspirants can be the surest way to lose an election. It's one of the reasons why the Congress tends to delay its candidate announcements to the very last minute.

'But our party has a different way of working. We have a different way of listening to people, explaining things to them; we have a different way of helping them out,' Sunil Yadav tells me decisively.

***

A lot of pre-election energy went in configuring the right candidates in the right seat; however, Akhilesh also directly oversaw the advertisement campaign for the party.

Faisal Fareed, in his *Express* article on the revival of the SP, writes about Akhilesh's brief to the ad filmmaker and content writer – he wanted a positive campaign, no personal attacks. More importantly he asked the creative team to travel the state for a month, speak to people on the ground and gauge what they wanted.[1]

Aspirations, everyday, tangible ones, became the theme of the election campaign: the aspirations of farmers, *zari* workers in Varanasi and school teachers alike for electricity, young girls for education, of a rickshaw puller for a rickshaw of his own, of the young in cities for jobs and higher education. The campaign was intimate, grounded, yet hopeful.

Former journalist and Bollywood lyricist Neelesh Misra was creative director of the SP ad campaign. Misra describes the first meeting with Bollywood director Arjun Sablok and Akhilesh over a long, casual lunch at his home on Vikramaditya Marg. Before the meeting, Misra had penned the campaign tagline '*Ummeed ki Cycle*' ('the Cycle of Hope'). Akhilesh liked it instantly. The SP advertisements for 2012 (available on Youtube) turned out to be touching, thoughtfully made films, the leitmotif of a man on a cycle woven through them.

With the nominations decided, the ads out, the *Kranti Rath Yatra*, was the last leg of the campaign. Former Radio Jockey Naved Siddiqui travelled with Akhilesh in the '*rath*' – really an air-conditioned bus, with a lift going up to its roof.

They would start early in the morning, the excitable Siddiqui tells me, and attend ten to twelve meetings a day. Siddiqui would open for Akhilesh. He'd tell everyone there was so much corruption in UP, he'd had to leave his radio job and join politics. There would be laughs. He'd recite buoyant couplets for the crowd, '*Parivartan ki lehar chali hai, charo or Pradesh mein, bas asha ki kiran dikhayee deti hai Akhilesh mein*' (there's wave of change in the air, all over Uttar Pradesh, we see a ray of hope in Akhilesh).

Akhilesh would speak, and then it was the local candidate's turn. In his speeches, which Shoma Chaudhary of *Tehelka* describes as a 'calm even-toned drizzle, in the abusive maelstrom of Uttar Pradesh politics,' Akhilesh promised loan waivers to farmers, education to girls, unemployment allowances, hospitals, electricity and roads.[2] Most famously, he promised laptops to students. (Whereas in 2009, the SP had campaigned against the use of 'machines', by 2012 the party had finally changed its tune.)

Akhilesh kept the campaign positive. 'Rahul made a mistake tearing that sheet of promises on stage. What are elections but a promise, a chance at hope?' he told Shoma Chaudhury presciently on the campaign trail, 'It remains to be seen if parties will deliver what they promise, but if you tear up that hope then what else is there?'

Akhilesh had refused to hire a PR agency for his *yatra*, Misra tells me. However, the crowds at his meetings, wherever his bus stopped, eventually pulled the media.

In another leg of the campaign, Akhilesh took out a cycle *yatra* from Noida, through Agra, upto Jalesar, near Firozabad. Over three days, he covered 250 kilometers, cycling 80 kilometers per day. 'Many people joined along the way. Almost everyone in the village can afford a cycle. And the cycle is our party symbol,' Bhadauria tells me. Without any visible 'security men', he cycled jostled by hundreds of party workers.

***

As evening comes, it's clear to all of us waiting outside his office that Gajendra Singh isn't coming today. Near the SP office, I share tea and chips with Abhishek Yadav and his wiry friend from Allahabad University.

They want to talk to Akhilesh about making Allahabad a model town, they tell me. Now, apart from the national university and the high court, the city is a dustbowl. They have a long list of ideas to give the CM.

If Abhishek is upset he didn't get a nomination to fight assembly elections, he doesn't show it. '*Bhaiya ney mere liye kuch na kuch socha hoga* (I'm sure *Bhaiya* has thought of something for me),' he shrugs good-naturedly. Everyone in the party calls Akhilesh '*bhaiya*' or 'brother.' Sometimes, especially in colourful political slogans, they also refer to him as 'Tipu', his nickname at home.

This is perhaps the most important distinction between Akhilesh Yadav and Rahul Gandhi – everyone in the SP seems to be on personal terms with *Bhaiya*, to have his number and to meet him regularly. Abhishek, a student wing member, not even a party office bearer, gives me Akhilesh's two cell phone numbers for Akhilesh and Anand gives me his house number.

Akhilesh is accessible, like Mulayam Singh Yadav has always been. In contrast, Rahul Gandhi is a private man; they say, while he's on tour, no one but his closest associates have access to him in the evenings and in between meetings.[3]But people joke with Akhilesh, spend hours deliberating in the party office with him; on tour, they join the family for breakfast at times. Journalists based in Lucknow all seem to have direct access to him.

Abhishek remembers having breakfast with *Bhaiya* and Dimple *Bhabhi* when they were on tour together for Dimple's election. Faisal recalls an SP politician had turned hopping mad at him over a piece he'd written. Worried, Faisal messaged Akhilesh at 2 a.m; Akhilesh called the next morning, telling him to relax.

'*Samajwadi Party parivar ki tarah chalti hai, Congress aur BSP company ki tarah* (Samajwadi party operates like a family, the Congress and BSP like companies),' Anand Bhadauria tells me, in summary.

'*Woh kabhi angreziyat nahi dikhatey hai (*He doesn't show any '*angreziyat*'*)*,' Bhadauria says. '*Angreziyat*' is an interesting word – it connotes arrogance or a feeling of superiority over one's command of the English language. Not just privileged politicians, but many urban Indians who've studied at English medium schools and traveled abroad can be accused of '*angreziyat*'. Somehow, Akhilesh doesn't seem to show it.

Akhilesh has had a low-profile upbringing – something he hopes to repeat for his three young children (Aditi and twins Arjun and Tina), shielding them from media photographers. He studied at the Dholpur Military School, Rajasthan, then at a University in Mysore. In an interview with Srinivasan Jain of NDTV, Akhilesh's friends from Mysore speak about how he'd ride a bike in Mysore through his college years and how no one knew he was a politician's son till his final year. Akhilesh did go to Australia for a Masters in Environmental Engineering, but the experience seems not to have affected him. He seems just as comfortable, if not more comfortable, in Hindi as in

English. Often, when asked questions in English on channels, he deliberately replies in a relaxed Hindi.

Abhishek Yadav calls me with good news an hour after we leave the SP office; he finally managed to charge his phone and messaged *Bhaiya* that he was in Lucknow. The Chief Minister messaged back, 'Tomorrow at 10.30.'

***

Meanwhile, day by day news pours of unemployment forms lying in the garbage bins of UP government offices and of jubilant SP workers harassing people.

Journalists continue to question the young Chief Minister's decision to fill his Cabinet with his father's old friends – many of them with cases pending against them. To this, SP workers tell me, 'if you joined the Samajwadi Party while Mayawati was in power, you would have a couple of cases pending against you too.' Many of the cases are political cases, or false ones.

Still, there are real *goondas*, real criminals, too in the SP, and across the board in the BSP, the Congress, the BJP and other parties in Uttar Pradesh. But the SP seems to have more such members than any other party.

Akhilesh has, in a way, inherited a party of goons in a highly criminalized state. At one time, inexplicably, Mulayam Singh let the high-profile murderer Atiq Ahmed become an SP candidate. D.P. Yadav, a notorious gang-lord and country liquor operator, was also sheltered by the SP. While Akhilesh has refused both from the party, he hasn't rocked the boat entirely. Raja Bhaiya, a controversial man with a host of murder cases and a one-time terrorism charge, is a part of the Samajwadi government now.

However, Akhilesh has also wooed a new brand of candidates for the party – Abhishek Mishra, an ex-Indian Institute of Management (IIM), Ahmedabad professor joined the party and fought for election from a Lucknow seat. (Abhishek's father, Jaishanker Mishra, is also a high-level Uttar Pradesh cadre IAS (Indian Administrative Service) officer who has been close to Mulayam Singh Yadav over the years). Abhishek will have clout in the new SP government.

Many ministries are still being handed out. Akhilesh has kept about fifty ministries (Home, Finance, Secondary Education, Higher Education, Sugar Mills to name a few) directly under him. Sunil Yadav, the SP student wing President, has been told to hold meetings to tell excitable student members to behave themselves and to keep rowdiness in check. As we speak, the government's character is still being formed.

'Becoming Chief Minister was not part of the script. Even in private, he always said Netaji would be Chief Minister,' Neelesh Misra tells me when I ask him to comment on the new government. It was only after the results that it hit everyone that the election had been fought in Akhilesh's name, that there would be disappointment if people didn't see him as CM. 'He's had to make some political compromises, but he will slowly come into his own,' Misra mulls, 'He has no coterie; he's on the ground. That's the best thing about him.'

For everything that she may not have done, Mayawati was said to have been good at keeping law and order in the crime-ridden state.

No one can say what mark the Akhilesh Yadav government will leave. However, most of us, when we see someone young go through a tough time, and work very hard to get somewhere, want him to succeed. And in politics, especially, we want to be inspired; we want to see someone do right.

He may have run this election exceedingly well, however, Akhilesh Yadav, with all our hopes heaped upon him, has many more expectations yet to fulfill.

Notes

1 Faisal Fareed, 'How the Cycle turned Full Circle', *Indian Express*, 11 March 2012
2 Shoma Chaudhury, 'Two Men and a Vote', *Tehelka*, 3 March 2012
3 Veenu Sandhu, 'Prince Un-Charming? What did Rahul do Wrong in Uttar Pradesh and What Does he need to do now to stop the slide,' *Business Standard*, 24 March 2012

The Man Without A Smile

In a turban, surrounded by trumpets and flowers, on a stage in Ajmer, Sachin is serious and unsmiling. In his office, at the Ministry in Delhi too, he keeps a straight face.

SACHIN PILOT

Indian National Congress (INC)
Ajmer Constituency, Rajasthan
Born on 7 September 1977
26 years of age at first election
Last victory margin of 76,135 votes

It's 6.15 a.m., on a Saturday in April 2011. Sachin Pilot sits in the Arrivals lounge at Jaipur's Sanganer airport. The young politician is clean-shaven, fit and long-legged, well turned out in a white kurta, white linen pants and fine, brown moccasins. Two officials from the Postal Department and some Congress associates are here to receive Pilot. G.R. Thakana and Mr Purushottam – old associates of Sachin's father, the late Rajesh Pilot – join Sachin for tea in the lounge, both in kurtas so white and crip that they rustle like fresh A4 paper.

The three chat about the goings on in the state. The *Gadia Lohars*, a traditionally nomadic tribe of iron-welders, want land to settle down. The *Saperahs*, a community of snake charmers, want water and electricity connections. And Gulabo, a folk dancer, has been in all the local papers for raising demands on behalf of her community of folk artistes.

A convoy of station wagons and jeeps is waiting outside. The day's itinerary involves a Sain community event in Ajmer, a Jain community meet before lunch, the launch of a new computer and internet classroom in a local school and a function at another school just outside Sachin's constituency. Then, there's the long drive to Jaipur where Sachin will catch a flight back to Delhi.

Sachin was elected from Ajmer, Rajasthan in 2009. He fought and won from Dausa before that, his father's old constituency, where the senior Pilot's reputation still loomed large.

Rajesh Pilot rose in the political scene of the 1980s – when Indira Gandhi and later Rajiv Gandhi helmed the country. Pilot's story is incredible. A farmer, he first came to Delhi to work as a milk-man in his uncle's dairy (Pilot loved telling everyone how he would deliver milk to 10 Akbar Road, the house he'd later live in himself). But Rajesh Pilot was ambitious. He put himself through flying school and became a pilot in the Indian Air Force; he fought as a Squadron Leader in the India-Pakistan war of 1971.

Years later, in 1979, Pilot wangled an appointment with then Congress President Indira Gandhi and told her that he wanted to fight elections. On a whim, Mrs Gandhi gave Rajesh Pilot a ticket. Pilot quit the Air Force and contested elections, winning first from Bharatpur and then from Dausa. It was before the Bharatpur election that he heard buzz in the villages that 'a Pilot is coming' and, on an impulse, changed his name from Rajesh Yadav to Rajesh Pilot. Pilot also served, at various points, as Minister for Telecommunications, Internal Security and Environment. He was an energetic member of the Congress Party, at the centre of every happening.

Pilot planned to contest elections for the post of Congress President, but died in an accident just months before the election. In June 2000, he was driving his jeep, in a great hurry from his constituency to the airport in Jaipur when he collided with a truck on a sharp turn.

G.R. Thakana, Rajesh Pilot's erstwhile Additional Private Secretary and confidante, introduces himself unceremoniously, '*Main* Thakana *hoon* (I am Thakana).' Thakana was waiting with Pilot's flight tickets at the Jaipur airport on the day of the accident. Like Thakana, many of Rajesh Pilot's aides and staff now surround Sachin. They are full of stories about the older Pilot.

Thakana tells the tale of how Rajesh Pilot, as Internal Security Minister, got a complaint from Som Chai, a Thai national, against the powerful 'god-man' Chandraswamy. 'We said don't do anything against this man; he's connected to the PM.' Everybody knew Chandraswamy was close to then Prime Minister Narasimha Rao. '*Chahe mainu jail jana padey, khel khatamb hoga* (Even if I have to go to jail, this game will end),' Pilot declared heatedly. He was a man of 'strong convictions,' Thakana recollects, his eyes clouding over, 'he insisted on fighting Chandraswamy.' As a punishment for taking down Chandraswamy, it's widely believed that Narasimha Rao moved Pilot from the Ministry of Internal Security to the then powerless Ministry of Environment.

Later, Pilot fought Congress stalwart Sitaram Kesri for Congress Party President, but lost. Most famously, he announced he'd next fight Sonia Gandhi for the same post. Everyone around him was skeptical, but Pilot refused to back down, believing he had grassroots support and would be able to work fast to win over the party. Apart from his fighting spirit and charisma, Rajesh Pilot was also known for his strong empathy with farmers and rural India.

Purshottam, who was at the last meeting Pilot attended before his accident, speaks of Pilot's initiatives with pride. He argued for credit cards for farmers and built roads to facilitate rural commerce. At the height of conflict in Jammu and Kashmir, Pilot visited the state as Home Minister.

At one of Sachin's stops, the Jain community meeting, we meet another Congress man who knew Rajesh Pilot. Eyes wide, he describes Pilot's feats, his instant connect. He narrates how, when Pilot entered a village that had elected him, he'd announce with panache, '*Baiman log jo hai, hat jao.* Rajesh Pilot *aa gaya.* (All the cheaters, trouble-makers here, back off now. Rajesh Pilot is here!)' He would sit with people in any small village in his constituency and say, grandly, '*Bicholiye nahi aaney chahiyey.* (No middle-men should come between us!)'

The senior Pilot was 'the kind of man who wouldn't bend before anyone.' He'd drive his gypsy at 100-120 kilometres per hour, the Congress man recalls with awe and affection. He'd get stuck in a river, and he'd say, '*Marney sey dartey ho kya?* (Are you afraid of death, or what?)'

Comparing Sachin to his father, '*Unsey zyada suljha hua bolte hai,*' the Congress worker says, thoughtfully, '*bahut, bahut meetha.*' Sachin speaks 'more moderately' than his father, 'much more sweetly.' Sachin, he reasons, is part of the 'new generation.' Where his father hailed from a strong rural background, Thakana mulls, comparing the two, Sachin has had a very urban upbringing.

People remember Rajesh Pilot like something out of a Western, like a cowboy who walks into the wild country and blows out all the miscreants. Everyone holds him in awe. Sachin could not be more different. Sachin is quiet and private; he speaks in serious, measured tones, and avoids controversy.

***

We're now on the road back to the Sanganer airport in Jaipur in a single file convoy of six station wagons. The long day that started at 4 a.m. has ended, and we're driving fast, late to catch our 7.30 p.m. flight back to Delhi.

The police escort vehicle in front of Sachin's slows, suddenly, at a speed-breaker. Sachin's car, unable to break enough, crashes into the escort car. The car I'm in brakes at the last instance, then crashes into Sachin's station wagon. The car behind crashes into mine and so on, till the entire file of cars comes to a standstill in a misshapen line on the Jaipur highway. Each vehicle is bent out of shape on the front and the rear, the windows cracked.

Everybody gets out gingerly, dazed. Sachin walks along the line, checking if everyone's okay. A Congress Committee Block President has sprained his arm and sits on the road. Thankfully, no one's seriously hurt.

A jeep that's been following further behind pulls up and everyone on the flight back to Delhi piles into it.

As the jeep moves towards the airport, Sachin calls his wife Sara to tell her he's had a small accident and had to switch cars. Within seconds, his mother, Rama Pilot, calls Sachin's personal assistant demanding details. Sachin smiles and takes the phone, reassuring her. Car accidents aren't taken lightly in this family.

I first met Sachin at his office in the Ministry of Communications and Information Technology, but didn't get much. Sachin is shy, instinctively private.

He shared the bare facts: He attended the Air Force School in New Delhi, then went on to St. Stephen's College in Delhi University. He was in the middle of an MBA at Wharton in the United States when his father died. Sachin didn't talk about his personal life at all, his relationship with Sara, former Jammu and Kashmir Chief Minister Farooq Abdullah's daughter, or their 2004 marriage, despite heavy opposition from Sara's family. He promised her when they married he wouldn't involve her in his political life, Sachin said, closing the subject.

Driving back to the Jaipur airport, the last hour, after the accident, I get another chance to ask Sachin a few questions. His personal secretary and I are in the backseat; Sachin is in the front seat of the car, staring out of the window. It's here, surrounded by close associates, after a long day touring and narrowly avoiding a mishap, that Sachin opens up.

About Rajesh Pilot, he says, 'I don't mind being compared to him at all, it doesn't bother me. It's natural for people to draw comparisons. I get so much benefit from being his son…it makes me work harder.'

'He started from scratch and made his own space in public life,' Sachin says, recollecting his father's bravado. 'Out of nowhere, just like that, he walked into Indira Gandhi's house.' As the road whizzes past us in the darkening evening light, Sachin adds, 'My father lived his life without getting mud on his shoes, which is a lot in politics.' Rajesh Pilot was never tainted by the corruption scandals of the 1980s.

'He was always smiling. I don't think I ever saw him not smile,' Sachin recalls affectionately. 'And me, I hardly smile at all,' he says, grinning slightly out the window at this irony.

'I had a wonderful twenty-one years with my father,' Sachin says, a lump forming in his voice, 'and then, suddenly, he passed away.' From the backseat, I sense there's nothing more to ask, right then.

***

Earlier in the day, Sachin speaks at the Sain Samaj meeting. The event is to honor young Sain students who've graduated from high schools with distinction, or from nursing and other higher vocational courses.

There are *dhols* (trumpets) on one side, women with *thalis* (plates) full of petals, much fanfare before the meeting begins. There are rows of medals, flowers, and certificates waiting to be handed out.

The Block President from Pushkar, Ajmer district, introduces Sachin, '*Yeh ganney key ras mein miley meethay sharbat hai.* (He's the sweetness in sugarcane juice.) In the middle of thunder, when you see a *diya* (lamp) lit,' she says, effusively, 'ask that *diya,* and you'll know Sachin *saab* was there.'

Sachin sits on the stage looking straight ahead, unmoved. Around him are community and political leaders, on sofas, leaning over each other and chatting. The young MP comes on stage and delivers a short, serious speech about how proud he is to see young people from the community graduate, and about the importance of education.

The Sains, traditionally a community of barbers, are now part of the Other Backward Class (OBC) list and get OBC reservations in the civil service and in government colleges. One percent of the population in Ajmer is Sain.

In the car with me, as we drive away from the Sain meeting, Mr Seni and Mr Narain from the Postal Department explain that while many Sains continue to be barbers, others have joined the civil service or other professions.

As we zip across Ajmer to another meeting, Seni and Narain talk about how most communities in Rajasthan are now either classified Scheduled Caste & Scheduled Tribe (SC & ST) or Other Backward Castes (OBC). Only the traditional upper castes, Rajputs, Brahmins and Baniyas, are not included in the OBC list. Now, it's almost easier to get a government job if you apply in the regular category, Seni says, grinning.

While reservations in the civil service and in colleges for SC & ST have existed since Independence, the OBC category was created in 1990 by the Janata Dal Prime Minister V.P. Singh. Since then, Gujjars, Meenas, Yadavs, and Rawats have been included in the OBC list in Rajasthan – even the Jats (who are considered a well-to-do community and not classified OBC in states like Haryana) have been added to this mix, as also the Ravana Rajputs, a sub-set of the Rajput clan. The OBC list has become so crowded now, that in 2009, the Gujjar community vied to move from the OBC list to the SC list, which is slimmer and offers more benefits.

Mr Seni, from the Seni, or *mali* (gardener's) community, also belongs to the OBC category. His father was an illiterate farmer, Seni tells me, and his own sons are today qualified engineers. One of his sons applied in the Civil Engineering Service with an OBC certificate. But, he got job offers in other states, in West Bengal and Punjab. Perhaps, if he'd applied in the general category, he would've gotten Rajasthan, Seni ponders. His son decided to forego the offer and is now working at Dell, he says, sounding quite proud of the outcome.

Mr Narain, in a well-stitched safari suit and *jootis*, tells me he's a Rajput. His father was also illiterate, but Narain finished school and joined the Civil Service. Today, his son and daughter are enrolled in MBA programs in Jaipur.

'There are enough opportunities for well-educated, hard-working young people,' he ruminates, as we trundle down the road to Sachin's next meeting.

***

'I'm a Gujjar, you know that?' Sachin says, suddenly turning from the front seat of his jeep. We're driving away from his last meeting and the Pushkar Block President and her husband are also in the car.

In Ajmer, he estimates, breaking up his constituency, there are 1 to 2 lakh Jats, 1.5 lakh Muslims, 3.5 lakh SC, 1 lakh Rajputs, 1 lakh Baniyas, 1 Lakh Jain Samajis, and about 1.5 lakh Gujjars. So Pilot needs to win votes from other communities apart from his own to win. This election, for instance, the Jats didn't vote for him, bringing down his margin. They were upset because some Jat candidates hadn't won Congress nominations for the MLA elections, Sachin explains.

Sachin is more comfortable talking about the math of caste than most Congress MPs, who skirt the issue. 'In Delhi, all the Bengalis live together in one area, Muslims live together; it happens everywhere in different degrees,' he says. He talks about caste upfront as a political reality, a matter of fact.

Rajasthan, like many Indian states in recent years, has become minutely stratified by caste. People tend to vote as communities (of caste), in blocs. They tend to clamour for benefits as communities, by way of reservations. Every community wants some kind of special status from the state. Political parties play up these various demands to get votes.

In the 1990s, the Bharatiya Janata Party (BJP) government in Rajasthan included the upper caste Jats in the OBC category. In 2003, just before the next election, the BJP began to promise Gujjars, who were already OBC, other special reservations. In 2008, the Gujjars, aware of their power to turn election results in many districts in Rajasthan, began to actively agitate for SC status and special reservations. The demonstrations took place in Sachin's family constituency, Dausa.

State police and Gujjar mobs faced each other on the rail tracks; the demonstrations turned violent. The Rajasthan state government, under Chief Minister Vasundhara Raje, announced 5 per cent new 'special' reservations for Gujjars, Banjaras, and Rabaris. It also announced fourteen per cent reservations for the economically backward upper-castes – Baniyas, Rajputs, Kayasthas. That brought the total tally of reservations to sixty-eighth per cent in Rajasthan, above the constitutional limit of fifty per cent for any state. The Rajasthan High Court stayed Raje's reservations. Since then, the government in Rajasthan has changed from BJP to Congress. 'The Congress is dealing with it now,' Sachin says, wearily.

The demand for, and disbursal of, more and more benefits by more and more communities is an unending political circus. Castes and Scheduled Tribes were first given reservations in India's constitution for ten years. But as Bhanu Pratap Mehta of the Centre for Policy Research (CPR) points out in his recent essay on welfare schemes, reservations once started are rarely stopped. In a society with great inequality, communities, ironically, want to one-up other communities to make themselves feel briefly superior; they vie for special statuses rather than real transformation in governance or society.[1] The comic end will, perhaps, come when, as Seni and Narain from the Postal Department joke, with every community getting itself included in reservations, the reserved categories will really become more crowded and harder to get into than the general!

Over the years, many academics have raised questions about reservations. What sense do they make when the rich among the castes eat up the benefits? Shouldn't reservations be based on economic criteria, or given only to the poor in the reserved castes?

'Even if you wanted to give benefits to the poor, in India, what criteria do you use? (to identify who's poor)' Sachin responds. 'You can't use land as a criteria. Because of the land ceiling laws, no one, on paper, has that much land.' Land is usually distributed under various names. He adds, 'Also, because agricultural income is non-taxable, you can't measure income on the basis of taxes.' (Below Poverty Line [BPL] lists in India identify the extremely poor based on local surveys, but these lists tend to be inaccurate, cooked up, in most states.) Without reliable criteria, how does one go about identifying the poor?

'I feel, if someone of a family has in the past availed the opportunity (reservation), they shouldn't get it again,' Pilot says slowly, untangling the problem on our drive back. 'I'm just thinking aloud... but there's no system to record that either.'

***

Later, at the Jain community meeting, Jain monks sit on a podium in white robes; they have white hospital masks on their mouths so they don't kill flies or germs by mistake and a *jhadu* (broom) at their feet. Rich Jain merchants, some in kurtas, others in shirts and pants, sit in rows on a platform to one side. Others sit on carpets in between. The Jain monks on the stage press Sachin to make a temple against female foeticide in the area. Sachin assures them he's against the practice, but, getting slightly irritated, postpones any promise of the temple.

At the next stop, a high school in Kishangarh, Sachin inaugurates a computer and internet classroom. As Minister of State for Communications, his initiative in Ajmer means almost 250 schools in this region will be equipped with computer classrooms, a project that will cost Rs 25 crores. Software services giant Wipro has been contracted to provide the computers, annual maintenance, and teacher training, Sachin explains.

In Kishangarh, we walk through the first classroom, newly tiled and equipped with four PCs, a printer and scanner, and also an LCD screen for teaching.

On the open-air stage, in the school grounds, somebody ties a colourful turban on Sachin's head. He sits on centre stage with it, looking ahead intently. The school ground, with rows of red plastic chairs, is full.

Sachin stands up to the mike for his speech. 'I can give you these amenities through this scheme, but you'll have to demand that your children get to use these services,' he says, in his speech. 'Keep a watch on this.' His stage voice is tempered and soft and he speaks without any paper to refer to.

'Now, even getting good marks is not enough. You can get good marks, but when it comes to getting a job, you need to know how to use a computer,' Sachin presses on, his voice straining. 'The kids in cities have laptops in their homes. They know how to use computers. Their parents have the money. I have put these computers here, so that our kids from the villages don't get left behind.'

Later, in the car, he shares, 'For me, even if these kids just play with the keyboard and mouse, and fool around on the net, it'll be enough, because at least they'll know what a computer is.'

Of course, the program may suffer the perils of teacher neglect, of ill-use, of limited access. Pilot is optimistic about the program, but he isn't a micro-manager. 'Someone from the office will follow up,' he says, as our car hurtles down the expressway, 'If I kept thinking about everything that could go wrong or everything that people will do to pull this down, I wouldn't be able to do anything.'

***

Sachin's final stop for the day is a private school, just outside of Ajmer district in neighboring Nagaur. Nagaur is the constituency of Jyoti Mirdha, another young Congress MP whose grandfather, Ram Niwas Mirdha, was a local Jat politician.

Sachin has been invited to celebrate the first year anniversary of the Shri Shiv and Ram school. A banner behind the stage announces the school is 'Future Ready"'with a digital classroom. There's a big *shamiana* (tent) up in the school grounds and a vast stage with big box speakers on either side.

An overzealous, natty presenter in a black waistcoat and jeans strides up and down in front of the audience. The speakers burst out the Vengaboys' *Brazil* at some point.

As everyone settles down, the presenter fills every quiet moment with a string of filmi dialogues and silly couplets. 'Who knows when we'll come and when we'll go,' he says, in a fast style, 'that's why we must live and love. *Pyar lo, pyar do*,' he sing-songs, striding up and down. 'Even the biggest Chanakyas are no more. Your life will pass in a flash!'

I'm standing right at the back of the big shamiana. Old men, women, young people look on at the stage, bored.

'I now call upon Sachin Pilot to bless the audience with his *amrit varsha* (holy shower)' the presenter now yells flamboyantly. In the back, a young man chuckles, '*amrit varsha!*'

Sachin, who's been sitting on the stage with a meditative air, removed from all the drama around him, gets up to speak. His voice is low, his demeanour composed.

At some point, Sachin begins to describe what kind of person the people of Nagaur should elect. 'When you think about what kind of person you want to pick as your leader, choose the right person, the right party. Choose someone who knows what crops grow in the fields here, when the rains come in, when the seed is sown here, what prices prevail in the markets here, someone who knows what problems you face here,' he counsels, his voice rising ever so slightly. 'Choose someone who knows this area well, who knows you and your needs, not someone who talks about community and caste to win votes and divide you.'

I watch the otherwise restless crowd become attentive as he speaks.

'You should watch over your politicians – watch what they're doing,' he adds. 'Politicians can't take people for granted. They've been elected for a short period. It's their job to bring schemes, to do things.'

Without vulgarly touting the Congress Party and all its jargon of 'development' and 'progress', without even naming the Congress or selling himself, Sachin Pilot makes a simple, commonsensical speech.

The applause filters all the way to the back where I'm standing. Old men, sitting in the middle, who've been looking on wearily this whole while, clap. Even the young boys standing at the back stop snickering and look on for a few moments.

***

Later, I ask Sachin about his speeches. How come he speaks in Hindi, not in the local dialect like many politicians do?

'That's that whole thing of being earthy,' Sachin muses, his elbow on the window, looking at the road ahead. 'People can see through that. It doesn't come from the stomach.'

'Nobody talks like that anymore,' he adds. 'You'll only hear that kind of talk in political rallies now, but you won't hear people talking to each other like that.'

Most MPs, young and old, sound different in Delhi and in their constituencies. In Delhi, they talk like technocrats, but in the rural constituencies, their speeches are emotional, peppered with local flavour. Sachin, even in his constituency, doesn't affect an accent, doesn't throw in bursts of local dialect, or talk about all the people as his brothers and sisters. He doesn't make familiar jokes, or, for that matter, any jokes at all. He is, always, self-conscious of appearing patronizing. He gives the same speech in Ajmer or Nagaur that he would've given in Delhi.

It's this quality that stands out most about Sachin Pilot as I follow him through the day, his reserve, rather than coming across as aloofness, signifies a need to be authentic.

Sachin lost his father all of a sudden at twenty-one. He went on to fight and win his first election five years later, at twenty-six. With all the pressure to live up to Rajesh Pilot's lovable, boisterous image, it says a lot about Sachin that he chose not to be a caricature of his father.

The older Pilot loved playing to the gallery. Journalist Vir Sanghvi remembers how, in every interview, Pilot never failed to mention he'd started life as a milkman. When Sanghvi asked if Pilot had ever mixed water in his milk, the politician laughed and immediately said 'Yes!' Another time, when Sanghvi wrote an article about how bad phone services were, Pilot, who was Telecom Minister at the time, promptly rang up Sanghvi and put him on the Delhi Mahanagar Telephone Committee.

Sachin still maintains some of his father's traditions. He holds the morning 'Open House' that Rajesh Pilot started; people from Sachin's constituency can drop by his house every morning, have tea and rest, before meeting him. The young Pilot also hosts a 'farmer's lunch' of *sarson ka saag* and buttermilk every winter, another of Rajesh Pilot's traditions. But, Sachin won't play to the gallery, act up or pretend to be his father in any other way.

Though Pilot's persona doesn't lend him 'earthiness,' that much sought after quality among politicians, it does lend him credibility. Whether he's speaking in his constituency, or awkwardly answering questions in his office, prickly when you ask him about his personal life, or at ease among a small group in his car, he gives you the feeling he's 'speaking from his stomach'. In politics, where most leaders, national and local, are smug showmen and gloss-over artists, Sachin Pilot's seriousness, his self-conscious evenness, is reassuring. It is, perhaps, his biggest strength as a politician.

Notes

1 Bhanu Pratap Mehta, 'The Politics of Social Justice,' *India 2011* (New Delhi: Business Standard Books, 2011)

The Man From The Badlands

In Anuragi's village, people are killed for the silliest of reasons. Anuragi himself narrowly escaped a bullet, running away to the district town at eighteen.

GHANSHYAM ANURAGI
Samajwadi Party (SP)
Jalaun Constituency, Uttar Pradesh
Born on 12 December 1972
32 years of age at first election
Last victory margin of 7,600 votes

'You'll never hear another story like mine. No other MP could have come from the place, the background, I've come from,' Ghanshyam Anuragi tells me, before answering any of my questions.

I first read about Ghanshyam Anuragi, the Samajwadi Party Member of Parliament (MP) from Jalaun, Uttar Pradesh, in an *Indian Express* article on candidates from central UP. It says Anuragi had been charged in a 'double murder' case in

Hamirpur (although the case has now been dropped).[1] I went to meet Anuragi at his official house on North Avenue in Lutyens Delhi, feeling a little on edge.

'*Hamara gaon kuch dabang type ka gaon hai* (our village is a fearless, ruthless kind of place),' Anuragi says, when I ask him about the murder case. '*Murder kya hai, hamarey kshetra mein?* (in our area, what's a murder?)' he asks, '*Aksar kisi na kisi ka murder hota hai* (frequently, someone or the other gets killed).'

For all the talk of murder, Anuragi is short and soft-looking. He still seems amazed to find himself where he is, at his own house on North Avenue.

'*Zara zara si baton mein ladai jhagda ho jaata hai, hamarey gaon mein. Zara zara si baton mein, logon ki jaaney bhi gayee.* (Over the smallest of things, people get into a fight in our village. Over the smallest things, people have been killed).' Land issues, stolen crops, inexplicable pride, the smallest dispute can lead to murder.

The *Express* article which included Anuragi mentions other candidates from central UP, former mafia, and others with all kinds of cases pending against them.

A list labeled the 'Bad Boys of UP' includes candidates from the Samajwadi Party (SP), the Bahujan Samaj Party (BSP) and one from the Bhartiya Janata Party (BJP). An SP candidate from Hamirpur has nineteen criminal cases against him, including a five person shoot out in the local market (he was later acquitted). A BSP candidate, formerly with the SP, has a total three dozen cases against him, including, shockingly, an attempted attack on Chief Minister Mayawati at a guesthouse. There are cases involving extortion and looting.

The incumbent BJP candidate, Bhanu Pratap Verma, who fought opposite Ghanshyam Anuragi from Jalaun, also has six cases booked against him, including cases for the destruction of ballot papers and one for falsely framing the chief of district police for the murder of a young boy.

The constituencies of Uttar Pradesh, at the heart of the country, are the badlands of Indian politics, where outlaws assist political power, and the landscape is bleak. The Hindi movie *Omkara*, Vishal Bhardwaj's masterful adaptation of Othello, was based here. Omkara is the head of mafia for a local politician, a member of the state legislative assembly; Omkara helps his boss get elected to Parliament by trapping his opponent in an MMS sex scandal. When his boss becomes MP, Omkara replaces his boss in the state assembly elections. 'In the brutal heartland of Uttar Pradesh,' *Omkara's* publicity ran, 'lives a Shakespearean anti-hero called *Omkara*...'

Central UP is also part of Bundelkhand, an area comprising some of the poorest, most fallow parts of the country. (Most farmers have tiny landholdings [less than one hectare] and only fifty per cent of farmed land is irrigated; gun-holding mafia divert irrigation water to their own fields.[2] Because of the state of the law, industrialization in the area is low. After agriculture, *beedi*-making is the largest source of employment in Bundelkhand.)

In Bundelkhand, droughts last for years together; animals, even people, Anuragi says, regularly die of thirst.

From time to time, Bundelkhand raises demands for a new state, for separation from the rest of the country, arguing that its problems aren't being heard in Delhi.

Anuragi is from Kheda Sila Jit village in the Rath *tehsil* (block) of Hamirpur district. His parents were ordinary people, he tells me, from the Kori caste, traditionally weavers, now part of the Scheduled Caste (SC) list. His father farmed. His five brothers and sister now farm or run small shops in the village. 'They just about earn their daily living'.

Anuragi's brothers and sisters studied up to middle school. 'Our parents hadn't studied, but they always wanted us to study. My brothers made excuses not to go to school, that they have a headache or something or other, but I listened to them,' he narrates. Anuragi, the youngest child of seven, is the only one to have made it through high school and college.

When I push him, Anuragi begins to tell me how he got around to becoming an MP. At first, he's vague; unsure what to reveal; later, as he relaxes, he tells his story animatedly.

In Kheda Sila Jit, Ghanshyam's village, an upper caste boy raped a lower caste girl. It was a serious, but not an exceptional crime for the area. Everyone in the village knew that the crime had been committed and who had committed it.

The head of the *panchayat* (village council), Pandit Bharatkumar Mishra, called a meeting to decide a punishment on the rape case. A drum was beaten through the village, calling a *panchayat* meeting at 10 a.m. the next day. The council met and by noon, announced the punishment.

The *panchayat* decided the boy who'd committed the crime would have to do four things as punishment, he'd do *uthak-baithak* (sit up and down holding his ears) ten times; he would do *ganga snan* (bathe in the ganga) to cleanse himself; he would apologize to the girl's family; finally, they said, '*usko muh kala karke gaon ghumaya jaye*,' Anuragi finishes – he'd have to blacken his face with soot and parade around the village to show his guilt.

It was a comprehensive but, again, not an exceptional punishment. It established the boy's guilt, but didn't penalize him in any other way.

Before the meeting, the family whose son had committed the crime had said they'd abide by whatever decision the *panchayat* took. But, once the *panchayat* announced its decision, the family said their son wouldn't do any of the above; they refused to recognize the punishment.

The *panchayat* then decried that if the punishment was not respected, no lower caste person would go to any upper caste family's house to work – in protest.

The village came to a standstill.

After a few days, the Pradhan Pandit Bharatkumar Mishra, Anuragi narrates, called another meeting of the village council. At that meeting, the *panchayat* decided to ostracize the family of the boy who'd committed the crime. The *panchayat* deemed the family 'untouchable': no one would drink water from their well or eat at their house; anyone who entered their house would have to bathe as soon as they came out.

The case began in 1984 when Anuragi was a small boy, just twelve years old.

Anuragi stops now, reluctant to dig up his story, but I beg him to continue. He was walking to the railway tracks one day, when he saw someone shoot at the Pradhan. He ran to the police station shouting, 'Pandit Bharatkumar Mishra *ko goli lagi* (Pandit Bharatkumar Mishra has been shot).' 'Police *bhagat aayi* (the police came running),' Anuragi remembers, lapsing into UP dialect.

The men who'd tried to shoot the Pradhan scattered; Pandit Bharatkumar Mishra was saved. The family who'd sent shooters to kill him pulled Ghanshyam in for questioning. They roughed him up, asking why he'd interfered and why he'd called the police. Anuragi said he had had no idea what was happening and managed to get off.

Soon after, Basir Mussalman, a close associate of the Gram Pradhan who'd lived with him, was killed. Later, over the course of two years, two other people, Ramprasad Ahlwan, an untouchable, and Gulab, a Rajput, were shot at and killed. Both were associates, supporters, of the Gram Pradhan. 'Finally, they killed Pandit Bharatkumar Mishra,' Ghyanshyam says. '*Main maukey pey tha*' He happened to be around at the time of the shooting, bathing outside, and witnessed the murder. 'About eighty people were present in the area. Many shots were fired. In the end, they dragged the body away.'

There were close to a hundred people standing around when Pandit Bharatkumar Mishra was shot, but no one was willing to testify in the murder case. No one wanted to challenge the family that had shot him.

Anuragi, about fifteen years old by then, went home and mentioned to his father that he had witnessed the murder. His father said that in that case, Anuragi should testify. 'So I testified,' Anuragi recalls nonchalantly. They were lower caste and the Sarpanch had been trying to deal justly with a crime against a lower caste family, so his father felt they must support the case.

The four murders happened separately, over a few years. Anuragi was present when two of the victims – Basir Mussalman and Pandit Bharatkumar Mishra – were shot, so he became the only witness for both the murders. However, no one was willing to testify in the other two murders; the family had turned all witnesses hostile. Anuragi decided to testify for the other two cases as well.

'Such *dabang* people had killed them,' Anuragi tells me, mulling over the case now, 'and no one was willing to testify in their trials. So I became a witness for all these murders.'

'Why were all these people killed?' I ask Anuragi, at some point, re-tracking, trying to make sense of the killings.

'I don't know why, in my area, people are killed for the smallest things,' Anuragi ponders slowly; he has no explanation for the murders, 'They had raped an untouchable woman and he, the Sarpanch, and some people, had gone against them, so they killed him. They killed a good man.'

The family behind the murders tried everything to make Anuragi withdraw his testimony. At some point, they accused Anuragi in another murder case (the charges the *Express* article mentioned). '*Usmey mujhe bhi farji bana diya, mujhe bhi fasa diya.* (They accused me, got me stuck also). I haven't slapped anyone to date,' he insists.

Anuragi went to jail, then got released on bail. He was adamant on appearing in court. 'I didn't care about the charges. At the time, I didn't have it in my head that I'd become MP.' That case got buried eventually, Anuragi tells me; other people testified he wasn't there and the case was dropped.

Then they tried to shoot Anuragi. The court hearing was in fifteen days and he wasn't withdrawing his testimony. 'The man standing behind me died. Half my body was paralyzed; I may have died, but I recovered.'

Ghyanshyam was eighteen when he got shot, in 1990, six years since the first shootings. He lay in the district hospital, recovering, for a month.

'Still, I testified. I even testified against the man who shot at me. He got life imprisonment. The man who I testified against for the Basir murder, he too got life imprisonment.' Another accused in the four murders, those of Basir Mussalman, Ahlwan, Gulab, and Pandit Bharatkumar Mishra, also got sentenced for life; some of the accused went free.

After he recovered, Anuragi moved away from the village to the district capital, Hamirpur town. 'I couldn't live in the village,' Anuragi says, 'they would've killed me had I stayed there. I couldn't fight them. I could only testify against them.' Power was on their side, political power (the then MLA was from the same community as the family who had perpetrated the murders and was a friend of theirs) and, therefore, the police.

Anuragi completed an MA from Varanasi. Later, he also earned a Law degree from Bundelkhand University.

***

The Gram Pradhan or Sarpanch election in Kheda Sila came in 1995 and the seat was reserved for SC-ST candidates. By then, the murder case had wrapped up. Anuragi was still living in the district town. 'People came to me and said,' Anuragi recalls, 'you fight the election.'

'*Us samay key Sarpanch hamsay ranjis mantey the* (the Sarpanch at the time considered me an enemy),' Anuragi shares, 'I said, who'll vote for me?' Up till then, in Kheda Sila Jit, the Sarpanch had always been from one community; the same caste had always won elections. '*Usi samaj key neta hotey the* (politicians were from that community, only).' That was how it was and it went unchallenged. The Kheda Sila seat had been reserved for SC-ST candidates, but the old Sarpanch was backing his own proxy candidate.

'They [the village people] said, you don't come to the village. Just file your nomination papers, we'll make you win. I filed my nomination papers and left immediately. Next, I went to the village the day votes were polled. The day of voting, I stayed in the village. Then, I came running back to Hamirpur.' By then, Anuragi feared for his life.

'When the counting happened, I won. All castes voted for me. I got 1,400 votes and the total votes polled in the village were 1,900.' Anuragi was twenty-three when he became Sarpanch.

In Kheda Sila Jit, Scheduled Caste reservation and the upheaval in political status quo it brought made room for new, unexpected alignments.

'People felt I had supported them in a time of weakness,' Anuragi says, remembering how the village elected him. 'They said he's such a small boy but he's not intimidated by them. *Marney ke baad bhi usney logo ka saath diya* (he supported people even after their death).' They said, '*risk liya usney* (he took a risk).'

'*Woh Zila ka sabsey charchit case tha jismey main gawahi,bana.* (That was one of the most discussed case in the district)', Anuragi explains.

Four people from different communities, including the head of the village council, had been flagrantly killed. Over six years, no one else had dared to testify in the cases. Everyone in the district had come to hear of Anuragi, the young boy who had had the guts to be a witness in the controversial murders.

***

'If something happens to someone and no one is with them, and they're feeling threatened, and, at that time, you support them, people talk about it,' Anuragi narrates. It has been, perhaps, his biggest learning in politics. 'They say, he supported us, gave us courage against people in power. This man who's from a small family, he's giving us strength.'

During his term as Sarpanch, Anuragi also become a local caste leader for his Kori caste. He'd speak at caste meetings, spread awareness amongst his community on the importance of children's education, on girls' education, on putting an end to dowry and other such social subjects. A retired DIG, Brigadier Muk Chand, then a member of the state legislative council and of the same Kori community, came to know Anuragi through the caste meetings and introduced him to 'Netaji' [(Mulayam Singh Yadav of the Samajwadi party), Anuragi narrates.

Mulayam Singh made Anuragi Area President of the Samajwadi party. He began organizing initiatives for the Party. Anuragi fought the *Zila Panchayat* (District Council) election from the SP and won. Next, he fought the election for *Zila Panchayat Adhyaksh* (District Council President), the biggest post in the District, and won. 'All the central government schemes go through the *Zila Panchayat*,' Anuragi explains, 'and are headed by the *Zila Panchayat Adhyaksh*.'

Then, when the 2004 Lok Sabha election came, 'Netaji (Mulayam Singh Yadav) said, you fight the election. I said, the Lok Sabha election is very big. He said, no, you fight it.' Jalaun, the reserved seat Anuragi was asked to fight from, was an entirely new district, 100 kilometres from Hamirpur where he lived.

In his first election, Anuragi managed to get 1.68 Lakh votes, but the two-time incumbent from the BJP, Bhanu Pratap Verma, won by 26,800 votes.

That Anuragi came under Mulayam Singh Yadav's radar sheds light on why the Congress loses to regional parties in UP – they have tentacles, contacts spread on the ground, to pick up local politicians like Anuragi and see them through district, then Lok Sabha elections. The Congress doesn't have its ears on the ground.

When Ghanshyam went to meet Mulayam Singh Yadav after his 2004 defeat, Mulayam Singh was unwavering. 'He said, "You should work hard and win the election next time."' Ghanshyam narrates. 'So I said, Sir, I'll stay there only.'

Anuragi took a house on rent in Jalaun.

Over the five years he was out of power, Ghanshyam lived in Jalaun, going from village to village, to public events, marriages, cremations, invited or uninvited. If he found about an event at someone's guest house, Anuragi tells me, he'd turn up there.

'I went to the post-mortem house regularly. If there's a road accident, or someone kills themselves, or someone dies, or someone's wife dies, at that time, people need support. Sometimes the doctor causes delay, sometimes you need help to move the body, sometimes there's no wood to even burn the body.' Anuragi would liason with doctors and the administration to provide support to the distraught and confused families at the postmortem house.

'I would also go the hospital every single day.' He'd talk to the patients and to the doctors. Someone would complain she wasn't being given medicines, or that he wasn't put on the drip and had high fever, or that no doctor had come to see him. Anuragi would stand around, talk to the doctor, make sure the patient was taken care of.

A band of people usually followed him about. '*Mujhe pone lakh vote miley the, log jantey the ki mere chahney wale the* (I had gotten about a lakh and half votes, so people knew me and I had supporters),' he says. He had been the SP candidate with the second highest number of votes; he had influence with the administration and the doctors.

He would also go to the police station almost every day, to find out if anyone needed support with a case. The police often trapped an innocent man, beat someone up. Other times, someone would get raped, someone killed, and the police would refuse to file an FIR. Some crime happens everyday, Anuragi says offhandedly, and the police often refuses to file an FIR. 'FIR *kya*? Police *kya*?' he recounts indignant. 'Police *key thaney mein ananya hota hai*! (What's an FIR? What's the police? Crimes are committed in the police station itself!)' Anuragi would arrive at the police station, with his band of supporters, put pressure on the police to file an FIR. He'd liason for families there and follow-up on cases.

Anuragi did regular rounds of the post-mortem house, the hospital, and the police station, the nodes of local power and vulnerability, for five years, till the next election.

Meanwhile, he collected donations (a sack of wheat, plates, a cupboard) and organized weddings for a hundred and fifty couples who were too poor to get married themselves. He also supported Bundelkhand University students in a protest.

'*Main charchey mein rahta tha* (I made sure I was involved in local discussions),' Anuragi adds. He'd give quotes to the papers and bytes to local channels on every local debate.

After a full five years in Jalaun, in the 2009 election, Anuragi managed to beat the three-time BJP MP Bhanu Pratap Mehta by a wafer margin of 7,600 votes. It was a huge win for Anuragi. His first election he'd gotten 1.7 Lakh votes, this time he'd gotten 2.4 Lakh votes. But when he hadn't contested in Jalaun, he tells me, the Samajwadi Party had gotten only 69,000 votes.

***

Anuragi looks back on his political career with satisfaction. 'I've come from the lowest political rung, the village panchayat, to the highest, Parliament. I've crossed every level and come. I've learnt how development can be done at every level. How you fight a fight.'

He talks about schools he's gotten built as a Gram Pradhan, under state government schemes, and since becoming an MP, about railway lines he's gotten sanctioned, about water issues, and a gutsy speech on the drought in Bundelkhand he gave in Parliament last year.

Anuragi describes the SP party's core issues as farmers debt, education for girl children and employment. I ask about the constant jumping back and forth of candidates between the Samajwadi Party and the Bahujan Samaj Party in UP and Anuragi laughs, '*Kabhi logo ko lagta hai ki yeh party kharaab hai, toh bhago. Kabhi lagta hai ki is party mein burey din aa rahe hai, toh bhag niklo* (Sometimes, people feel this party is bad, so they run. Sometimes, they feel bad days are ahead for this party, so get out of it.)'

Recently, the Samajwadi Party has been undergoing some turmoil in its top leadership, with the exit of Amar Singh and the entry (and also exit) of Kalyan Singh.

Akhilesh Yadav, Mulayam Singh Yadav's son, thirty-eight years old and MP from Kannauj, is heir to the Samajwadi Party. Akhilesh has been appointed UP President of the Samajwadi and he showed his mettle in the 2012 UP state assembly elections. The election took down Mayawati (and the Congress) and brought the Samajwadi to power with an unquestionable majority. Before the election, Akhilesh traveled through UP, often riding on a cycle, the SP symbol. He talked about education, offering free laptops to school children. After the big win, Akhilesh spoke on TV about not breaking Mayawati's statues and about supporting the Congress at the center in a manner that showed he hadn't lost his head (yet). Throughout, he surprised by coming across as a clear-headed guy – no inflated self-image or vindictive edge. Anuragi, predictably, showers praises on him. 'He's very knowledgeable, very easy to get along with. Everybody in the party is eager to meet him.'

I ask Anuragi what he thinks of Rahul Gandhi, the supposed heir to the Congress party; I mention his organization building in the Youth Congress, his Youth Congress membership drives in UP, and his effort to give tickets to new, grassroots candidates. At the time, the conclusive UP 2012 assembly election hadn't happened yet and the Congress still had hope in the state. '*Itni tezi nahi dikhayi de rahi unmey* (I don't see that sharpness in him),' Anuragi insists.

He asks bemusedly, 'What issues has he (Rahul Gandhi) taken up? Sometimes, he's going to a university, saying "hello, hi." Sometimes he's at this one's house, he's eating their food, he's drinking their water; he's here, he's there. Are these issues?' Anuragi asks chuckling, 'Okay, you tell me. Talking about farmers, is that considered work?'

In the 2010 spring session of Parliament, Anuragi recounts, he gave a speech on Rahul Gandhi's Bundelkhand *yatra* (march). Rahul Gandhi said he'd do something for Bundelkhand, but he came, travelled extensively in Bundelkhand, ate and drank our water there, but ultimately did nothing, Anuragi said in his speech, he has not even returned to us the food and water that he and his 50,000 followers consumed in Bundelkhand. 'Is Rahul Gandhi a liar?' Anuragi asked sensationally in Parliament.

Rahul, Congress President Sonia Gandhi, and the Prime Minister were present in the House, he says. Sonia got up and asked him to apologize. You're using unconstitutional language, she said; as Ghanshyam narrates this episode now, he marvels over the flurry he'd caused. Meanwhile, Mulayam Singh and the SP started protests outside Parliament over the ineffectiveness of the relief package. (Championed by Rahul Gandhi, a Rs.7,500 crore Drought Relief Package to Bundelkhand was announced by the Congress Party in November 2009 for the year 2009-2010; but it was reported in 2010 that, at most, only 9 per cent of the central funds allotted had been utilized. The Congress blamed the BSP state government for not making use of the funds, while state parties blamed the Congress central government for not deploying the funds properly.)

***

Anuragi's family now lives in Hamirpur town, he tells me, an hour's drive from Jalaun. His wife, Kalpana, also fought the elections once and was elected to the district council, but she's now a professor in Hamirpur College. She's stood by him, encouraged him like a friend, Anuragi says. His daughter, whom Anuragi is extremely fond of and considers lucky (he won the *Zila Panchayat* elections right after she was born) is a boarder at the Navodyaya Vidyalaya, the government school for gifted children, and his young son is in school in Hamirpur. Anuragi's private secretary, a former neighbor, now travels with him everywhere.

Even today, Anuragi tells me, he tries to keep himself in the news. He gets involved in everything. He visits everyone. He still turns up at weddings uninvited and goes to the hospital and the police station. 'If I want to start a cleaning drive, I pick up the broom and start cleaning myself. I come from nowhere, so it doesn't bother me to do these kind of things.'

Anuragi's journey is, without a doubt, unique. He is the only young MP I met to have started at the village panchayat, the first rung of Indian elections, and made his way to Parliament, the last. Others – Meenakshi Natarajan, Ashok Tanwar – had started out in the Student Congress, made it to the Youth Congress, but they'd eventually been picked up by Rahul Gandhi to fight directly for Lok Sabha elections. Anuragi is the only one to really know life in a village first-hand. The others, even those who'd grown up in rural areas, had lived most of their adult lives in cities. Anuragi has experienced first-hand how government, law, and administration pans out in rural areas. He speaks openly of the whimsical and brutal way the police works in the districts, about the carelessness of government hospitals. Most MPs address their constituencies in large meetings and, sometimes, briefly, in smaller groups. Anuragi is the only one who seems, over the years, to have met and collected his voters almost one by one.

As soon as I'd first sat down with him, Ghanshyam Anuragi had told me I wouldn't find any other MP with a story like his. I thought he was just being melodramatic, but his claim holds true. Anuragi's story turns out not only stranger than that of other MPs I meet, but stranger still than fiction.

Notes

1 Alka Pande, 'Phase III: A third of drama and action,' *Indian Express*, 24 May 2009

2 A.K. Verma, 'The Badlands of Bundelkhand,' *Indian Express*, 8 January 2010

The Exacting Minister

The Senior Superintendent, Posts, Jaipur, remembers how Scindia would chase numbers and operational metrics. Every week, at a fixed time, without fail, he'd hold a review over video conference of the Jaipur post office's performance.

JYOTIRADITYA SCINDIA

Indian National Congress (INC)
Guna Constituency, Madhya Pradesh
Born on 1 January 1971
31 years of age at first election
Last victory margin of 4,50,000 votes

'Can I expect some efficiency from you? The *least* I expect of you is efficiency,' Jyotiraditya Scindia sputters, annoyed, talking to an assistant over the phone. He is tanned from travel, in a *kurta* the colour of denim and white pyjamas. The young Member of Parliament, despite a brow furrowed with whatever's going on during the work day, still looks like a school boy. We're meeting in a room full of framed family portraits and photographs: Jyotiraditya's father, the late Congress politician Madhavrao Scindia, sister Chitrangada,

wife Priyadarshini, and their children Mahanaryaman and Ananya. A stiff, silver-haired servant, probably from the Scindia palace in Gwalior, Madhya Pradesh, brings in tea and a bowl of *poha*. 'Maharani has sent it,' he says formally.

Jyotiraditya puts down the phone, looking preoccupied. 'Okay, let's begin,' he says suddenly, the expression on his face now demanding. He has exacting standards – of himself and of everyone around him. It's evident from the fastidious way he dresses, the rigor with which he runs his office and the method with which he conducts interviews – never too guarded but also never revealing too much.

'How did you first hear you'd be Minister of State (MoS) for Commerce?'

'The same way you did. From the news channels.' Scindia is known for his no-nonsense, dead-pan responses; I press on. 'You didn't lobby for it? Did you expect this department?'

Scindia switches to a formal, measured tone. 'It's primarily the purview of the Congress President and the Prime Minister. I had no clue that I would be a Minister. But I was very happy and very grateful for getting this opportunity, to serve not only my constituency, but to serve a larger interest in terms of India's interest. I try and shoulder it to the best of my ability.'

I've seen Scindia play pranks and shake up sit-down dinners. Before he became Minister, I once saw him start a game of throwing ice-cubes at unsuspecting people across a long, formal dinner table. He can crack jokes and have a sombre group in splits within minutes. I'm expecting him to be light-hearted and funny, but here, in the middle of the work day, he's serious and precise in the words he uses.

On the wall, I notice a particularly cute portrait of Madhavrao Scindia holding up baby Mahanaryaman, Jyotiraditya's son.

Madhavrao Scindia was a doting grandfather; he was an indulgent father to his daughter, but he was tougher on his son. He piled high expectations on Jyotiraditya. 'My father was clear about the distinction between being loving and strict,' Jyotiraditya remembered in the *Times of India* a few months after Madhavarao's death. 'I was never pampered as such, growing up with clear cut guidelines.'[1] 'But whenever I performed well,' he recalled, 'be it academics or anything else, *Baba's* joy was apparent.'

The younger Scindia pushed himself to study economics at Harvard as an undergraduate, and then through Stanford Business School. Back home for summer holidays, he'd hear about his friends' jobs and feel he wasn't 'performing enough.' He worked at the investment bank Merril Lynch and then at Morgan Stanley, in financial services, moving from New York to Hong Kong and finally, to Mumbai.

When his plane crashed in 2002, Madhavrao had been Member of Parliament (MP) from Gwalior or Guna, in Gwalior-Chambal, for over thirty years. Just four months after his father's passing, a grieving Jyotiraditya stood for his first election and became Member of Parliament from Guna. He was thirty-two at the time, fresh out of Morgan Stanley and Mumbai. 'The only precondition that my father and myself both put on my life together was that I would want to do something for my region,' Jyotiraditya says, when I ask him if his father had expected him to join politics. 'Now, that could be not necessarily in politics – politics must not be an end, but it must be a means. It could be through politics, it could be through business – by making sure that there are employment opportunities. It could be by just doing social service non-politically. So the means are varied, but the end goal was very clear in my mind.'

However, in the piece in the *Times* in June 2001, a few months after Madhavrao's death in September, the young Scindia said simply, 'My dream is to make Baba proud of me.'

***

Once, at a dinner, I overheard Jyotiraditya announce melodramatically to a friend, 'I'm just not ambitious. They say my father wasn't ambitious,' he said, in a black bandh-gala, a red handkerchief sticking out of his pocket, 'neither am I.'

I ask him about this now. 'I am very ambitious for my people and my region. But I am not very...,' he pauses. 'I think that's maybe the genetic code in this family. My father was always accused of not being ambitious for himself.'

Following Rajiv Gandhi's assassination in 1991, Madhavrao Scindia had been touted in the Congress as the next possible Prime Minister of India. Scindia had the education and subdued charisma of a statesman. But with Narasimha Rao – who eventually did become Prime Minister – and fellow Congress MP Sharad Pawar already in the fray, Scindia appeared to have stepped aside. Refusing to fight for the PM's post, he came across as rather meek. But Madhavrao apparently hated the intrigue of party politics. Even years later, when he could have easily become the Chief Minister of Madhya Pradesh, Madhavrao told the party he wasn't interested. He couldn't be bothered with managing alliances, negotiating with and shepherding MLAs in the state. So a sense of mystery and unfulfilled destiny has always enveloped the senior Scindia.

What Madhavrao really enjoyed was turning around ministries. In their biography of Madhavrao Scindia, journalists Vir Sanghvi and Namita Bhandare comment on the extensive work Scindia did as Minister of Railways in the Rajiv Gandhi government. In his first eight months, Madhavrao travelled widely to diesel locomotive factories and coal units to understand the breadth of the Railways. He then focused on how to make systems in the ministry more efficient. He reduced the turnaround times for freight trains, implemented the computerization of train reservations with custom software. He introduced new model railway stations all over the country. Later, in 1988, he launched his brainchild: the fast commuter train, the Shatabdi Express, which would compete with airplanes for inter-city passengers.

Sanghvi and Bhandare describe the zeal with which Madhavrao managed the ministry, the late nights he spent there. During Scindia's tenure, files in the ministry were cleared in four days instead of the weeks it usually took. George Fernandes, Scindia's successor as Railways Minister is said to have thumped Madhavrao's seat and said, 'The man who sat on this chair for five years has done a bloody good job!'

Later, Scindia brought as much energy to his assignment as Civil Aviation Minister. He recruited a new Chairman from the private sector to revitalize the national airline. Air India posted profits of one crore rupees a day in 1993, under Scindia. (Today, many Ministers later, the national airline is abysmally bankrupt.)

No one had expected the 'fun-loving Maharaja' to turn into such a capable and effective minister, Sanghvi writes.

The Scindias seem to define success and ambition by their own unusual, stubborn standards. Madhavrao hadn't worried about how high he rose in the pyramid of politics, or about his closeness to so-and-so. He had gotten a kick out of measuring and improving the operational efficiency and the financials of his ministries.

Jyotiraditya defines himself by his father's yardstick. 'I have taken my zeal and my passion very much from my father,' he says. His 'lack of ambition' translates into a strange hunger for results. The young Scindia puts an enormous premium on his work in his ministries. He's tense, almost edgy with self-imposed pressure.

***

Back in 2008, towards the end of the first Congress term, Jyotiraditya was made MoS in the Ministry of Telecom, Information technology (IT) and Posts. In the ministry which handles all mobile and internet initiatives, he was given independent charge of the unfashionable Postal department.

In his ten month term in the ministry (general elections came in 2009), Jyotiraditya put together a core group of talent – including the flamboyant advertising chief Piyush Pandey, known for his unique, mass appeal campaigns and business consultants – to develop a new strategy for Posts. 'I believe in forming a group that is dedicated to a particular project,' Scindia explains. 'They ate, slept, and worked on nothing else but Project Arrow.'

'We have a wonderful network, probably the largest distribution pipeline of any organized system in the country – 1,40,000 Points of Presence (PoPs) across 600,000 villages,' he says, laying out the spread of the postal network. While the Postal Department revenues have waned in cities with the coming of the internet and private couriers, in villages it is still the only network in villages. In far-flung areas, the fabulous distribution network can 'be used to sell everything.'

'How to really update it and make it a twenty-first century product is what we looked at.' The re-structuring was not only for look and feel, or a simple re-branding, but also evaluated back-end operations.

'We did a sort of structured review of the standard post office – what are the efficiencies that need to brought in, the latencies?' They established 'the rigors of a performance metrics review,' Jyotiraditya explains. The team set up web-based technology to monitor the systems in post offices – 'I could tell you in a particular day, how many letters came into this particular post office, how many were delivered, what time the postman checked in, what time he checked out.' Every day at 5 p.m., Scindia poured over the metrics on efficiency and volume.

Piyush Pandey's team also developed the slick 'India Post' brand.

'We started off with fifty post offices as a pilot,' Scindia says, almost mirroring the method used by his father in the Railways Ministry. 'Then we multiplied it by ten, went up to 500 and rolled those out to see the response over six months. I was contemplating rolling out another two thousand,' he adds, but after the 2009 general elections, Sachin Pilot became MoS for Communications and took over Posts. Scindia started his term as MoS for the Ministry of Commerce and Industry.

Scindia isn't ruffled by the cyclical changes in ministries. 'The ability to be able to envision something and start seeing its effects is one challenge. But the change carries on,' he says. 'The project is still going on full steam.'

***

I imagine bureaucrats in the ministries shaken up by all the data collection and monitoring.

'How resistant is the old system and the bureaucracy to these changes?' I ask.

'Well, I don't have any sort of hidden mechanism,' he looks irritated by the question. 'I don't think diktats or orders work in today's environment, whether it's in the public sector or in the private sector. I think it's important to infuse energy to get people on board.'

'Once you get that level of energy going and you get that commitment on board, then it's a self propelling system and it perpetuates itself, which is what I've seen in Project Arrow.'

I have the common perception that bureaucrats drink tea, push files and slow things down.

'Well, you know, I think in India we tend to generally be very wide in terms of painting people with a brush. In India, generally all politicians are labeled corrupt and useless and all bureaucrats are resistant to change. Neither is the case,' Scindia retorts. 'There are politicians who are very committed, dedicated, passionate public servants and similarly, bureaucrats that are very committed to their job and produce astounding results. In my experience in the last decade I have found, if you show a tremendous amount of passion, people in the bureaucracy are more than happy to help you out in whichever way they can.'

***

A few weeks later, on my way to Sachin Pilot's constituency, I happen to pass through Jaipur. Here I meet the Senior Superintendent, Post Offices, Jaipur District. Jaipur has one of the first 200 model post offices refurbished under Jyotiraditya. The Senior Superintendent talks without any prompting about the changes in Posts. He describes how the postal system was computerized, how data began to be collected on turn-around times. A citizen's charter is up today on every post office wall; it guarantees a maximum five minute wait for speed posts.

A video conferencing facility was set up in the Jaipur Post office through which, he recalls with some amazement, the Minister then, Jyotiraditya Scindia, would actually monitor the numbers every week.

An Assistant Superintendent, Posts adds, 'You can now access the internet in a kiosk at the post office. You can track the status of your letter on the India Post website.' (It works 90 per cent of the time, he warns, not cracking a smile.)

The refurbished post offices – about 400 now with 150 added every year – were branded in white, with a red arrow across the top. New office layouts were designed to maximize efficiency. New steel furniture was made as part of the project to comply with standard measurements. 'You know how the post offices were – old wooden tables placed any which way. Now, you don't feel like you've entered a Post Office,' the Assistant Superintendent tells me, 'you feel good.'

There were, he adds, plans afoot to introduce ATM cards at Post Offices and special machines with bio-metric recognition for the illiterate.

***

Scindia combines the vocabularies of very different worlds.

Having worked at Morgan Stanley, he has an analyst's bent of mind and vocabulary. He compares 'verticals' to 'horizontals,' and describes removing 'latencies' (delays) and bringing in 'efficiencies' in everything he does. However, breaking his work down, he also manages to speak simply, to sift through complexity and explain his projects in layman's terms.

At other times, he speaks with a lilt of emotion, with the poetics of someone who's used to appealing to a large gathering of people. Jyotiraditya will be talking about performance metrics and, all of a sudden, he'll describe the postal system as a 'carrier of emotions'; the *dakiya* (postman) is still the most trusted man in the village because he 'delivers people's secrets,' he'll say.

Campaigning in his constituency Guna, Madhya Pradesh, he'll talk about his *dil ka button* (the button to his heart). '*Aap voting ka machine nahi, mere dil ka button daba rahe honge. Kisi aur ke dil ka button mat dabana*,' he said during his last election.[2] (That's not a button on a voting machine you're pressing, it's the button to my heart.) He also appealed to people as their King, saying, 'Let our old bond be strengthened… When votes are counted on 13 May, you should be saying, *Maharaj*, have you ever seen so many votes being cast?' Finally, he appealed to people on the Congress Party platform of development: referring to rival parties, Scindia said, 'They will come and go. Our battle is for development. *Yahi hamara dharm hia, yahi hamari jati* (This is our religion; this is our caste).'

In the villages of the Gwalior region, Jyotiraditya relates to people on many levels, at once a local King and a Congress Minister. He dons multiple identities, like his father did. In rural, feudal India, old bonds still endure; people respond. In the assembly elections in Guna, the Bhartiya Janata Party won most seats. Still, Jyotiraditya won the Parliamentary seat from the Congress with a huge margin. It's said in Guna, the Congress can lose the election, but not the Scindias.

To the international press, fixated on his royal lineage, however, Jyotiraditya says with impatience, 'All this Maharaja business is cosmetic.'[3] Instead, he talks about the Lifeline Express, a train equipped with surgical equipment and doctors that he takes into Guna every year. Large private companies and the best doctors have partnered to deliver the Lifeline Express, and on each visit, it treats upto 10,000 patients and provides free operations to about 1,500 people. 'I believe in India that people are willing to give, they want to give, but I think the greatest apprehension that people have is whether that money is going to be utilized for the manner and for the purpose which they have determined it to be.'

In assessing himself, Jyotiraditya talks about his passion for Gwalior Chambal because of his family's 300-year old bond with the region. Journalists sometimes give Scindia flack for being an erstwhile Maharaja, for an assumed uppitiness, for royal titles that linger. Without a doubt, Scindia doesn't make a warm and cosy interviewee – at times, he can be dismissive. Yet, his is far from a laidback, lofty sense of responsibility. The family's ties with Gwalior may supply passion, but Scindia is pragmatic and professional, intent on results, constantly assessing himself against specific deliverables. Having learnt the drill of corporate reviews and systemization, Scindia brings a rare management discipline to the public sector.

***

On transitioning from Posts to Commerce after the 2009 elections, Scindia says, 'I believe that before you expound on issues, it's important to get a very clear, deep understanding of your subject. That's why for the first few weeks, I actually took very detailed briefings. Our bureaucratic set up is extremely well versed and they bring you up to speed fairly quickly. They are outstanding in the way they put presentations together.'

In the Ministry of Commerce, he got an 'allocation,' by way of a job description. 'My work allocation is mainly the areas of plantations, so tea, coffee, spices, rubber, all of that.' It is a large allocation by most standards, enveloping entire industries and a few continents such as West Africa and Latin America.

Throwing himself into the job, Jyotiraditya went to the country's north eastern tea-producing region and to the tea centre of Calcutta. He then travelled in the south of India to understand spice production. While the world loosely associates India with spices, spices 'made in India' are not coveted over others. 'I think a lot of work needs to be done in terms of our positioning, our branding, and also our value addition in these areas.'

Eventually, as he'd done in Posts, Scindia put together a 'core team' to understand how Indian tea and spices could be branded and promoted for export.

'I love being a change agent. That's what excites me and that's what I'm passionate about,' says the young politician, now warming up. 'To get my hands around a problem and see what the possible solution could be and to get people's support and enthusiasm so that we can work towards that solution.'

For the tea project, Jyotiraditya again threw together adman Piyush Pandey, along with fifteen other leaders from the industry and executives from Hindustan Lever, Tata Tetley, and Britannia.

In the wider ministry, Scindia is working on other measures to facilitate trade. A group of twenty specialists are examining how layers of transaction costs in India – from the factory to the port – can be minimized. (The average cost of moving a container of goods in India is, apparently, double that of China.) 'We're trying to understand the latencies, redundancies, and bottlenecks in terms of transaction costs so that Indian exports are cheaper,' Jyotiraditya explains. Some measures like around-the-clock customs clearance and a reduction in levies were announced as part of the 2011 annual budget.

Scindia is also exploring how to use technology to cut costs and speed up transactions. He's working on 'a horizontal and vertical portal' that'll ease the cost of doing business and reduce facilitation hassles.

The vertical portal, a service he's excited about, called E-biz, being developed with Infosys will cut through the forest bureaucracy and try to be a one-stop solution for all government permissions an entrepreneur needs to get – from the *nagar palika* (local municipality) right up to the Central Government. It could be, Scindia says, 'to get a shop and establishment license or to get an electricity bill paid… just a single vertical that any entrepreneur or business man would access for any processes done across the board.'

The horizontal portal, called e-trade, will coordinate facilitation across ministries. So, any exporter that needs permissions from Customs, Ground Transport, or Civil Aviation to transport his goods will apply here, instead of running between different agencies and putting in multiple applications.

Scindia's projects are complex, and a departure from the usual fanfare announcements. I ask him how he arrived at these particular ideas. 'Through discussions,' he says off-handedly, 'with officials, with the private sector, and it also depends on what areas you have a flavour for, what you are interested in.'

Jyotiraditya enjoys delving into the details of the ministry. For all his concern with efficiency, he doesn't, for a moment, mourn inefficiency in the country's administration. He doesn't give in to lamentation, or throw his hands up and look to the private sector. He talks, instead, of problems in the ministries as problems of management, of data that needs to be collected, of systems that need to be managed, of chains of processes that need to be monitored, and of people who need to be given real incentives.

***

A few weeks later, I meet Jyotiraditya Scindia's wife Priyadarshini who is from the royal family of Baroda. She's waif-like, her face always aglow, framed by a mane of long hair; she's wrapped in a chiffon sari and speaks in a soft, graceful voice. Priya grew up in Bombay, so despite her delicateness, she has the confidence and irreverent sense of humour of a big city girl that puts me at ease.

Priya has slowly become entrenched in Gwalior. She's restoring the Jai Vilas palace museum, holding local craft *melas* and health camps, and organizing extra classes for school children. She spends increasingly less and less time in Delhi, she says. 'You have to be in Gwalior,' she tells me. 'You can't organize these things in proxy and later ask – *Kaisa hua? Kitney log aye*? (How did it go? How many people came?)'

Priya talks of the women in Gwalior. 'For me, sometimes, I think why are these women complaining to me constantly? But I realize they just need someone to listen to them. *Nobody* listens to them.' The women tell her about problems with their crop, of the fights within their families. 'And they feel,' Priya says, in her soft voice, 'if through me, they can get through to him (Jyotiraditya), something in their lives might change.'

'He's so busy, he goes straight to his constituency, Guna, but I ask him to stop in Gwalior,' she says of her husband. 'He used to wear dark glasses. I told him don't wear dark glasses. These people have been standing here in the heat for hours to meet you – you need to look into their eyes and acknowledge them.'

Priya's family lived in Bombay but they constantly visited Baroda, their home state. 'Baroda, for us, was the place we went to run wild. It was where we have some of our happiest memories,' she remembers.

Priya is adamant that her children grow up with a strong connection to Gwalior. Their son Mahanaryaman goes to the Doon School in Dehradun, where his father studied, and their daughter Ananya is currently at school in Delhi. But Priya draws them to Gwalior regularly. 'If they don't come here, bring their friends here, spend time here, if they only come for holidays like Dussehra or Diwali, to dress up and take a picture, they'll remember it as something they have to do. They'll hate it,' she says, her voice soft yet urgent.

If that happens, Priya suggests, a crucial sense of responsibility, conveyed across generations and transferred across shifts in political systems, will be lost. Their father and their grandfather's lives were shaped by this bond, with a feeling of belonging and responsibility towards Gwalior-Chambal. If the kids lose that bond, Priya knows, it will be, for them, a tremendous loss in their sense of themselves and the meaning of their lives.

Notes

1 'The Evolution of Jyotiraditya Scindia,' *The Times of India*, 2 June 2002

2 Saroj Nagi, 'Jyotiraditya Scindia strengthens bond with Guna voters,' *Hindustan Times*, 5 May 2004

3 Sophie Campbell, 'Maharajas: Back to the Rolls-Royce days in India,' *The Telegraph UK*, 10 October 2009

The Foot Soldier

Natarajan was a tough Madhya Pradesh Youth Congress leader before she fought Lok Sabha elections. She coined slogans that spread like wildfire around the country.

MEENAKSHI NATARAJAN
Indian National Congress (INC)
Mandsaur Constituency, Madhya Pradesh
Born on 23 July 1973
36 years of age at first election
Last victory margin of 30,000 votes

It was a winter day in 2009 when Meenakshi Natarajan's phone rang. It was Congress' Rahul Gandhi, asking if she'd like to contest elections. For Natarajan, it was a bolt from the blue. 'I had not made up my mind. I said yes, I said no, again I said yes; I was confused.' Natarajan, as General Secretary of the All India Congress Committee (AICC) and advisor to the Youth Congress, had thought she should focus on organizational work. Like most Congress ground workers without lineage, she had not expected to stand for Lok Sabha elections at just thirty-five years of age.

'I very clearly remember what he (Rahul) said then. He said, this is not for just this particular thing, but if in your life, you keep getting confused you won't be able to set a path. You won't be able to, then, further pursue that path. He then actually forcefully said, you have to take a decision just now. Then somehow,' Meenakshi smiles, very slightly, 'intuitively, I said yes.'

Natarajan got a ticket from Mandsaur, some distance from her home town Ratlam in Madhya Pradesh. Opposite her was the eight-time Bhartiya Janata Party (BJP) winner from Mandsaur, a septuagenarian Member of Parliament (MP), Laxmi Narayan Pandey.

Natarajan modestly attributes her success to mileage from the United Progressive Allies (UPA) achievements like NREGA (the National Rural Employment Guarantee Act) and to Rahul Gandhi's big public meeting in Mandsaur before the election. For the Congress, however, the outcome in Madhya Pradesh, even of Rahul Gandhi's rallies, was lukewarm. The state leaned toward the BJP, which won sixteen seats; the Congress won only twelve seats. Rahul Gandhi himself visited eight constituencies in Madhya Pradesh, out of which the party got mixed results. The Congress won in four of the eight, Hoshangabad, Dewas, Ujjain and Mandsaur, and lost in four, Khajuraho, Khargone, Balaghat and Bhind. Congress schemes, even Rahul's rally, could not have ensured Natarajan's victory.

Natarajan won because she opened all fronts in her campaign. After getting her ticket, she moved base from Ratlam to Mandsaur (Pandey, who'd been MP in Mandsaur since 1971, had still not made Mandsaur his home). She rallied together Congress workers, many of whom she knew from her time as head of the Madhya Pradesh Youth Congress and gave strong speeches on her development agenda for Mandsaur. A former debater, Natarajan speaks fiercely in both English and Hindi. Unlike most MPs who focus only on the rural poor, Natarajan scoped young people from Mandsaur on the social networking site Orkut and mailed them 'scraps'; she introduced herself as a Congress Party candidate and invited their suggestions.

Natarajan became MP by a slim but clear margin of 30,000 votes, two percent of the total votes polled in Mandsaur.

***

Since then, there has been a wave of curiosity about the young Meenakshi Natarajan. But she barely meets the press, or gives interviews, so the few articles on her say very little about Natarajan. It's said she's close to Rahul Gandhi, a member of his 'core team' along with Ashok Tanwar and Bhanwar Jitendra. One newspaper article mentions she coined the sharp slogan '*Gau Hamari Mata Hai, Atal Bihari Khata Hai*' and compares her to the populist female politicians Sushma Swaraj and Uma Bharti of the BJP. The slogan sticks in my mind.

When I ask around about her, other MPs respond with a puzzled look. Everybody claims to know her but can say little about her. For the most part, Natarajan is an enigma, an elusive foot soldier in the Congress flanks.

Then, after months of emailing, calling and badgering her secretary, I get lucky with an appointment. On an afternoon in late 2010, I find Meenakshi Natarajan in her Delhi office on the AICC grounds, casually sitting in front of her desk, not behind it, and flipping through a report.

She's dressed in a printed *salwar kameez*, with thick glasses over small, sharp eyes, her hair in a neat plait. Her appearance is plain and no-nonsense.

I try to break the ice with small talk. How come she hasn't been in town during Parliament?

'Even during Parliament, there are many other kinds of party work to be done,' Natarajan says firmly. She sees herself less as a Parliamentarian and more as a ground worker, more involved in her constituency and in the various Congress organizations she's part of than in Parliament or speaking to the media. Her life revolves around her political work; she lives alone, shuttling between Mandsaur and Delhi.

***

While in college, Meenakshi joined the National Students Union of India (NSUI), the student body of the Congress Party. Then later, as a bio-chemistry post-graduate at Holkar Science College, Indore, she became very involved with debating. 'You know, in student life you tend to get attracted to these kind of activities,' she says, in her even way. The politically charged world of debating led to student activism and to the decision to drop bio-chemistry for law. 'I was interested in working for the country, not through biochemistry or science, but definitely by working for the rights of the people,' she says.

At the NSUI, Natarajan's active, vocal role in student causes started to receive attention and in 1999, Congress MP PK Sangma (who would later quit the party over Congress President Sonia Gandhi's 'foreign origins'), is said to have made Meenakshi the National President of the Congress' student body when she was twenty-six years old.

Three years later in 2002, at twenty-nine, Natarajan became President of the Madhya Pradesh Youth Congress. This time Congress stalwart Digvijay Singh is said to have picked her for the role.

It was during this phase, while she was President of the MP Youth Congress, that Meenakshi was credited with the raw, hair-raising slogan involving the then BJP Prime Minister Atal Behari Vajpayee: *Gau Hamari Mata Hai, Atal Bihari Khata Hai* (The Cow is Our Mother, Yet Atal Bihari Eats Her Meat). It rose like a hard slap out of Madhya Pradesh and resounded across the country. Cows are sacred in Hinduism, eating their meat banned. Natarajan's wild slogan accused the Hindu-centric BJP of hypocrisy, with a direct shot at the BJP Prime Minister's well-known eating habits.

Meenakshi pauses, then comments with a twinge of embarrassment. 'Uma Bharti had launched an anti-cow slaughter campaign in Madhya Pradesh,' she explains. 'That was completely communalized. They started targeting Muslims and other communities. And we wanted to counter that.'

The BJP hadn't banned cow slaughter in Goa or Nagaland where a large number of people eat beef. But in Madhya Pradesh, they were targeting communities that ate beef, tooting that they were 'the sole cow protectors of this country.' Of course, it was not the issue that mattered to them: whether or not people ate beef all over India. By raising the beef issue in a largely Hindu state, Uma Bharti and the BJP hoped to incite Hindus, to activate them in support of the BJP.

'What I'm trying to say is that we didn't want the BJP to communalize people on this agenda. And that is exactly what the BJP wanted to do,' Meenakshi says. Delving into the history of cow-related politics, Natarajan points out, 'It was Mahatma Gandhi who had started this [anti-cow slaughter campaigns]. And he had started this with the help of Abdul Gali Saab, who was the first one to ban all slaughter houses in Parliament.' The issue was championed by Gandhi and a Muslim leader during the independence movement, so, she explains, they would not tolerate anyone communalizing the issue and using it to target minorities.

In response to the gust of Uma Bharti's anti-beef campaign, the Madhya Pradesh Youth Congress under Natarajan started its own campaign, canvassing for people to see through the hollowness of the BJP's tactics. The official Youth Congress slogan for the campaign, Natarajan says, was *Pehle Ram Naam Bech Satta Pai, Ab Gau Maiya Teri Bari Aayi.* (First They Sold Ram's Name For Power; Mother Cow, It's Your Turn Now.) The slogan referred to how the BJP had raised the Ram Janmabhoomi issue at Ayodhya and theatrically positioned Hindus against Muslims to win power. Now, they were using the cow as a symbol to do the same thing. The slogan was resounding and thought-provoking; it gained circulation throughout Madhya Pradesh.

The *Gau Hamari Mata Hai, Atal Bihari Khata Hai* slogan, Natarajan clarifies, came only later, from some wing of the Youth Congress in Madhya Pradesh, and spread. 'We had an official slogan, but, of course, when you start a movement, then,' Natarajan lets out her breath, with a laugh, 'you know, all kinds of people in their own blocks, in their own villages, they might start things.'

Natarajan was State President of the Youth Congress, so the slogan was attributed to her. The BJP retaliated by creating havoc. They said that the Youth Congress was maligning the Prime Minister. They slapped a court case against Meenakshi which the media covered avidly.

'We were not trying to make value judgements on anybody's eating habits,' Natarajan says. However, she adds, 'We definitely did launch a *serious* offensive movement against the campaign which they (the BJP) had initiated.'

Though the *Gau Hamari Mata Hai* slogan wasn't officially condoned by Natarajan, the entire movement started by her and the momentum it took on catapulted her to fame in the Congress; it established her notoriety as a firebrand. To Uma Bharti's communal movement, the MP Youth Congress had given a cutting reply. Meenakshi, just about thirty at the time, demonstrated she had a flair for political theatre on the ground, something which very few Congress leaders seem to have.

At the time of the BJP's grand *Rath Yatra* in Ayodhya, for instance, the Congress's response towards diffusing the growing communal tension had been weak. Narasimha Rao, the Congress Prime Minister at the time, was severely criticized for not calling in Central Forces, for not dismissing the BJP Chief Minister of Uttar Pradesh, Kalyan Singh, and for believing the word of the BJP's LK Advani that the march would pass without harm to the Babri Masjid. The security response was, however, only part of the problem. At the time, the Congress didn't do much to turn the tide of public opinion. Against the backdrop of the BJP's big communal road show, with Advani at its helm, there was no Congress leader on the ground, no retaliatory campaign, no slogans, no theatre.

Taking off from its success in Ayodhya, and soon after Uma Bharati's anti-beef rally, the BJP issued a list of mosques all over the country that they claimed were built on demolished temple sites. In Madhya Pradesh, they began to rally against the Kamal Maula Mosque in Dhar, saying there should be a Saraswati temple at the site instead. Rashtriya Swayam Sevak (RSS) activists organized an *arti* (prayer) in the Mosque compound, blocked roads, beat drums announcing their campaign.[1] Communal tension was brewing in Dhar and throughout the state of Madhya Pradesh.

In response, Natarajan and the Youth Congress planned a 26 day *yatra* from Ujjain to Dhar to build solidarity around an inclusive Indian nationalism. The campaign involved walking through six or seven districts and all the villages on the way. In each village, people joined the march and attended gatherings. Here, Natarajan and the Congress talked about the perils of *Sanskritic Rashtra Bhav* (Sanskritized nationalism). 'We did say that people belonging to all communities, all regions, speaking all languages, they have all been sacrificing for the sake of the country. You cannot be talking about Hindu nationalism.'

The nationalism campaign started on 31 March 2003 and ended on 26 April. Digvijay Singh, one of Natarajan's supporters in Madhya Pradesh, and many other notable Congress politicians in the state attended the closing ceremonies.

'That was a good movement,' Meenakshi remembers.

It was through such antics, such nuggets of political showmanship, that Meenakshi came to Rahul Gandhi's attention. In India, in the villages and districts, politics is often played out in dramatic shifts – not via newspaper columns. People are won with theatre that brings issues alive, that involves them and draws out their emotions. But most Congress MPs are educated, polished speakers, able administrators and managers of Ministries. They don't have the temerity to shape movements on the ground. The ability to shape public opinion, to back and enact a strong stance on the ground, is a much needed skill set in the refined English-speaking Congress.

While talking to some of the young, second generation MPs across various parties, I'd ask if they used any interesting slogans, or *nadas*, during their campaigns. 'No, no slogans,' they'd say flatly. To them, slogans are too populist, too crude to use. We talk about development and progress, most of them said.

Natarajan, however, understands the power of slogans as efficient tools to communicate a message. She has coined slogans that encapsulate an issue, a point of view, and spread quickly. To sway, in the cow and Nationalism campaigns, for example, thousands from an extreme to a moderate nationalism.

***

The name Mahatma Gandhi comes up a number of times as Natarajan talks. He undertook 'self-penance' with his forms of peaceful protest; he taught 'patience and fearlessness' which come from being on the 'path of truth and honesty.' The Mandsaur MP admires grassroots social workers Anna Hazare and Baba Amte. Anna Hazare is a social activist from Maharashtra, a former army officer, a self-professed Gandhian. Hazare has taken up water and dairy projects, cultivated strict Gandhian norms, to make his home village, Ralegaon Siddhi, a 'model village'. Hazare is best known now for his anti-corruption fast in 2011 and for his agitation on the Jan Lokpal Bill. (When Natarajan spoke to me of Hazare and Amte, however, Hazare had not yet begun his anti-corruption movement on a national scale.) Baba Amte, another social worker, has set up homes for people with leprosy. Natarajan worked at his centre in Maharashtra for several months.

'Politics is basically that,' Natarajan says, indignant, when I ask her if she can marry social work with the demands of big party politics. 'Politics is working for the people. What they do is… I don't see a disconnect between the two.'

'How relevant are Gandhi's methods today?' I try to get a sense of Natarajan's views on the raging debate over Naxals in India. 'The dispossessed, the urban poor, the tribal poor, the Naxalites, those without access to the media, could they solve their problems with his methods?' I ask her.

'I would only say that if you are into seeking rights – that cannot be done with violence and hatred,' Natarajan says firm, citing Gandhi yet again, a spark in her eyes. 'But I would not like to comment on the larger Naxalite issue because it has complexities. In some places, there is administrative failure, there's an empowerment issue, there is also law and order involved. It is multi-dimensional.' Everyone has an opinion on the Naxals and their movement, but Meenakshi, interestingly, refuses to comment on it until she's delved into it thoroughly.

'Inquiry,' Natarajan says straight, looking me in the eye, 'is the way to lead change. That was fundamental to the Gandhian movement. Gandhi never just started a movement. When he was invited by the Champaran people of Bihar, he said he would only come to hear all parties concerned. That would also include the British, the government of the day. When we follow this mode, we get better insight on the issue.'

'It's very easy. First of all, politicians have to come out of, what I call a Santa Claus syndrome, that I am the all powerful and I am here to distribute... sweets,' she says, pin-points of fire in her eyes, her voice still even. 'And once you are out of it, out of that, I think you can definitely conduct a serious inquiry into issues of that time. And that might lead to a movement; that might also lead you to a situation where you feel that a movement is not needed and maybe just a discussion with all the people concerned would resolve it.'

Natarajan has been trying to understand and inquire into the problems of opium farmers in her constituency – Mandsaur is India's biggest legal opium growing area. The Central Bureau of Narcotics (CBN) buys opium at a rate that is miniscule compared to what the black-market pays, so most farmers sell in black; many also run ramshackle heroin producing units. Natarajan has been interacting with the opium farmers, trying to understand the problem, campaigning to increase the government purchase price of opium and its by-products.

Not surprisingly, Meenakshi Natarajan seems calmly indifferent to – and almost bored by – convention. With travel and work taking up most of her time, she's happy to find time to read on the evenings she has to herself. She's told her parents she has no time, or inclination, to get married and have a family. Meenakshi tells me about her current reading on the 1857 Indian Rebellion. She also mentions being deeply inspired by a book on the life of the Buddha, *Old Path, White Clouds*, by Thich Nhat Hanh.

***

In 2008, Natarajan became Secretary of the All India Congress Committee (AICC), the main body of Congress members. She's been part of the drive to give the NSUI, the Youth Congress and the AICC, the party's various membership flanks, 'a new meaning.' To make them live routes to electoral politics, 'hardcore leadership training platforms,' rather than sleepy, chaotic cogwheels.

'It used to be, generally, a process, finding out more about the person, giving them some tasks,' she explains, talking of how she picked leaders in the Youth Congress. When she was heading the Youth Congress in Madhya Pradesh, she would ask people she thought capable to design a movement around an issue – 'any program which they are able to not only frame, but also execute.' For instance, she once asked YC workers to design a program on the Right to Forest Land for tribals. Much like she had put together the march for nationalism as a response to the communalization of politics, the YC members had to understand the issues around forest land, then fashion a movement to educate people and get their support.

'So they passed your test?' I ask. 'I would not say exactly my test, but I would say that they proved themselves to be leaders. It's not the question of my being able to understand or pass judgments on people,' Meenakshi, slightly indignant, clarifies with her thoroughness. 'It's for them to lead movements and be leaders.'

Most people get lost hanging about in the Congress channels, or old, hankering for a ticket. Very few actually fight elections as a result of membership in the NSUI, Youth Congress or AICC.

However, Natarajan is hopeful that the process of elections in the Youth Congress will eventually lead to democracy in the Party as a whole. 'Today, with the right kind of surname, you can go up to any position,' Natarajan says, breaking down the current shape of the Congress. The Party would be truly democratic 'when all their leadership, the organizational leadership, gets elected from amongst its members.'

'Democratization is not a simple thing,' Natarajan warns.

To date, the State level heads and the Presidents of the Youth Congress and the NSUI, are picked out – they tend to be favourites nominated by influential people in the party. 'Yes, we practice democracy, when it comes to elections – Assembly, Lok Sabha, and so on,' Meenakshi says, 'but, none of your political parties are in the real sense of the term democratic internally.' Even as a member of the Congress, she points out, 'You do not have a choice about whom any political party would be fielding as an MLA candidate or an MP candidate. You do not know their merits or anything.' 'We have started this internal democratization movement within our youth wing of the organization,' she says. 'Till that spreads and becomes a kind of passion, till then how can you say that our organizations are open?'

Despite the difficulties of democratization, the remoteness of it, despite the nepotism, the rot which tends to settle in the machinery of democracy, Natarajan is captivated by the thought of internal party reform. Having come out of the NSUI-Youth Congress herself, she is excited at the thought of these organizations creating the next generation of leaders in the Congress.

At the same, I realize, Meenakshi is pragmatic; not an idealist. When I ask her if P.K. Sangma and Digvijay Singh were mentors to her, she says, tactfully, 'All have always supported me. I seek guidance from all senior leaders... I don't come from a political background, so had it not been for informal mentoring by all senior leaders, it would not have been possible for me to progress. Of course, it was the Congress President (Sonia Gandhi) herself and then Rahul ji who have given us the liberty to work, given us the freedom to exercise what we can do,' she adds, neatly focusing credit on the Gandhi family, who, she feels, have taken progressive stands. She doesn't name P.K. Sangma, who walked out of the Congress, or the often controversial Digvijay Singh.

Inspired by activist ideas yet an active politician, Natarajan is a bit of a paradox. Internal democracy, a transparent party, are ideals she talks about – they throw up constant challenges that hold her interest; yet she's also committed to party politics as it is.

Perhaps, Natarajan is just not impatient. She's determined to be politically relevant and active, yet hers is not a hunger for conventional power – after becoming MP, even more than when she was in the Youth Congress, she has shunned the public eye.

When the Anna Hazare anti-corruption protests began and turned anti-government and anti-Congress, I thought of Natarajan. With a strong response, a slogan, she may have been able to capture the imaginations of the protestors on the street and take a stand on the movement for the Congress. But Meenakshi was invisible through the movement. For now, she remains a hidden talent in the Congress rank and file.

Notes

1 Naunidhi Kaur, 'Building hatred around Bhojshala,' *Frontline*, 26 April 2003

The Police Man

As Superintendent of Police in Bihar in the nineties, Kumar chased out the mafia and cleaned up the police. The Ajay Devgan movie, *Ganga Jal*, is inspired by his work in Jamshedpur.

AJOY KUMAR
Jharkhand Vikas Morcha
Jamshedpur Constituency, Jharkhand
Born on 10 August 1962
47 years of age at first election
Last victory margin of 1,55,727 votes

Ajoy Kumar seems to re-invent himself every ten years. In 1986, at the age of twenty-four, he graduated with a MBBS (a Bachelor's in Medicine and Surgery) from the Jawaharlal Institute of Postgraduate Medicine and Research (JIPMER) in Pondicherry. He'd spent more than six years studying sciences to become a doctor. But then, instead of practicing or studying medicine, he gave the Union Public Service Commission (UPSC) exam, which recruits for the Indian Foreign Service, the Administrative Service (IAS) and the police.

Kumar took the UPSC exam in history and zoology; he made it through. His first choice was the Foreign Service, but he didn't qualify for it, so he joined the Indian Police Service instead.

'You'd finished your MBBS, you were a doctor: what made you join the police, all of a sudden?' I ask Kumar, pulling the brakes on his roller-coaster story.

'My dad was in the civil service, so I just took the exam,' Ajoy says nonchalantly, 'I had some time after my medical school exams, so I just floated.' He adds, 'I was floating; you know what Steve Jobs said – "you can only connect the dots later."'

Kumar trained for a year at the National Police Academy in Hyderabad. He trained on the field in Bihar for another year. He rose quickly in the Bihar police. Kumar was in the Indian Police Service precisely ten years. He served as Superintendent of Police, Patna, Bihar's capital, for four years and as Superintendent of Police in Jamshedpur for another two. He was then Bihar Chief Minister Lalu Prasad Yadav's favorite. He served as Superintendent of Police, Patna, Bihar's capital, for two years and as Superintendent of Police, Jamshedpur, for four. He suddenly quit the police in 1996.

After the police, Kumar did a business degree at the XLRI School of Business, Jamshedpur and joined the Tata group, as a General Manager in Tata Motors and Tata Sons.

Kumar spent the next decade in corporate India. He became CEO of a multi-national diesel engines company. He did a post-grad in medical informatics at the Apollo University in Chennai and was Head of Operations for Apollo Hospitals. A few years ago, he was recruited to Delhi as CEO of Max Neeman, a contract medical research company.

Around 2007, Kumar began to scope out political parties. He'd been running an NGO in Jamshedpur for years and he had a home there. Jamshedpur was now in Jharkhand, not in Bihar, and the Bhartiya Janata Party was in power there.

However, the BJP turned Kumar down in 2009. So, about a decade and some after, he'd joined Tata Motors as a General Manager, Kumar joined the Jharkhand Vikas Morcha (JVM), a tiny breakaway Party started by ex-Bharitya Janata Party (BJP) politician Babulal Marandi. The Jamshedpur Lok Sabha seat came up for by-election in 2011; Marandi nominated Kumar. Kumar was elected Member of Parliament (MP), Jamshedpur, by a shattering margin in July 2011.

Ajoy Kumar now sits at the Max corporate office in the Okhla Industrial Area in Delhi half the week. Though Kumar is MP from Jamshedpur, he continues to be CEO of Max Neeman. He zips between Jamshedpur and Delhi through the week.

Steve Jobs had advised Stanford University graduates to 'stay hungry, stay foolish,' to explore what they gravitated towards, to float and 'follow their hearts' even if it led them in unexpected directions.

In the now famous commencement speech, Steve Jobs, towards the end of his own rollicking life, had said, 'You can never connect the dots looking forward. But when you look back, you'll be able to connect the dots.' Ajoy Kumar connects the dots now, surprised by his own life, as he looks back.

***

At his office in Okhla, Ajoy Kumar hands out two cards – one with the Government of India 3D gold lion seal that says he's Member of Parliament, Jamshedpur and spells his name 'Ajay' instead of 'Ajoy'. The other card says he's CEO, Max Neeman.

Kumar is the only MP I met who is still holding down a job.

'I need the job,' Kumar tells me. Since he won in 2011, Kumar spends about one and a half to two lakhs every month to run his MP office in Jamshedpur; the money comes from his CEO salary.

'It's run like a corporate office,' Kumar says. A lawyer in the team handles all the legal aid – he gives legal advice to poor constituents and files Right to Information (RTI) claims. Another person tracks, and follows up on, the progress of government schemes and development programs with the Jamshedpur District Commissioner's (DC) office. (The MP has five crores at his disposal, but the District Commissioner has 300 crores for all kinds of government schemes, Kumar points out.)

Another person handles the MP's health related initiatives. Kumar has enlisted 500 doctors in Jamshedpur to see one patient per day free, with medicines. He's set up a small call center, which receives calls from patients and books appointments with the right doctor. Kumar had the technology developed for the program. The project is close to his heart; it connects with his medical background. It now gets about 150 to 200 calls per day, he says.

There's also a solar lighting project underway. Fifteen hundred villages will get a solar light each. 'I would get lost in the villages at night during elections,' Kumar explains, 'I also noticed without light, in the evenings, villages became dull and quiet.'

The solar light, usually under a big tree, becomes the village hub in the evenings, brings the community together – women bring their sewing, kids their homework; everybody hangs out. The first solar lights went up in November, 2011. Tata BP is supplying the lights at a subsidized rate. Ajoy's raising the remaining funds for the lights from private donors, whom he canvasses directly. (While I'm at his office, Kumar tries to get me to sponsor a Rs 40,000 light as well.)

A few months in, Kumar already has a fixed schedule in the constituency: He travels the rural block of Jamshedpur on Tuesdays. On Saturdays, he meets people in the urban *bastis* (slums). On Sundays, from 12 noon to 8 at night, he keeps office hours in the city, for those who want to drop in for anything. On Mondays, he calls on the District Administration offices, to coordinate and follow up with them. On Tuesday nights, he zips back to Delhi and spends Wednesdays, Thursdays, and

Fridays are his corporate job.

Kumar runs every morning when he's in Jamshedpur, through a different area each time. 'I run and finish at a tea shop,' he tells me, 'I get to know what's happening.' People join him for tea and he picks up on what people are talking about. Many politicians have done the tea shop routine, trying to act casual before elections or on visits. For Kumar, however, it's a regular stop-over, a kind of 'feedback' forum for his work, every morning after his jog.

***

Kumar's father had been in the foreign service, so he grew up moving place to place. After his stint as Superintendant of Police in Jamshedpur, however, Kumar made Jamshedpur his home. He bought a house there. After he left the police, he started his NGO, *Subhash Yuva Manch*, and organized health camps and sponsored kids' education.

When Kumar moved from Chennai to Delhi for a job, and was closer to Jamshedpur, he thought of joining a political party. 'I've always been politically inclined.' He'd called up the BJP with the idea of fighting in Jamshedpur some years ago, but, he says, they decided to go with a safer candidate, Abha Mahto, who was former BJP politician Shailendra Mahto's wife.

Many years later, Kumar called Babulal Marandi. Marandi had been ousted as the BJP Chief Minister of Jharkhand in 2003. Under strange circumstances, five MLAs from the ally Samata Party had rebelled against Marandi while George Fernandes, the then head of the Samata Party, had supported Marandi. For fear of the coalition breaking, the BJP-led government forced Marandi to step down from Chief Minister.

Marandi left the BJP angrily in 2006 and formed his own party, the Jharkhand Vikas Morcha, with five BJP MLAs. Since then, Marandi has been a loud voice in Jharkhand, criticizing the BJP government for corruption in the state.

The Jamshedpur by-election was on the first of July, 2011.

Arjun Munda, the Jamshedpur MLA, vacated the seat to become the BJP's Chief Minister. Marandi announced Kumar would fight in June. Kumar had been a lion in the area, everybody knew the former SP. When he ran out of funds and was planning to sell his house, all kinds of people, tea stall owners, shop owners, raised money.

Ajoy Kumar won by a huge margin, over 1.5 lakh votes, a margin even larger than the Chief Minister Arjun Munda who had earlier held the seat. The BJP lost what they felt had been a sure seat. They called Munda and others in to Delhi to break down what had happened.

As Superintendant of Police, East Singhum, Jamshedpur from 1994 to 1996, Kumar had taken down big mafia and drastically cut crime. For many years after he left Jamshedpur, the city was free of crime gangs. People remembered Kumar well.

When Kumar came in as SP, Jamshedpur was run by mafia, with the police often serving as accessories in crime. Contracts for roads were taken by the mafia. No one else bid, for fear of being shot down. The Tata's operate out of Jamshedpur; even contracts to pick up Tata Steel scraps were reserved for the mafia.

'They'd kill the Tata official in charge if they didn't get the contract. Kill one and the next guy will give you a contract,' Kumar explains. The town was so run over by contract killers, contractor mafia, and scrap mafia, that people didn't leave their houses after 6 p.m.. Anything might happen. And the police wasn't known to be of much help.

'You follow the 80-20 rule, on what impacts society. You need to focus not on small thefts but on professional crime. You need to go after them.'

Kumar began by pulling out case records gathering dust in the police station. For criminals who'd been convicted but were absconding, he began going after their property, because Kumar explains, 'you can attach the properties of criminals if they abscond'.

One of the first things the police did under him was

demolish the house of a big mafia head, nearly destroying it to the ground. 'We'd demolished a big symbol of criminality in the area,' Kumar says. After that, people became more cooperative. They realized the police was serious. Also, when they thought they'd lose their houses, the criminals would often surrender. They'd go into jail for the next eight to ten years, or they'd take flight and run away to other states.

As the police became active, there were many shoot outs in Jamshedpur between the police and gangs, raids on mafia hide-outs. The big gangs, as well as petty gangs, in the area slowly broke up as mafia were shot down, driven away or locked up.

The Bollywood movie *Ganga Jal*, in which Ajay Devgan plays a Superintendent of Police called 'Amit Kumar,' is said to be based on Ajoy Kumar's work in Jamshedpur. Devgan overhauls a corrupt police force and cracks down on gangs. In the movie, however, in a macabre twist, the city's people and police officers start taking the law into their own hands and use *ganga jal*, or acid, to blind criminals. That part of the story, Kumar clarifies, was taken from the Bhagalpur blindings in UP in the 70s. No such thing happened under him.

Kumar recounts what he saw when he came into the police in Bihar, 'You can rape a girl and walk around and nobody registers an FIR. Somebody's land gets stolen by a powerful landlord and the police does nothing. There's a dowry death and they (the police) will write the case report as if the girl was at fault.' Cases would be filed and when an arrest warrant was issued, no one would get arrested, because the police made money for sitting on warrants.

Kumar started monitoring cases, following up closely. 'You change the investigating officer if he sits on a case, you monitor the case.' He made sure no one was in the police lock-up without a good reason and actual warrants didn't lie around unused. He pushed officers to dispose cases within a fixed period of time. He pushed cases in court. 'When a case is stuck, you also need to talk to the judge, to expedite the case, and get them convicted.'

Kumar introduced the idea of 'community policing', encouraging people to help the police. He made himself accessible: 'If I heard a complaint, I would take action.'

Jamshedpur is a large district, 140 kilometers across. Kumar would camp at different stations from time to time to understand what was going on in different parts of the district.

In Jamshedpur city, he'd drive around the city on his motorcycle incognito. He'd walk up at tea stalls in plain clothes and listen to the talk there (the tea stall habit started back then). He'd listen in and find out what was happening in the city, what the police men were doing. 'People wouldn't recognize me. They just don't they expect the SP to be out there.' He'd hear about constables troubling people, taking bribes from shopkeepers, and so on.

'You can't expect to raise the morality. You can only make sure corruption is difficult,' the former Superintendant of Police tells me squarely, 'they don't stop doing it (being corrupt), but it (corruption) goes down.'

Apart from monitoring and cracking down, Kumar took positive steps to raise morale. 'We applied management principles to policing, though we didn't know it,' he says. Kumar started preventive maintenance of police equipment to prevent break-downs. He commissioned new toilets in the police quarters, made the barracks beautiful, cleaned, and white-washed police stations.

In a move to make police stations less intimidating, he put volley ball courts in police station compounds and encouraged local kids to play there.

***

Kumar remembers other challenges during his police tenure. During the Ram Navami and Muharram processions in Jamshedpur, the administration would be on tenterhooks for two days, afraid that communal tension would flare up.

'When a huge procession covers five kilometers in 18 hours, energies flying high, there's the chance people could molest someone, taunt someone, shout something at a temple or a mosque.' The SP had the right on paper to regulate processions, but no one had ever tried. Every SP in the past had been too scared of offending religious sentiments. During his term, Kumar declared that the processions 'will start at this time and finish at this time.' Without much protest, for the first time in Jamshedpur, the procession started at 8 a.m. and was done by the afternoon. 'We showed them we weren't afraid of religious fervor… I feel that reduced communal tension in the town. It continues to this day.'

Even as SP of Patna, earlier, Kumar hadn't been afraid of challenging even the Chief Minister Lalu Prasad Yadav when it came to law and order. Through the nineties, while Lalu Yadav was Chief Minister of Bihar, Kumar was SP of Patna and then of Jamshedpur. 'I used to talk straight, he liked my attitude. I had no trouble. He allowed me to work properly,' Kumar recalls.

When Kumar had just become SP of Patna in 1990, L.K. Advani led his Hindutva *yatra* through Patna. 'There were 4 lakh people on the road, the country had gone mad, imagine thousands of women doing arti of the *rath*.'

A few people in Lalu Prasad Yadav's government felt they should arrest Advani before he addressed people in Gandhi Maidan in Patna. Kumar recalls, 'I said, "I'm not afraid of arresting him. What's there in that? I am scared of the consequences for innocent people."' If he doesn't reach the meeting ground, people will spread rumors that he's been shot dead or something. There'll be riots.'

As Superintendent of Police, Patna, Kumar told the CM that his advice was to arrest Advani the next morning, after his speech. The Chief Minister finally took the SP's advice. 'You need to have the courage to say no to the CM of the state,' Kumar tells me, 'I don't know if you've seen four lakh people together: it's scary.'

Over time, Kumar won the Chief Minister Lalu Prasad Yadav's trust.

In the early nineties, when Kumar was SP of Patna, the Mandal Commission gave reservations to a new class of 'Other Backward Castes.' As a result, society became divided along anti-Mandal and pro-Mandal lines. In Bihar, a bloody war raged between upper caste gangs who were against the Mandal recommendations and the backward castes that would benefit from them.

Lalu Prasad Yadav was looked upon as a backward castes' leader. Kumar, as SP of Patna, is said to have killed Nunu Singh, an upper caste Bhumihar gang lord who'd been terrorizing OBC groups, in an encounter. The police force under Kumar also apparently came down heavily on other upper caste criminals in police encounters.

Even before he became SP of Patna, Kumar had gotten the President's gallantry award for service as a junior officer. He had led a shoot-out against a major gang that had been regularly robbing a village. It was an eight hour shoot out, from four in the morning to twelve noon. When the sun came out, the gang members realized there were only six police officers there and about forty to fifty gang members surrounded the police. Luckily, reinforcements arrived from the police station and Kumar and his team were saved. Four of the robbers' gang and one police died.

Kumar became known as Lalu Yadav's blue-eyed boy. He could do no wrong. Ajoy pushed his boundaries and talked straight to the Chief Minister. The Chief Minister respected him because he was unflinching in his work.

After Tata executives were killed and threatened in Jamshedpur, the Tata Steel Managing Director, J.J. Irani, asked the Chief Minister Lalu Prasad Yadav to urgently control crime in the Tata's headquarter city. It was Lalu Yadav who then moved Ajoy Kumar from Patna to Jamshedpur.

With the Chief Minister's backing, Kumar came down like a

hammer in Jamshedpur. Not only did he shake up the police, he didn't stop even when crime involved politicians. He conducted raids on Bihar Assembly Members' houses when he thought they were hiding criminals. He prosecuted cases against MLAs, put them behind bars. They would get out on bail and, often, get re-elected, Kumar tells me, but they did have to face the brunt of criminal proceedings.

Some time before he quit the police, however, Kumar ordered a raid on a Bihar State Minister, whom he suspected of hiding mafia. 'The raid was conducted by an Assistant Superintendant of Police, but ordered by me,' Kumar says. The Minister was a Rashtriya Lok Dal politician, a senior member of the Chief Minister's party. It was the first time he'd ordered a raid on a Minister's house. The police raided the house, but no criminals were found there.

Kumar felt the heat of what he'd done. He was called in by the Chief Minister; he was told, 'You have no idea what you're doing. You have no sense of proportion.' 'I could see where things were headed. I knew things wouldn't go my way for long,' Kumar says.

So when Kumar quit the police, the Tata group, which had benefitted so much from his work in Jamshedpur, snapped him up and he joined them as a General Manager.

***

After stories about encounters and shoot-outs, I can't believe that Kumar is the same man sitting in front of me now – in a formal grey suit with two kinds of business cards.

How did his wife and children dealt with being the SP's family, I ask Kumar.

'They'd threaten my wife a lot. We'd get a lot of blank calls and they'd try scaring the kids. They'd say we're going to kill you, or one of the kids,' he narrates. 'But Reena is left of center. She says you must do something with your life; your life must have a larger meaning,' Reena, Kumar's wife, is also in the civil services. 'Her uncle was the first IPS officer in India to be shot dead,' he adds, 'So she was very cool about it.'

The police was, really, Kumar's first rung to politics (though he could not have connected the dots back then). Anyone can imagine why Kumar would have wanted to enter politics. Power, for whatever noble or ignoble reasons, is a high. However, it's difficult to imagine why Kumar would have wanted to serve in the police in Bihar, when he could have become an orthopaedic surgeon; a much higher paid and more respectable job.

In Jamshedpur, too, rumors go around about why Kumar joined the police. Kumar joined the police after his brother was killed by the mafia, someone who lived in Jamshedpur in the mid-nineties tells me. People try to guess what motivated him to drive the police so passionately, court danger so maniacally.

'Sometimes they kill my wife, now it's my brother,' Kumar tells me, rubbishing the stories. 'These are all rumors. I joined the police because I saw the situation in Bihar, I was zapped and I thought I could do something for the country.'

Instead of studying to become a surgeon, Ajoy Kumar spent a year at the Police Academy on a whim. However, he still thought of returning to medical school. But when he got posted in Bihar for his field training, Kumar says, he saw what a terrible state the police was in. 'I decided to stick around and try to help. I saw this crazy amount of injustice – I was totally zapped by it! I said, this is India, so, I thought, let me stick around.'

There is, it seems, no other explanation for why Kumar did what he did. Perhaps he actually followed his curiosity and did what felt interesting at the time.

Ajoy talks about his future initiatives; he's trying to get the twenty-seven unregulated, low-quality private schools in Jamshedpur supported by DPS. 'My grandfather was a sharecropper, an illiterate farmer. I was the first generation who really had the chance to study properly, so I know the value of education.'

'I run and I read,' Kumar says of himself. He's organizing a cross-country run in every block in his constituency. Children will get free shoes and Bachendri Pal, the first Indian woman to climb Mount Everest, will inaugurate the run. 'You don't know what children take in, you don't know what impacts a kid's life,' Kumar shrugs, as he explains the event.

When Kumar's father was posted in Japan, in the Indian Foreign Service, he once brought home a John F. Kennedy piggy bank for his kids. It had the famous JFK quote: Ask not what your country can do for you, but ask what you can do for your country. Kumar shares thinking back, 'You never know what sticks with you, what affects you, years later.'

ASHOK
TANWAR

MANICK
TAGORE

The Rahul Clique

Tanwar and Tagore were among the first Student Congress and Youth Congress members to be picked by Rahul Gandhi for Parliamentary elections. They describe what its been like working with Rahul in the Youth Congress back-rooms.

ASHOK TANWAR
Indian National Congress (INC)
Sirsa Constituency, Haryana
Born on 12 February 1976
33 years of age at first election
Last victory margin of 35,499 votes

MANICK TAGORE
Indian National Congress (INC)
Virudhanagar Constituency, Karnataka
Born on 1 June 1975
34 years of age at first election
Last victory margin of 15, 764 votes

Ashok Tanwar says a shy hello as he walks slowly into his drawing room. His wife, Avantika Maken, welcomes me warmly as she breezes in and switches on the lights. Ashok, dressed in starched white, sits straight-backed on a sofa. Avantika, in a T-shirt, track pants and flip-flops, a big red patent-leather bag next to her, relaxes on the opposite side of the room. They make a contradictory, and yet endearing pair.

Ashok Tanwar is one of the five candidates from Rahul Gandhi's inner circle who was elected to the fifteenth Lok Sabha. Dubbed members of 'Team Rahul,' Jitendra Singh, Meeankshi Natarajan, Manick Tagore, Vijay Singla, and Ashok Tanwar, were elected to Parliament in the 2009 general election. All except Jitendra Singh had fought and won elections for the first time, hand-picked, as they say, by Rahul Gandhi.

Other players in Rahul's core group are said to be fellow politicians Prakash Joshi, Shakir Zaidi, Usha Rani, and Vishnu Nath.[1] Rahul and his core group have taken up the task of restructuring and strengthening the various organizations of the Congress party – the National Student's Union of India (NSUI), the Indian Youth Congress (IYC), and the All India Congress Committee (AICC).

Ashok Tanwar is Secretary of the All India Congress Committee and a former President of the Indian Youth Congress and the National Students Union of India. He's the first Youth Congress President to have been given a ticket to fight national elections.

Avantika Maken was formerly with the NSUI; that's how she and Ashok met. Given her political background and experience, Avantika is an energetic partner. Charged with opinions, she chips in as Ashok pauses over answers, finishing his sentences, contradicting him dramatically and, in a moment, scolding him with an easy affection.

Ashok Tanwar fought and won his first election from Sirsa, Haryana in 2009, defeating his main opponent, Sita Ram.

***

Sirsa is a difficult constituency, Ashok explains. Touching Punjab and Rajasthan and lying close to the Pakistan border, the region is fractured into many sub-communities and has a mottled social landscape.

'Many of its people migrated from Pakistan after the Partition,' Tanwar says. 'Then when the Bhakra Nangal dam was constructed, those displaced were rehabilitated here.'

There is also a large Scheduled Caste population, which again is comprised of many sub-castes and divisions. Within the Jats in Haryana, there are opposing groups called the Bagdis and the Deshwalis, a 'Rohtak and Sonipat mix.' The Bagdis and the Deshwalis clash on ideas of same-gotra (clan) marriage. The Bagdis want a narrow definition of same-clan marriage, while the Deshwalis want to ban all same-clan marriages. Most areas have either Bagris or Deshwalis, but, Tanwar says, both communities live in Sirsa.

Sirsa is also known for being the origin of the Dera Sacha Sauda (DSS), a social-spiritual organization that yields plenty of influence in the area. The Deras are a sub-sect of Sikhs that have amalgamated ideas from Sufism and Bhaktism. The DSS runs a large drug rehabilitation centre in Sirsa, a hospital, schools and colleges. They have a strong, structured leadership and tend to be at loggerheads with the mainstream Sikh Akal Takht, for their out-of-the-box representations of the Sikh religious head Guru Gobind Singh. 'In addition to the Deras – I have not seen such a mix – there are 150,000 other Sikhs,' Tanwar sighs.

Then there are the Radha Swamis, a fairly new faith that propagates spiritual awakening through *mantras* (chants), *satsangs* (singing) and devotion to a living s*wamy* (master).

'Until I entered Sirsa, I did not realize the complications of that constituency,' Ashok remarks. Most constituencies have a majority of one or two social groups who share the same aspirations and determine elections. Sirsa, on the other hand, is a patchwork of the new fangled, the displaced and the traditional, with strands of mutually incompatible religions, clans, and communities.

Politicians do talk about development and progress during elections. But in most constituencies in India, blatantly or more discreetly, candidates still connect with particular communities, reaching out to them and speaking to their demands. In Sirsa, the patchwork made this a challenge. 'To take everybody along with you is difficult,' Ashok says.

In the end, Ashok and Avantika say, Rahul Gandhi was the panacea who, with his bright, shining face full of promise, raised everyone's hopes. In the six weeks that led up to the 2009 general election, Rahul held 125 rallies across the country and one in Sirsa.

'Sirsa was such a difficult seat, that even senior leaders said,"If you are getting a ticket, say no!"' Avantika chuckles. 'And when we got to Sirsa, it was like – we know we're losing.' Ashok echoes his wife somberly, 'We were losing by 100,000 votes.' Then, Rahul Gandhi held his rally in Sirsa. 'All the people came from their villages just to see him, just to get a glimpse of him. That was the kind of magical thing he did,' Avantika says dramatically. 'The election turned after he came. We won only because of him.'

***

Ashok Tanwar comes from a modest family in Jhajjar, Haryana, not far from Sirsa. He mentions briefly that his father worked for Indian airlines; one of his brothers is a commercial artist and the other works for a private firm. Ashok himself thought he'd join the Indian Administrative Service or teach.

The Tanwars are Dalit, from the lowest caste community. 'People comment '*dekho woh chamaar hai*' (see, he's an untouchable) and I get very angry,' Avantika says. 'When you are in an important position *thoda sa kum hota hai* (it's a little less),' Tanwar reasons of the prejudice and harassment.

Traditionally, Dalits worked with leather as tanners and butchers; some cleared rubbish, others cleaned toilets and cleared carcasses. They were at the bottom of the social order, illiterate and shunned by other castes. Since independence, Dalits have been classified 'Scheduled Caste' and about one fourth of Parliament and Assembly seats, government jobs and government university seats in India are reserved for Scheduled Castes and Tribes (SC/ST). In the 2009 elections, for instance, out of a total of 543 seats in the Lok Sabha, eighty-four constituencies were reserved for SC candidates and forty-seven for ST candidates. Sirsa, Ashok's constituency, was one of the reserved seats in Haryana.

Dalits have become politically relevant, many have won political power; they've become educated and moved out of their social class. Yet, in rural India, caste remains an inescapable stigma.

'You are born in a community, you don't realize how important community is,' Ashok says quietly. 'My only advice to him was never lose your identity as a Dalit. Help your people. That should be your topmost priority,' Avantika adds passionately, 'You are a Dalit, and you will remain a Dalit, never be ashamed of it!'

Avantika's background could not be further from Ashok's. She comes of Congress lineage – her maternal grandfather was Shankar Dayal Sharma, the former President of India. Her parents, Lalit and Gitanjali Maken, were both active in the Congress party (in the early 1980s, her father Lalit was elected to the Lok Sabha from Delhi; her mother Gitanjali served as President of the NSUI). (Avantika's cousin, Ajay Maken, with whom Avantika has an antagonistic relationship, is also a Congress MP and current Sports Minister.)

In 1985, when Avantika was just six years old, Lalit and Gitanjali Maken were shot and killed by three Sikh Khalistani militants outside their home. Lalit Maken had been one of 200 names on the People's Union for Civil Liberties (PUCL) list – PUCL had listed the names of people who allegedly led mobs and killed Sikhs after Indira Gandhi's assassination by her Sikh bodyguards in 1984.

An only child, Avantika grew up fiery and emotional, often talking of how she was going to 'kill her parents' murderers.'[2] Then, in a strange turn a couple of years ago, she decided to forgive one her father's killers and appeal for his release. (The other two had already been hanged.) Kuki Gill had been an eighteen-year-old science student when he planned the Maken murder. When Avantika met Gill, he'd been in prison for seventeen years. She says she met his family and felt a rare sense of compassion, a need to forgive and to allow herself to 'move on.'

Avantika had known at a young age that the Congress – the party her parents had been dedicated to – would be her inheritance and her future. When she was only fifteen, against her protective grandfather's advice, Avantika joined the NSUI school students program. In college, she became NSUI National Secretary at nineteen and General Secretary at just twenty-three.

At the time, Ashok was studying History (he did a BA from Delhi University and was doing an MA at the left-leaning Jawaharlal Nehru University, known better as JNU). At DU, Ashok says, power alternated between the Congress-led NSUI and the Akhil Bhartiya Vidya Parishad (ABVP), the Bharatiya Janata Party (BJP) student wing.

'But when I joined JNU, I felt the NSUI there is very weak. I must contribute. I thought I must give some time. And when I started giving time and I contested elections, I just got into it and I just could not take myself out.' In JNU, the Communist Party tends to win elections. Over the last four decades, JNU has seen the Congress and the ABVP each come to power only once. Tanwar became the Congress Unit President of JNU and contested the Student Union elections. He didn't win, but he got the most votes an NSUI candidate had gotten in JNU in eighteen years.

The campus, he says, was crucial in shaping him. 'Now, they don't say it as much, but they used to say that JNU *mein toh har aadmi* politician *hai* (in JNU, everyone is a politician). The culture there was full of debate and discussion and I think that openness gave me confidence.'

'You weren't influenced by the Left at JNU?' I ask. The university has produced Sitaram Yechury and Prakash Karat of the Communist Party of India (Marxist), or the CPI(M), the grand old men of the Left. 'There are a few good things about the Left but they just talk. They don't implement. That is the problem with the Left. But otherwise, it inspires you, it attracts you *ki bahut achchi baat kar rahe hai* (what they say sounds very good). That's why they've had power for a very long time.'

Avantika and Ashok met when Ashok was made an office bearer in the NSUI.

'I used to hate him!' Avantika says excitably, short of breath. 'He was a very simple man and he used to come in the bus. And he used to wear *kolhapuri* chappals and a shirt and pants. I used to host dinners and Meenakshiji (Meenakshi Natarajan) used to tell me, '*Yaar,* Ashok *ko bhi bula lo*' (you should invite Ashok). And I used to say, '*woh bolta wolta to hai nahi, chodo na* (what's the point, he barely speaks!)'

'After he became President,' Avantika remembers, heating up, 'even I wanted to become NSUI President. I was competing with him, I wanted to become President, he wanted to become President, and we both were in the race, but he ended up winning,' she smiles. 'After that, I think he didn't want to accommodate me as General Secretary' she says hotly. 'He was docile and I was very aggressive.'

Avantika grins, 'Under a lot of pressure, Ashok appointed me General Secretary and he gave me the worst states. I wanted Punjab or Bombay-Goa; he gave me the North-East. Travelling to the North-East for a woman is very difficult. And he attached a secretary to me who was from the North-East. So, naturally, the Secretary knew more than I did and I felt I'd be a big failure in front of a junior,' she says, still burning at the thought.

'What happened is, during the long process,' Avantika shares, calming down, 'during the last Delhi University elections, we worked together very closely. Both of us wanted that by hook or by crook, we (the Congress) should win this election. That's the time we became very close. That's when I realized he's a very simple man and that in today's day and age I won't find anybody like him.'

Their courtship was sudden and romantic. They'd go for long walks, Avantika says, remembering 'the liberal JNU atmosphere, lots of trees and *vada pao*.'

Aside from the differences in family and upbringing, Avantika – at the time she started seeing Ashok – was also a divorced mother of two.

'This hardly happens, that two colleagues get married,' she pauses, 'I have not heard of any of our other colleagues marrying each other. My parents did that and maybe one or two other people.' People tend to marry within their community, however, Avantika's parents had met and married in the NSUI, so the decision made sense to her.

She switches gears and jibes Ashok for being too simple and too much of a workaholic, talking about how he 'does the *jhadu pocha*' (dusting and sweeping) when he wakes up every morning, how they have no security and how Ashok sometimes walks home at night with his cloth *choga* slung over his shoulder, all the way from the Youth Congress office.

Ashok is largely quiet, very still as his wife speaks. He watches her intently, listens and smiles at her teasing. He seems to enjoy her carefree glibness and the drama of her version of their story.

'Did you actually put her in charge of the North East for revenge?' I ask Ashok.

'Not going to say anything,' Ashok mutters sportingly.

***

In the 2009 elections, nine people from the Youth Congress, chosen by Rahul Gandhi, were given Congress tickets to fight elections; five of them won. Some months after I meet Ashok and Avantika, I catch up with Manick Tagore from Tamil Nadu. Like Ashok Tanwar, and Meenakshi Natarajan, Tagore is one of the first time MPs from the Youth Congress clique.

Jitendra Singh, the General Secretary of the AICC and a close aide to Rahul Gandhi, first called Tagore and asked him to meet the Election Screening Committee head. 'Rahulji called later and asked, "How is the Virudhunagar election going to be?"' Manick grins broadly as he recalls the moment, the phone conversation almost drowned out by a chopper in the background. Manick replied confidently, 'I will win, Sir.' Rahul Gandhi laughed and said, 'All the best, man!'

Though he's worked his way up, Manick is not without political lineage. Tagore's grandfather had been a Member of the Legislative Assembly (MLA) in Karnataka. His father was a school teacher. His uncle, EAS Natchiappan, however, was also an MP, and defeated the Congress' stalwart P. Chidambaram, (then with the Tamil Maanila Congress), in the 1999 election from Sivaganga.

In 1988, when Manick was twelve, then Prime Minister Rajiv Gandhi visited his school and made an impression on him. At seventeen, Manick joined the NSUI, and in 1998, at twenty-two, came to Delhi as the 'back room' man for the Delhi University elections. Tagore was later moved from the NSUI to the Youth Congress and, in 2007, was noticed by Rahul Gandhi for his dedication to the party. He was entrusted with building the Youth Congress in various states, including his home state of Karnataka. Somewhere along the way, Tagore also managed to get a law degree from Tamil Nadu.

In the Virudhunagar election, Tagore defeated V Gopalswamy (also known as Vaiko), a two-term pro-LTTE (Liberation of Tamil Tigers) Lok Sabha MP alternatively called a 'giant', a 'champion' and a 'monster' in the area. It was a narrow and shocking win.

'Vaiko used to only talk about the Lankan Tamils,' Manick said after his election, 'It led to voter fatigue on the issue... Voters are more interested in what they will get out of the elections, not larger issues. Our panchayats are more interested in getting the colour TV sets promised by the state government, and in NREGA.'[3]

Tagore is plump, confident, and relaxed. He doesn't embellish his words.

Before Rahul Gandhi came in, he explains, everything was done on 'recommendation' by senior leaders. 'Nobody (in the Youth Congress) was assured of their future.' Any top leader – the President of the Congress Working Committee, the President of the AICC, the party leader of a state – could nominate his or her favourite to a Youth Congress post.

There was no concept of grooming for leadership. 'If some leader is unhappy with me, he doesn't like my face, he likes your face, you will be given the opportunity.' The dominant culture, as Manick tells it, was of cultivating sycophants.

After Rahul Gandhi took charge of the Youth Congress in 2007, there were days of brainstorming. 'He (Rahul Gandhi) has spent days and days together to just involve everybody,' says Tagore's cohort Ashok Tanwar. He'd have office bearers from the Youth Congress and others, professionals with experience building organizations, come together.

Soon, the Youth Congress started on what Tagore calls its 'leader producing mission.' New rules were laid out and a state-wide talent hunt began.

Earlier, the Youth Congress elected Block and District Presidents. The system was changed to elect *Panchayat* (village), Assembly and Lok Sabha Presidents to mirror actual elections. The *Panchayat* level was added to bring the Youth Congress to the grassroots. The *Panchayat* posts, Tagore explains, are the most accessible. Each *Panchayat* is only about 1,000 people, so if you can convince a couple of hundred people you know to vote for you, you can win. Now, the *Panchayat* President post is the first rung of leadership in the Youth Congress.

All the *Panchayat* representatives then elect the Assembly leaders and the Assembly elects the State Presidents. All the State Presidents elect the Lok Sabha representatives, who will then, all together, elect the Youth Congress President. It will, eventually, be a bottom-up chain.

'Very, very few people,' Tanwar mulls thoughtfully, 'have ever been given tickets in the past.' Manick adds, 'It was hard to believe. Where is the opportunity? Which party gives you opportunity? You tell me, how can you become a leader? You don't know how you can enter the democratic process' he asserts, explaining the momentousness of the Youth Congress stance.

With the idea of a democratic overhaul, the Youth Congress had its pilot membership drive in Punjab. From 30,000, the membership in Punjab rose to 3,50,000 as they broadcast the new system; in Gujurat the numbers swelled from 50,000 to 6,50,000. In states where the Congress has been weak, Tanwar and Tagore talk about how the Congress upped the ante for other parties – the Akali Dal in Punjab, the BJP in Gujarat, the Dravida Munetra Kazhagam (DMK) in Tamil Nadu. Out of the blue, the Congress seemed to be handing out opportunity.

The Youth Congress is suddenly flush with new members but the challenge now, according to Ashok Tanwar, lies in keeping them engaged. 'Most people are coming in with great expectations. How do we involve them? How do we channel them?'

To organize the tide of new members, the IYC brought in the Foundation for Advanced Management of Elections (FAME), an organization started by former Election Commissioners. FAME has been training Youth Congress members to manage booths at internal elections. It has been trying to excite the new recruits on government welfare programs – the Right to Information Act and the Employment Guarantee Act – as part of the Congress *Aam Aadmi Ke Sipahi* (Common Man's Soldiers) campaign.

Of course, the voluntary work and social training are not the main attractions to the IYC. The IYC will attract large numbers only if it is seen as a recruiting ground for future politicians. In the 2011 State Assembly elections in Kerala, West Bengal, Assam and Tamil Nadu, Rahul Gandhi handed out tickets to Youth Congress members and office holders. (In Kerala, five of the seventeen IYC candidates won. In West Bengal four out of seven won, in Assam six out of seven. In Tamil Nadu, despite its 14,00,000 Youth Congress membership, Chief Minister J. Jayalalitha swept all ten IYC candidates out.) But the fact that these Youth Congress members are in the running, according to Tanwar and Tagore, has given the organization real credibility.

Manick describes Rahul Gandhi's management style. 'RG's greatest strength is that he doesn't set your targets. He is a democratic person. He lets you set your own goals and decide how you're going to achieve them.'

The young Gandhi has been criticized for a lot – for not leading from the front, for being a shy and hesitant speaker, for not being visible in times of crisis for the Congress. Manick gives a window into Rahul's strengths – Rahul Gandhi may not be a lot of things, but he is a benevolent manager, a low-key locker-room strategy man.

Despite the efforts of FAME and its guidelines, internal elections in the IYC have not been smooth. There has been all the pandemonium and hoodwinking of a regular election, with both heroes and hoodlums emerging from the process.

'One of the biggest challenges is still the influence of local leaders.' Tagore shares. 'If I am a *sarpanch* (village head) or an MLA, I can work to defeat a person, or I can promote my brother or sister.' Local politicians can easily exercise their influence on people to manipulate the Youth Congress elections. So, in some states, candidates who are sons of somebody or other and have had nothing to do with the Youth Congress have somehow been elected to the Youth Congress Lok Sabha seats.

And of course, there is the issue of funds, with flush candidates spending extravagantly on Youth Congress elections to ensure their wins. Candidates have reported spending upwards of forty-five Lakhs to fight elections for Youth Congress Lok Sabha President.[4]

Still, for now, there is a swell of pride in the Indian Youth Congress. 'There is a vast difference between the fourteenth and fifteenth Lok Sabhas,' a pleased Tagore points out. 'The fourteenth was all about the big leaders' sons. The fifteenth Lok Sabha includes names like Meenakshi Natarajan, Ashok Tanwar, Manick Tagore, people who've worked without lineage, people who've been given an opportunity by Rahul Gandhi.'

Rahul Gandhi calls many of the Youth Congress nominees himself to tell them they will be fighting elections. How these names are chosen no one seems to know – it is not a transparent or democratic process (Tanwar and Tagore had no idea they'd be asked). Even as the Youth Congress strives for democratization, its mother-ship Congress party is not democratic. Real decisions – who will get tickets for elections, even from the Youth Congress, who will be allotted what ministry – are still taken mysteriously.

'Why do you think Rahul Gandhi chose you?' I ask Manick.

Tagore answers promptly. 'There must be a system, parameters. I don't know what they were. I worked fifty-three days nonstop in Punjab and forty-eight days in Gujarat; maybe he chose me for my commitment. What I can say is that Rahul Gandhi doesn't go by emotions; he goes by a greater logic. Without the groundwork being done, he would not have given this opportunity to me – not because he likes my face or something.'

For now, despite the grey zones, in the Youth Congress, there is a feeling that the commitment to change systems, to create opportunities, is real. 'In our meetings,' Manick Tagore adds, 'he (Rahul Gandhi) says, this is only ten per cent of the change you have seen. There will be more.'

Notes

1 Aurangzeb Naqshbandi, 'Rahul's Team Opts Party Work over Ministerial Berths,' *Hindustan Times*, 28 May 2009

2 Avantika Maken, 'I said, hang him… now, I want him freed,' *Tehelka*, 23 April 2005

3 'Mom made payasam on learning about Prabhakaran's death,' *Mumbai Mirror*, 21 May 2009

4 Samarth Saran, 'It's not lineage that matters in the Youth Congress, it is the moolah,' *Tehelka*, 24 August 2011

The Maverick

Swamy dropped down from the tech worlds of California and Bangalore to join politics. He took an experimental 'year-off' to fight elections.

JANARDHANA SWAMY

Bharatiya Janata Party (BJP)
Chitradurga Constituency, Karnataka
Born on 4 June 1968
41 years of age at first election
Last victory margin of 1,35,571 votes

Swamy has a big grin, a round optimistic face, and sturdy, broad shoulders. He looks at home with a thick laptop open in front of him on an otherwise empty desk.

Few, even among members of his own Bharatiya Janata Party (BJP) seem to have heard of him. I first heard of Swamy when I called Arun Jaitley, the BJP's election strategist, to ask which of the party's under-forty MPs I should meet. 'There's Janardhana Swamy in the South,' he said. There was a twang of curiosity in the way Jaitley said 'Janardhana Swamy' that made me think I must track him down.

Swamy comes from humble beginnings and has had a meteoric journey. Trained as a scientist, Swamy speaks of his election and his life like a wild experiment, one that could have gone this way or that, and laughs incredulously at everything.

Swamy grew up in Chitradurga in the southern state of Karnataka, an only child. His father was a retired primary school teacher, his mother a home maker. (Swamy's family, I learn later – he doesn't mention this – are also Dalit or Scheduled Caste.) Chitradurga was, in Swamy's words, 'a very rural and very poor, very small village.' His family, like all the others in the village, lived without electricity until Swamy was in the tenth grade.

Swamy doesn't speak with bitterness as he recounts the difficulties he had studying without proper light. He buzzes with a nervous, buoyant energy, and clicks through his computer to pull up old speeches he's given to students to inspire them.

Academically curious and bright, Swamy studied engineering and specialized in a subject called Instrumentation Technology, before moving to the Indian Institute of Science (IISC) in Bangalore to do a Master's degree in electronics and communication engineering. After IISC, Swamy worked in Bangalore for about four years in what he calls 'integrated circuit design,' applied to cellular phones, computers, and other compact technology. After a couple of years there, he got recruited to California.

On the west coast, in California, Swamy worked at Cadence Design Systems, a large electronics systems design company. He focused on system and chip design. 'Mainly,' he explains rapidly, 'how do you put the entire computer into one single chip?' He made a couple of inventions and got one patent for a system that tests 'complex integrated security systems.'

Swamy did a stint at Sun Microsystems, where he was promoted to take care of an array of servers. 'It was a very successful program. I was heading the entire engineering for this high volume server, taking care of the electrical, mechanical, thermal, manufacturing, software, testing – the entire thing. It was a very enjoyable and rewarding job. There were about 50,000 engineers and just four or five engineers who were the brains behind this very sophisticated computer. I was one of them,' Swamy says, matter of factly, a current of energy running through him.

In America, Swamy was struck by the slick wide roads, the public spaces, the infrastructure, the quality of people's lives. What impressed him most of all was the amount the country – government as well as private companies – invested in the research and development of new technologies.

A turning point came in 2009, when Swamy, well entrenched at Sun Microsystems, decided to quit the US. 'All this time, while I was enjoying my job, I was always thinking about where I came from, and who made me what I am today, and what are my obligations?' It gnawed at Swamy that the technologies he was working on were so confidential and proprietary that they could not leave the US and be shared with engineers in India. It made him question himself: 'What am I doing? Is it in the right direction in helping my own people? The answer was: No. So then my immediate question was how do I prevent this?'

Back in India, Swamy joined Dell as the head of its hardware division in Bangalore. Later, he was recruited to set up a new hardware division at the Computer Information System Company, CISCO.

'Then, one year, it occurred to me, I should join public governance,' he narrates. Swamy throws this out as if it's something that just occurs to people – 'I should join the group which decides the future of this country and its people.'

'I didn't know all the answers, so then, I started the questions: What *is* politics?' The questions tumbled out. 'How is it going to work? How do I get my ticket? How do I work on winning? I didn't even know what I didn't know! I thought, I'm forty years old, I'm going to retire at about sixty, I will have ample time. I can afford *one year* in my *entire* working life to experiment. So, that's how I came into politics,' Swamy finishes, grinning broadly.

***

'So one thing is clear, why I joined politics?' Swamy asks, leaning back in his chair. 'Because I was obligated to serve this country, because I took so much from ordinary people who made me what I am today, so is there anything I can do to give back?' he recaps, zipping over his logic.

'I did not build the engineering college; I did not build the Indian Institute of Science. It's the tax payer's money. And who pays tax? All of us, including a farmer who does not have the basic income to sustain his life. He goes to a medicine store and buys cough syrup for his sick wife. He pays a tax on that.'

'And why politics?' Swamy asks himself. 'Why not other avenues?' Swamy has this Socratic way of thinking through questions – he'll ask himself a question and reverse into a crate of other questions to clarify his original question.

'I thought this was an ultimate demonstration of leadership and you can impact wider segment of society,' he answers himself, matter-of-factly, 'If I'm in the corporate world, I will be impacting a product there and I wanted to do a lot more than that.'

'It was 3 June 2007 – June 4 was my birthday – that was the day I decided to go into politics.'

Swamy had already joined the BJP by then. On his birthday, a couple of his relatives and friends from his home town were visiting in Bangalore. They jibed at him. 'People like you, get educated and leave the country. We're glad at least you came back.' '*Yeah*, that's the most I could do,' Swamy replied. 'Why not come and help us? Why don't you consider the upcoming parliamentary election?' his relatives persisted.

'Just a blind idea, Okay, today, how about we climb the

Mount Everest?' Swamy grins. 'Such a remote idea. But then, after a while, I thought – why not?'

That was when Swamy, in his maverick style, decided to take a shot at the General Election, without having a clue how he'd go about it. 'I thought,' he says, 'okay, what is this election? It is something called a *Parliamentary election.*' He grins. 'They call it Member of Parliament, MP... I started educating myself, I went to Wikipedia and started reading, what is an MP? And what is the distinction between an MP and an MLA, a Member of the Legislative Assembly? How do these things work?'

'And then, people started telling me, there are so many *taluks* (district subdivisions)...I started writing down, o*kay*, how many *taluks* are there in Chitradurga, tell me? General knowledge, right?' he chuckles. 'I had the urge and the good intentions to help, but I was like an expert driver in a new town. So I had to look at the map all over, right?' he says, gloating fondly over the madness of the time.

'So then it started like, what is this ticket?' he says, 'In the US, you get a ticket when you do traffic mistakes!'

'And then they said nomination is called the ticket and you have to get it. I was wondering what colour it might be?' he quips, getting into the swing of things.

'Before going to the US, the only ticket we knew was the movie ticket,' Swamy adds. 'And after going to the US, you know why they give you the tick-ate. Talk of the tick-ate – you have done something wrong. The police have given you the *tick-ate*! And here, they were telling me you have to get the ticket again!'

'So then?' I ask, grinning.

'So then, I called up my friends to say, you know, I'm trying to do this. They were all so scared,' he laughs, remembering the moment, 'They thought, for a minute, what are you talking about? Are you okay?'

Eventually, they pulled together. 'Fine, what does it take to win an election? Or how do you get a ticket? Why should anybody give you a ticket? That's the question we started asking ourselves.'

Swamy reverses the question. 'Let's say you are the person who is supposed to give the ticket, what are you going to look for? Okay, you have winnability – that means if they give you the ticket you should win. Okay, what makes you a winner? Do you have a political background? *No*. Do you have lots of money? *No*. Do people know you? *No*. Did you ever contest before? *Noo*. Was your father an MP or MLA? *Noo*! Then, um, are you doing any social work? *Noo*.' Swamy is chuckling now. 'Then you have, you know, little chance of really getting it.'

'But deep inside, the question I had was,' he continues, now in a more serious vein, 'if you are good, if you are educated, if you are young, if you are concerned, why would people *not* choose you?' However, the real obstacle remained: 'How do you convince the authorities that you are a good product, therefore people will choose you, therefore you should get the ticket?'

By this time, Swamy had already narrowed in on the BJP as his political platform. A few years earlier, he'd wanted to meet with the BJP Chief Minister (CM) of Karnataka, B.S. Yeddyurruppa, to discuss technology and farming. The CM had given him time and listened to his ideas.

He'd joined the party in Bangalore and had been recruited to start its Information Technology wing.

Eventually, Swamy and his crew of relatives and friends went to the BJP leaders. 'What is the probability? Can you give us a ticket?' The BJP asked all the anticipated questions, and said, in Swamy's words, 'you scored zero.' Swamy laughs. 'Because the traditional winnability factors are what I mentioned before, I was nowhere close to any of them.' 'Then we said it is the *people* who should demonstrate that they want you. Then the leaders would feel, you know what, this is the guy people want, let's give him a *tick-ate*.'

They didn't, however, have a lot of time. It was a big constituency, and people had never heard of Janardhana Swamy. Some thought he'd just dropped down from America and stuck his foot in the election. There was bad mouthing; people said, 'this guy doesn't even know Kannada.' Even though, Swamy grins, 'I probably know better Kannada than many people there.' There was a lot of competition – twenty-five aspirants from within the BJP itself were vying for a nomination ticket.

Swamy, and his relatives and friends, started pottering about the constituency. They'd go to Chitradurga, about three hours from Bangalore, and hang around. Ten, twenty people would gather and they'd start talking. 'I had to do this while I was working,' Swamy says, 'so it was during the weekends, like a hobby.'

But then he realized that weekends wouldn't cut it and decided to quit his job. 'I told CISCO that I'm quitting my Senior Engineering Manager position.' And, Swamy remembers, 'in the whole division, people were laughing, like, you know, what are you doing? You're quitting your job for doing these things? I said, like I told you, it's a controlled experiment, I have to do it.'

Swamy traveled around Chitradurga relentlessly. 'Slowly,' he says, 'I think people started noticing what I had to offer.' In all the ad-hoc meetings, he'd tell people who he was, his concern for Chitradurga, where he'd been, why he'd came back. 'I think people saw the sincerity in my statements and they started aligning themselves towards me. I think they considered three factors – young, educated, concerned.'

Swamy finally got his ticket, just fourteen days before the election. 'The BJP had never ever won in Chitradurga, it had always been the Congress Party. And I had no political background. Within the State BJP, there was a clear assumption that we would lose.'

However, Swamy – and the BJP – won, that too by a huge margin. And that, perhaps, explains the twinge of wonder and curiosity in Arun Jaitley's voice when he said 'Janardhana Swamy' on the phone.

During the elections, Rahul Gandhi came to canvass for

the Congress candidate, around the same time BJP leader LK Advani came to support Swamy. 'Advaniji talked a lot about me,' Swamy says, smiling unabashedly. 'But, those were tense moments...nonetheless, it was a great honour.'

'I have his speech,' says Swamy and moves towards his laptop. A video shows a big podium, lots of background noise. L.K. Advani talks in Hindi about Swamy, a '*hon haar* (whole hearted) engineer' who can do a lot for the country. Swamy grins. Like most people in the audience, he didn't – and still doesn't – understand a word of Hindi. Advani continues his long-winded speech on the invention of the wheel, the internet, and so on. A Kannada translator pipes up after Advani.

Swamy managed his campaign with his own funds, and those of his family and friends. 'I didn't know what actually makes you feel you might win; I had no prior experience. I was only saying, I just want to win with one vote minimum. If I get two votes, it'll be a bonus.'

Janardhana Swamy was hugely surprised. The margin of his win in Chitradurga, Karnataka, was one lakh, thirty-five thousand votes. 'The second largest for the BJP,' Swamy murmurs, and pokes into his computer. 'Yaa, one lakh, thirty-five thousand, five seventy-one.'

***

Swamy says he was drawn to the BJP because of former Prime Minister Atal Behari Vajpayee – his National Highways program, the nuclear tests, the scientific approach of his initiatives. He felt the BJP was intellectually oriented; he saw it as valuing 'true contribution rather than father-son kind of politics.'

A lot has changed since Vajpayee's heyday in power. In 2004, Vajpayee lost the general election. In 2009, despite Swamy's win, LK Advani and the BJP lost the general election again.

Recently, the BJP government in Karnataka has stewed in

controversy. The party, in the state, is driven by the Reddy brothers of Bellary, a district bordering Andhra Pradesh. One brother is MP from Bellary and also Revenue Minister, Karnataka. The second brother is Mayor, Bellary and the third is Tourism and Infrastructure Development Minister, Karnataka. The Reddy trio control thousands of crores of mining in iron-rich Bellary, bordering Andhra Pradesh and Karnataka, and apparently support, and control, the BJP's candidates in the Bellary district elections and the Karnataka Assembly.

In late 2009, the Reddys bickered with CM Yeddyurrappa over his taxes on mining and his 'interference' in the state's Ministries. They demanded that he step down. (The BJP stood by Yeddyurrappa and mollified the Reddys.) Then, in early 2010, the Reddys were again embroiled in a scandal over illegal mining in Bellary. The Opposition demanded they quit. Eventually, Yeddyurrappa issued a statement that backed the Reddys and insisted that the allegations were rubbish.

In late 2010, Yeddyurappa himself landed in a scam – for selling 500 crores worth of state land cheap to his two sons. In a strange dance, the Karnataka state MLAs, the Rashtriya Swayamsevak Sangh (RSS), even the Reddy brothers (who didn't want to risk the BJP government in the state being dissolved), supported Yeddyurrappa. Yeddyurrappa, in his own defense, insisted previous Congress and Janata Dal CMs had been far more corrupt. After hectic flying back and forth from Delhi and meetings with the BJP 'high command,' the BJP asked Yeddyurrappa to stay and everything went back to normal. Later, in mid-2011, Yeddyurruppa was finally pushed out of the Chief Minister's chair, when Lokayukta Justice Santosh Hedge submitted a report indicting him *and* the Reddy brothers in a major mining scam. Yeddyurrappa finally resigned, installing his own man as CM as we went.

Later, in October 2011, *The Bangalore Mirror* broke a story that figured Swamy too in one of Yeddyurruppa's land dealings.[1] Almost immediately after he was elected MP, Swamy was allotted a 4,000 Sq. Ft. piece of land in upscale Bangalore under then Chief Minister Yeddyurruppa's preferential quota, *The Mirror* said. To get the land, Swamy swore that he had no other property in Bangalore, whereas, *The Mirror* reported, he has three other plots in the city. Swamy reportedly paid 7.6 lakhs for the land worth 4 crore. 'Politics changed the man who had promised to change the polity,' *The Mirror* stated. Swamy defended himself in the paper saying the other land he had was a 'total waste' and he wanted the new land to build a home.

When I first met Janardhana Swamy in early 2010, the Reddy brothers' public battle with Yeddyurrappa was in the news. The BJP itself was in a shambles, after their defeat in the election and the new head of the party (Nitin Gadkari) was yet to be named.

Swamy attributed the resounding blow to the BJP in 2009, to 'confused branding.' 'What does India stand for?' Swamy asked. The BJP, at the time, hadn't managed to answer this question and work it into their campaign. 'See, you have to produce a product people want to buy.'

'We didn't bring out the deficiencies in the Opposition. Some of the other things which I notice,' Swamy reflected, 'are consistency in our messaging and coherency. At the end of the day, we were lacking clarity – why people should vote for the BJP.'

'Sometimes a Party has distributed leadership and distributed decision making,' he opined, 'That sends mixed signals to the voters.'

When I met Swamy, however, the news about his own land dealings had not broken and I haven't been able to reach Swamy for comment since. As I think about it, it was an unfortunate slip up by a man who seems to have a lot of energy. I can only hope he doesn't prove himself lazy in years to come, fattened and jaded by politics.

***

After the adventure-filled story of his campaign, Swamy seems drained of energy. Comedic till now, he collects himself and becomes quiet and serious, talking about his work in the constituency.

He peers into his computer, that most organized archive, and clicks through files. 'My constituency,' 'Development,' – each file is neatly labeled. From one of a myriad folders, Swamy opens up an excel spread sheet with a grid of projects and stages. 'So myself and our DC,' he says, thoughtfully, 'we are tracking several things here.' The DC is the District Deputy Commissioner, head of the staff at the district level in Chitradurga.

Swamy stabs at the chart. 'Look, there's the improvement of the water supply for the entire district, a water table study, there's an Upper Bhadra Project, a six and a half thousand crore project.' The Upper Bhadra project involves bringing drinking water from a dam to *taluks* in Chitradurga. 'There's railway connectivity from my place to the capital city. An engineering college, a Kendriya Vidyalaya. There's tourism-related activity, healthcare-related activity, the construction of a trauma center.' Swamy says, meditatively quiet, 'There are also several things not on the list.'

'So, on a higher level,' Swamy says, with barely held excitement, 'the Indian Institute of Science, which is hundred years old and the number one institution in the country, has decided to open its second branch. In South India, in Karnataka, in my constituency.'

Swamy went to IISc and he attributes a gigantic part of his success to the training he had there. 'You know the Indian Institute of Technology (IIT)?' he asks. 'Well, the IIT is ranked 30 or 40 in the world. The IISc is ranked 20 in the world.'

It's the first time, he says, an IISc alum, has become a Lok Sabha MP. 'It is a science and engineering oriented community, so they don't really get into active politics... So it's a rare opportunity, right? I want to makes sure it takes good shape.'

Another academic institution, the DRDO (Defence Research and Development Organization) with an Unmanned Aircraft Testing Center is coming to Chitradurga, Swamy says. And BARC is coming, the famed Bhabha Atomic Research Center.

Chitradurga has thousands of acres of government land available, Swamy explains, and it's also very well connected by road to Bangalore. 'It has been told several times to the CM also,' he says, glowing, 'that it's good that we have the right MP there who can oversee these things. These are substantial projects. This is the first time,' Swamy intones, 'that these things are happening in my constituency.'

***

Swamy had come into politics to help farmers, to bring technology to farming in India. He'd first gotten in touch with Karnataka CM Yeddyurrappa years ago to talk with him about this. What happened to that initiative? I ask him.

Swamy shuffles through folders, concentrated on his computer. As he clicks on an icon, dramatic show music fills the room. 'The name of the game is speed and efficiency,' booms an American presenter's voice, 'whatever the crop, there's truly a custom machine to harvest it.'

The video shows a huge cotton field in California and an aeroplane flying over it, spraying something. 'Digital Globe Information Company operates the world's highest resolution commercial photography satellite,' the commentary explains.

'That's the company where I was working,' Swamy interjects, 'I was the Chief Engineer at Sun Microsystems.'

Before harvest, cotton farmers in the US apply a chemical called diffolio to their crop to make it shed its leaves, Swamy explains, pausing the video. Now, the satellite pictures let them know where the crop is more or less dense and a plane, linked to the satellite and a GPS (Global Positioning System), automatically squirts the right proportion of diffolio on the crop.

The satellite pictures allow farmers to take 'management decisions,' to identify weak and strong spots on the fields and to respond accordingly.

'This is the farmer we have to compete with, right?' Swamy points out.

'Even if a hundred farmers get together they cannot solve this,' Swamy laments. 'Who is going to launch the satellite? This is not solved by farmers. It is solved by government and scientists for farmers. That outlook is missing in our political scenario today.'

India has the highest area in the world – nine million lakh hectares – under cotton production, yet the lowest yield per hectare. Cotton productivity has climbed somewhat with new varieties of Genetically Modified (GM) seeds, but India still yields less than half of the cotton that the US, China, Turkey, Australia, and Israel yield per hectare. (In 2007, the Indian yield per hectare was 1.03 tons of cotton, whereas the US produced 2.83 tons and China 4.21 tons per hectare.)

'Rather than saying, okay, we will give you more crop insurance, we will give you drought coverage, we will waive your loans, rather than these kind of artificial, election oriented tricks, they need to think much more seriously. Why did we not invest in technological innovations in this country?' Swamy asks frantically. 'At least at this point, we have to consider intellectual development, innovations and discoveries made in India by Indians on Indian soil.'

'They solve very tough problems with technology,' Swamy tells me; he fast-forwards through videos that show machines husking rice while it's still in the fields, machines shaking trees just the right amount to make only ripe fruit fall out of them, machines catching and sorting all the ripe fruit that falls.

'You have to institutionalize. Put the right people to do the farming. Put scientists, engineers, and MBA graduates in farming!' Swamy holds forth passionately. The fragmented land holdings, he says, could be leased by the government into a company, with farmers holding shares in the company. 'Let's say you were getting 20,000 rupees per acre, these people should be able to guarantee you 30,000 rupees per acre.'

Swamy is against GM crops because he's not sure about their long-term effects. Still, he hankers for more research on hybrid crops, on new technology and techniques. He brushes off the annual Parliament debate on farmer's debt and farmer suicides – the kind depicted in last year's sleeper hit Hindi movie *Peepli Live* – and instead envisions smarter, broader changes.

Private companies have tried to consolidate land holdings, but have always run into problems with land acquisition. Swamy imagines government, flanked by researchers, institutional backing, and technology, working on a real, non-cyclical transformation in Indian agriculture.

Swamy's friend's secretary (we are in the New Delhi house of a fellow Member of Parliament from Tamil Nadu) wanders in to watch the action on video. He scratches his chin with a long fingernail and asks, 'With all this technology, what about this thing, employment?' The invention of the many machines were prompted by labour shortages, Swamy admits, something India doesn't have.

'See, we won't start farming like this from tomorrow morning. See, it will take *decades,'* Swamy says, getting a little worked up. He adds excitably, 'In America, it took a hundred years to bring the population in agriculture from seventy per cent to a mere three per cent. *One full century*. So, you had ample time to find better opportunities. It did not happen overnight. Let's not get scared that way.'

'The first thing is, we have to make sure the children of farmers do not remain farmers. Put them to alternate, more productive, more useful employment. Make sure they get an education,' Swamy thunders. 'Today, what happens is, land gets divided and each of the sons is poorer than his father...'

'When the computer came into the country,' he tells the secretary, who's now standing at the desk, holding his chin and smiling in amazement at Swamy's excitement, 'there was a massive demonstration in Bangalore. People thought the computer is going to take away all the jobs because it will do *everything*.'

'Yes, something like that,' the secretary muses.

'I don't think we would have built the National Highway, if we had said only people will build it. I don't think we would have built any skyscrapers..,' Swamy continues, pulling the argument to its most ridiculous conclusions. 'Should we employ people to pull a bus and shut down the engine?'

I squeeze in a question: How does he view the National Rural Employment Guarantee Act (NREGA), the Congress Party's much publicized program to increase employment in rural areas? Swamy doesn't hesitate. 'It is a good program. But we should also question whether, if it takes ten rupees to do something by machine, would you like to invest a hundred rupees to get it done by people?' he asks. 'Take ninety rupees and give it to people free and put ten rupees in getting the job done – otherwise, it's draining resources, money, and time.'

We need to create employment in areas where human skill is necessary and machines don't work, like in the jewellery industry, he adds, thinking aloud.

Many MPs have management backgrounds, others have risen from student activism. Swamy is the only MP I met with science and research experience. Having moved from studying under lamplight in Chitradurga, through the IISc, to inventing path-breaking new technology at Cadence in California, he has firsthand experience of the transformative power of science and technology. It allows him a wild imagination, one that soars above executive issues, and beyond small, stop-gap measures.

***

'Some time back, I did try this topic in Parliament,' Swamy admits, slowly.

At the time, the hot topic under discussion was crop insurance.

Somebody had asked whether the government was planning a national insurance scheme for farmers. Somebody else asked whether the government was planning an employment guarantee for farmers.

Swamy, in his question, pointed out that India has been trying to help farmers by giving them loans, subsidies, and waivers for decades. Still, our per hectare yield is low. 'So we work hard but we don't get the results we deserve,' he'd said. He'd said modernization of agriculture involves 'scientific research, good infrastructure, proper irrigation, sophisticated machines...which require serious investment.' Swamy had straight-forwardly asked if the government had plans to improve agricultural production. He'd also asked what plans the government had to provide alternate livelihood to those dependent on subsistence agriculture.

Swamy admits his question petered out in Parliament. It was too broad and it didn't set off any immediate triggers – it was much too long term.

Within the BJP as well, Swamy hasn't made much headway with his ideas. 'Of course, the BJP is not ruling also,' he's quick to point out.

At that, Janardhana Swamy shuts his thick laptop. We get up from the bare table and he strides restlessly around it. I thank Swamy for the interview and am half way out the door when he shouts out, grinning irrepressibly and leaning forward, hands in his pockets, 'Say hello to Mr Jaitley.' 'And if you tell him one thing,' he adds saucily, 'tell him to make *use* of us while we are still young!'

Notes

1 Hemanth Kashyap and Chetan R, 'Techie Politician Proves he is no Different,' *The Bangalore Mirror*, 13 October 2011

The Performer

When Prasada speaks in the usually chaotic Lok Sabha, with 220 opposition members shouting at him, he, somehow, manages to make himself heard.

JITIN PRASADA

Indian National Congress (INC)
Dhaurahra Constituency, Uttar Pradesh
Born on 29 November 1973
31 years of age at first election
Last victory margin of 1,84,509 votes

Jitin Prasada took over as Minister of State (MoS) for Road Transport and Highways in the cabinet reshuffle of January 2011. Earlier, he'd been MoS in the Ministry of Oil and Natural Gas since 2009. Prasada had also been MoS for Steel briefly in 2008, towards the tail end of the first Congress government, however, it was really in the Oil and Gas Ministry that Jitin first made an impact. He began answering questions in Parliament (the reticent Oil and Gas Minister Murli Deora delegated question-answers in Lok Sabha to Jitin) and, immediately, a whorl of excitement rose about him – here was a young man who, well informed

and plucky, could hold the House in his grip. (It was while Prasada was in Oil and Gas that Arun Jaitley, the leader of the Opposition in the Rajya Sabha, a formidable speaker who tends to look out for young talent, first told me I must look him up).

4 March 2010. Spring Session of Parliament. There's bedlam in the House.

More often than not, in Parliament, there's pandemonium, with the opposition thronging the pit and shouting slogans against rising prices or rampant corruption. Sometimes, there are violent shows of emotion – chairs and shoes are thrown, MPs nearly choke with anger shouting.

Peaceful days in Parliament are rare, days when everyone speaks in turn and listens quietly to what's being said.

Then there are the somewhat in-between days, days that begin in mayhem and subside into a rumble of small interruptions.

Today is one of those in-between days. In the beginning, there's bedlam – MPs protest lightly, not aggressively, over a question. The Deputy Speaker, with headphones hanging over his head, pleads uselessly, 'Please sit down. Please, *please*, go to your places.' He repeats himself like a harried school master, 'Sit down, SIT DOWN!'

'I'm not asking my question,' a frail-looking Congress MP from East Delhi says, annoyed by all the interruptions.

'No, no, please ask your question,' the Speaker pleads.

'What is all this? I'm not asking,' the MP nods his head, acting miffed.

The commotion subsides. The MP from East Delhi finally asks why production of LPG (cooking gas) is low when demand in homes is growing. How will the Minister fulfill the demand?

Jitin Prasada, the Junior Minister for Oil and Natural Gas, springs out of his seat. He answers with gusto that LPG connections have gone up from 3 crore in 1999 to 11.5 crore in 2010; the Ministry is building more refineries and is also trying to extend LPG access to cover eighty per cent of urban India.

There are murmurs of protest all over the house. The East Delhi MP responds that poor areas, like his constituency in Delhi, are still not being supplied.

Prasada, in defense, talks about a new line of piped natural gas for urban areas that's under development.

A man in a saffron kurta, who's been shouting protests throughout, gets up, and argues that during the National Democratic Alliance (NDA) government, LPG was free. Now, there's a lack of it. People stand in line *during holidays* for gas, he says piously.

Prasada responds that during the NDA government, LPG prices in fact rose by 80 per cent, that the United Progressive Alliance (UPA) has kept them constant even though the real price of gas has risen the world over.

A slew of people from the opposition stand up, offended by this. There's a din of protesting voices.

The Deputy Speaker pleads, getting perturbed, 'The Minister is trying to explain, let him answer. Listen to him. *Please*, listen to his full answer.'

Kalikesh Singh Deo, another young MP from Orissa, adds a rejoinder: Why are they talking about subsidies when in actuality people have to pay 500 rupees as premiums in the black market to get a gas cylinder? What about that? And can the 'honorable minister' specify what refineries are coming up to increase production of LPG, he asks. Meanwhile, why are imports of LPG going down?

Prasada replies with courage, 'Imports are going down but at the same time indigenous production is being increased, so that compensates.'

Kalikesh laughs in his seat, as if he doesn't believe a word of this.

Prasada continues that three new refineries are going up and lists them out.

The question finally ends and Prasada sits back down, intact and triumphant.

On another day, the same week in Parliament, Prasada fields three questions back to back. There's one on the fire in an IOC depot in Jaipur, another on the safety of off-shore drilling in Mumbai. An MP from the Communist Party of India (Marxist), the CPI (M), asks Prasada why the public sector is retracting from oil exploration in favor of private companies.

Prasada readily jumps out of his seat for question after question. He pulls out figures, dates, arguments, numbers, and assurances. He spars with energy.

Murli Deora, the Cabinet Minister for Oil and Gas and Prasada's boss, sits next to him, nodding from time to time. While most decisions in the Ministry – on allocation of blocks and refineries – are taken directly by Deora, he doesn't enjoy the limelight. He lets his Junior minister handle the talking.

Jitin doesn't speak with eloquence. The crowd in Parliament is, anyway, far too restless and misbehaved for long and subtle speeches. Jitin has a more dogged style. He throws out statistics, looks his opponents in the eye and blusters through like a rugby player, the ball held close.

Of the 543 MPs in Parliament, 262 are from the Congress (Jitin's own Party), sixty more are somewhat allied with the Congress, and 220 others are in viral Opposition. There are grumbles all over the house and from the Opposition, but people listen when Jitin Prasada speaks, arrested by his ready supply of arguments, his moderately aggressive style.

One almost imagines Jitin taking a bow after he finishes, just as the semi-circular Parliament – the country's best political theatre – erupts in both cheers and protests.

***

Down the corridor from Prasada's office in the Oil and Gas Ministry, his right hand man and secretary, A.K. Pandey, sits in a nest of papers, phones and computer wires. A tiny television, suspended from a corner of his cosy office, is permanently tuned onto Lok Sabha TV.

'How is the Minister?' I ask Pandey. I've stopped by his office to pick up CDs of Prasada speaking in the Lok Sabha.

'The Minister has been answering questions in Parliament nearly every day,' Pandey says glowing, 'Yesterday, he spoke for the full one hour, fifteen minutes.' Pandey is a large, officious man, who clearly loves the MP. 'He's speaking much more now, and also much more confidently,' Pandey tells me, brimming with joy; I feel we could be talking about his twelve-year old son.

We chat for some time about how Prasada respects his staff, how straightforward and polite he is. 'Maybe because he is young, there are no barriers between us. We can give our suggestions, in fact, he asks us our advice, in all political and professional matters. You know how it is with Ministers of older years – they keep their distance from their staff,' he shares.

***

When I first met Prasada in early 2010, he'd just returned from the morning session; he was still whirring with the adrenaline of Parliament. There was already a neat stack of files in his office, questions coming in for next week.

Behind his large desk, Jitin Prasada threw his hands up. 'Just think, we've had so much of this by now. We've said so many times, all this... constituency, campaign, how does it feel, what were you doing before,' he rattled. Prasada is lean and rod-like; his long face is all angles, with a pointed nose and glasses. 'How many times are we going to talk about the same stuff?' he asked moodily, hovering above his chair.

'Now it's all about the Ministry,' Jitin said, plunging into thought, 'How can I prove myself in the Ministry? How can I contribute?'

Jitin's core allocation within the Ministry was the marketing and the distribution of oil and oil products. 'Downstream,' he said, in a word. 'It's about taking oil and oil products to this country – petrol, diesel, kerosene, LPG, which are in every house. Pricing, delivery of oil products, will affect you, a poor man in a village who's using kerosene to cook his food, and a middle income housewife in a Mumbai flat who uses gas. Any change, anything to disturb or change that pattern, affects the whole country, every house. From a person driving a scooter, to a person driving a Mercedes, to a person transporting a truck... so, it's a sensitive portfolio.'

Jitin's job involved ensuring better distribution of oil and oil products through the several public sector oil marketing companies – the Indian Oil Corporation (IOC), Bharat Petroleum (BPCL) and Hindustan Petroleum (HPCL). Public Sector Oil distribution companies, because of their monopoly, are notoriously lackadaisical in customer service. In big cities and in the districts, you have to beg, bribe and wait endlessly for a gas connection.

Prasada's effort, as an MoS, has been towards trying to make the PSUs more accountable towards customers. One of Prasada's initiatives was SMS bookings for gas cylinders. The service was launched in September 2009; where customers would earlier chase distributors for refills, now dealers had to respond to the SMS booking by confirming the date and time they would deliver. Another initiative was toll-free numbers to register LPG customer complaints.

Prasada worked on what was named the 'Rajiv Gandhi LPG Vikrak Yojna,' a scheme to increase gas connections in rural areas. Only 50 per cent of India is covered with gas connections and most of the connections are in urban areas. Half of the country still collects firewood or uses kerosene, a dangerous fuel, for cooking. The LPG Yojna promised gas services to small villages with a capacity of 600 gas refills. As a result, there have been over 2,000 new gas agencies in rural India.

The system of allotting gas agencies itself faced allegations of corruption. Gas agencies were allotted by public sector companies based on certain parameters, including an oral 'interview'. There were invariably officials who were accused of awarding the discretionary 'interview' points to their own people. Prasada eliminated the 'interview' process and switched to a lottery system.

Prasada's effort has been towards making public sector oil companies more service friendly and accountable – to the middle income urban housewife and to the poor man in the village.

'Our job is really just that of a… regulator,' Jitin mulled, in his snipped, faraway way. 'It's the PSUs that have to deliver. We just chart the policy to try and make sure they do.'

***

Jitin's confidence today, his impatience with the same old questions about his first election, masks his somewhat hard ride. Prasada hasn't inherited power easily, though he comes from a strong political lineage. Jitin's father, Jitendra Prasada, MP from Shajahanpur, Uttar Pradesh, was a former Vice President of the Congress (Jitin's grandfather, Jyoti Prasada had also been a Congress Party member).

Jitty bhai, as Jitendra Prasada was known, had been a UP landowner, well-educated and fond of poetry. In the Congress, he was political advisor to Rajiv Gandhi (in 1991) and later to Prime Minister Narasimha Rao (in 1994). He was always in the thick of Congress politicking. However, in 2000, Jitty bhai pitched himself against Sonia Gandhi for the post of Congress President and lost badly. Sonia Gandhi won with 99 per cent of the votes – of the 7,771 votes cast, Sonia got 7,448.

Even so, at the time, columnists like Harish Khare in *The Hindu* had written woeful editorials on the Congress becoming 'a property of the Gandhi-Nehru family' and had praised Prasada for fighting an 'unequal battle' in the face of dynastic politics.[1] (Harish Khare is now media advisor to the Congress Prime Minister Manmohan Singh, while Sonia Gandhi continues as Congress President.)

Prasada had actually been banking on Rajesh Pilot to fight alongside him, but Pilot died in a road accident that same year. What made his loss in the party elections brutal was that Jitty bhai was, in the end, largely alone, ostracized in the Congress at the center and in the state. A year later, Jitty bhai died from a sudden stroke.

Jitin's mother, Kanta Prasada, fought by-elections from Shahjahanpur just after her husband's death in 2001, and lost. 'It was a huge, huge setback,' Jitin told Sushmita Bose of the *Hindustan Times* in an interview after he first became MoS, 'Our people had voted us out.'[2]

Jitin had attended the Doon School in Dehradun, and then the Sri Ram College of Commerce (SRCC) at Delhi University. Later, he did a Masters in Business Administration from the International Management Institute in Delhi. Jitin worked first at Merrill Lynch and then, with BPL net. He was initially drawn to the corporate sector over politics, he's said. But, his mother's loss in his father's constituency must have shaken Jitin up – suddenly, the ground seemed to slip under his feet.

Jitin quit his job as an investment banker and returned to the family's lost constituency. The Prasada home was deserted, devoid of the Uttar Pradesh Congress members who used to hang around; the Prasadas were now out of power and out of favour with the Gandhi family. 'People in the world are usually very pragmatic. They are with you if you have power; otherwise they disappear,' Jitin said, in an interview with Nadine Kreisberger of the *Indian Express*.[3]

Jitin took the setback as a challenge. He realized, as he told Bose in the *Hindustan Times*, that there had been 'no first-hand interaction... we (his family) had, without realizing it, distanced ourselves from the grassroots.' Prasada spent time in his constituency, getting back in touch with the local

Congress and getting to know his people and their issues. He also reached out to the Gandhi family, and, by end 2001, got his first political break when Sonia Gandhi made him General Secretary with the Youth Congress.

With his reprieve from Sonia Gandhi and his appointment in the Youth Congress, Jitin overcame his bad patch. As he told Kriesberger, the psychologist-journalist, later, 'There are a lot of people opposing you and gunning at you constantly. You can't run away from it, you have to face it, you have to get used to the fact that people will point their finger at you, that all sorts of accusations will flow... You need to try and do your work without getting bogged down by the nitty-gritty of people constantly trying to pull you back and pin you down.'

Since then, Jitin hasn't lost a notch. He won from his home constituency Shahjahanpur by 80,000 votes in 2004. He was the youngest Minister of State in 2008. He got dealt a tough hand when Shahjahanpur became a reserved seat in 2009, but he won again from Dhaurahra, a new constituency, by a margin of 1,80,000 votes. He's been handed important portfolios in various Ministries one after the other. Now Jitin Prasada is so much in favour that it's said – were the Congress to rise in Uttar Pradesh, Jitin would be groomed as Chief Minister.

In 2009, Jitin also got engaged to an attractive journalist from Lucknow. In February 2010, the week of the couple's wedding, newspapers carried cartoons of the young Minister dressed as a rakish groom. Jitin is, apparently, the first Indian Minister to marry while in office.

***

Jitin's wife, Neha Prasada, is warm and lovely; I meet her a few months after their wedding. We sit on the terrace of the Café Coffee Day in Khan Market in Central Delhi. It's a Sunday and Jitin is away visiting his constituency.

Neha reported on government and administration for the CNN IBN network before she married Jitin. She's covered state elections in Delhi and Uttar Pradesh and she's enthralled with the 'colour of elections,' well-versed with what they entail. She recalls the 2007 UP state elections in particular. 'The whole atmosphere is electric. There's excitement in the air. It's one big festival,' she says. She describes trailing Rahul Gandhi, witnessing his style of mingling with people. He'd sit at a *dhaba* and have cups of tea; if there was sugarcane growing in the area, he'd have a *ganna*. In contrast, she describes UP Chief Minister Mayawati's phalanx of bodyguards, her aura of power, her 'birthday rallies,' with tiers of cake, silks, and diamonds.

Neha also volunteered, for a brief period, in the media department of BJP leader Vasundara Raje's election campaign in Rajasthan. (She'd always wanted to work with a woman politician, she says, and Raje gave her the opportunity.)

Jitin and Neha met through common friends and dated for a few years before getting engaged. 'If I have a question, I try not to ask him,' she says, 'He doesn't like talking politics at home, maybe because that's what he does twenty-four hours of the day.'

Neha had already quit her reporting job by the time she and Jitin married. At present, she's writing on food, culling together recipes and stories from royal households around the country – Rajasthan, Kashmir, Mysore, and others.

Neha hasn't visited Jitin's constituency yet. 'Election time is when everybody gets involved, so I suppose that's when I'll go,' she says, sounding nervous and excited at the same time.

Meanwhile, the couple likes to take short breaks to wildlife preserves and to their home in the hills near Nainital. Jitin loves the outdoors and is a bird-watcher and an animal enthusiast. 'He can sit still for hours on a safari,' Neha says. Otherwise, she describes Prasada as 'restless.' 'You know, his mind is always ticking, even when he's at home. He doesn't take any achievement for granted, so he's always at it.'

Neha says she has no idea what Jitin does day-to-day at the Ministry. 'The Constituency is primary, but when you're given a responsibility like this, it's huge. What I do know, is that he is one of the few young ministers handling questions in Parliament,' she muses, 'You have to be prepared for multiple questions. His is such a vast subject, you have to know what you're talking about.'

***

The Cabinet reshuffle in early 2011, in the wake of the 2G corruption scandal, came as a surprise to everyone.

Ministers were moved around without much reason. Prasada was shifted from Oil and Gas to the Ministry of Roads and Road Transport without warning. The new Roads and Road Transport Cabinet Minister CP Joshi deputed right away that all questions put to the Ministry in the Lok Sabha would be answered by Prasada. This wasn't surprising – Prasada's performance in the Oil and Gas Ministry had created a buzz around him.

I call Prasada's secretary, Pandey, to ask him about the shift. The move out of Oil and Gas was 'unexpected', Pandey admits; but in Roads, he adds, always willing to look at the bright side, the MP's work will likely be more 'visible'.

Jitin has been given charge of all road development in the state of Uttar Pradesh. Even the smallest new road will be inaugurated; there will be photo opportunities and press releases in the media; the Minister's work will be more publicly celebrated.

At the same time, Prasada will continue volleying questions in Parliament. Road Transport, like Oil and Gas, is a Ministry that gets a lot of flack, one that raises lots of questions from MPs all over the country.

Whatever his other accomplishments, Jitin has clearly earned the reputation of someone who can be relied upon to speak for a Ministry, someone who can effectively push back the Opposition.

Barely weeks into his posting, Jitin Prasada began fielding questions on delays in national highway projects, on unfinished roads all over the country. It speaks well of Prasada's future – that he's able to absorb a dozen punches, that he's able to take in assault like a sponge, process it silently, and come back with an assured, unapologetic response.

For in India, in politics, to be plausible, to stand tall and retain a note of bombast while being assaulted on the floor of the House, to hit back with enough intelligence so that people are wary rather than critical of you, is to be a man to be reckoned with.

Notes

1 Harish Khare, 'In Praise of Jitendra Prasada,' *The Hindu*, 15 November 2000

2 Sushmita Bose, 'The Reinventor,' *The Hindustan Times*, 12 April 2008

3 Nadine Kreisberger, 'You need fear to keep you under control,' *The Indian Express*, 9 August 2009

The Little Fish In The Big Sea

His small, Uttar Pradesh-based party, survives on nostalgia and family loyalty. Jayant mulls over driving a small party in a very large state.

JAYANT CHAUDHARY

Rashtriya Lok Dal (RLD)
Mathura Constituency, Uttar Pradesh
Born on 27 December 1978
30 years of age at first election
Last victory margin of 1,69,613 votes

'Right now, with every election, we're looking to grow the number of seats, to be credible,' Jayant says frankly. He scans his state's gargantuan landscape, the moves of heavyweights like the Congress and the Samajwadi Party, noting the exits and entries of new players. Chaudhary talks with dashes of hope and weariness about the electoral importance of UP and the twists and turns in UP politics.

At eighty seats, Uttar Pradesh holds almost double the number of spots of any other state in Parliament (Maharashtra elects 48 seats; Andhra, 42; Bihar, 40; Madhya Pradesh, 29; and Punjab, 13, in comparison). If a national party wins with a substantial majority in UP, it swings to the centre; if a regional party wins the state, then that party is invariably needed to make the coalition at the centre. The entire Gandhi family, celebrity cricketers and Bollywood superstars, are thrown up in the bid to win UP. Uttar Pradesh is the 'state of king-makers,' it is said; here, elections are hotly and dramatically contested.

For the Congress, the erosion of its majority in Uttar Pradesh through the early 1990s has been devastating. Things reached a head with the Bharatiya Janata Party's Rath Yatra, a march led by the BJP's L.K. Advani, to crusade for the Ram Mandir in place of the Babri Masjid in Ayodhya. Advani fanned Hindu sentiments throughout Uttar Pradesh, sentiments that soon reverberated all over the country. In the process, he culled out Hindu voters. In 1991, the BJP managed, for the first time in its history, to win fifty seats of eighty in the state of Uttar Pradesh. The Congress shakedown in UP, its slide in the 90s, the rise (and fall) of the BJP and upstart regional parties, is every seasoned journalist's favourite subject. The torrid changes in UP politics make for fabulous intrigue and analyses.

In 1992, Congress Prime Minister Narasimha Rao committed a blunder by failing to send in army troops to protect the Babri Masjid (in December 1992, the mosque was attacked by the BJP's *kar sevaks*, or volunteers, leading to the worst communal riots ever seen in Uttar Pradesh).

As a result, the Congress, seen as ineffectual and soft on right-wing Hindus, lost the Muslim vote in the state. Senior journalist Shekhar Gupta has written about how Narasimha Rao looked back on the Babri Masjid debacle in UP – in one conversation, Rao haltingly tells Gupta that he didn't call in the Army because he was afraid the Hindus in the Army would defect to the Hindus in the crowd, all chanting '*Ram, Ram*'.

Bitterly, Rao adds that L.K. Advani had promised him the procession would pass without harming the Masjid. (Many argue that Rao, while still Prime Minister, later framed L.K. Advani in the country's *hawala* (money laundering) scandal for his betrayal.

Around the same time, in the nineties, politics in Uttar Pradesh were being transformed by caste. 'Rajni Kothari wrote a book called *Caste in Indian Politics* in 1970 and said that Indian elections would be fought along caste lines,' old-time political commentator Vir Sanghvi recounts. 'But the 1971, 1972, and 1984 elections were elections where caste didn't make a difference at all, so, at that time, we all thought caste didn't matter.' The Congress had dominated those elections in Uttar Pradesh and elsewhere.

But when the Janata Dal and V.P. Singh's government came to power in 1989, it created caste-based reservations in government jobs and colleges for a new category of Other Backward Castes (OBCs), and triggered widespread protests, together with a new era of caste politics.

As India began doling out more and more benefits based on caste identity, the country as a whole began to vote along caste lines. In Uttar Pradesh, the Bahujan Samaj Party (BSP), a Dalit party led by the present Chief Minister of the state, Mayawati, grew in strength as a representative of the Scheduled Castes.

The Samajwadi Party (SP), led by Mulayam Singh Yadav, proclaimed itself leader for Other Backward Castes or OBCs. The SP also put up Muslim candidates for election and won over the Congress's disgruntled Muslim voters. The Congress went from holding eighty-one seats in Uttar Pradesh in 1984 to an embarrassing total of zero in the general election of 1999. That year, the BJP won fifty-seven seats, the SP twenty and the BSP, four seats in the state.

It was in this predatory political jungle that the Rashtriya Lok Dal – the small homegrown farmer's party led by the raffish Ajit Singh – re-emerged by winning a single seat in 1999, two seats in 2004, and then five seats in 2009. Somehow, it held its sway in the state.

In the 2012 UP assembly elections, the RLD scraped through with eight seats, two seats less than it had won in 2007.

The RLD doesn't vie for Hindu or Muslim votes per se, as do the big sharks, the BJP and the SP, but it does get a large section of its votes on caste. The Jat community, which Jayant's family belongs to, is clustered in Western Uttar Pradesh, the RLD's stronghold. Chaudhary denies that caste is his party's main talking point. 'No, no, in fact, we never say that,' Jayant says. 'If we talk about caste, it's limited to maybe a couple of seats. There's Mathura, there's Bagpath... only nine per cent of all UP is Jat, and so caste-based politics can't be our forum for growth. I have to appeal to a pan audience,' Jayant insists.

Yet outside ofWestern UP, the RLD has no sufficient identity. Vir Sanghvi has called Ajit Singh the 'flip-flop politician.' Shekhar Gupta calls him a 'serial defector', commenting on how the RLD has opportunistically woven its way through alliances with every party. More than anything else, in Uttar Pradesh, the RLD is remarkable simply for surviving.

***

In the 2009 national election, Uttar Pradesh was shaken all over again with the Congress, this time, winning twenty-one seats – the most it had won in a quarter century. Initially, credit went to Congress's Rahul Gandhi, who spent a lot of his election time campaigning in the state. The Samajwadi Party skid back by ten seats and seemed to fall apart with internal bickering, the BSP stayed at twenty seats and the BJP, ironically enough, totaled a new low of just ten seats. For a short time, the Congress seemed to have been vindicated.

'The Congress has grown this time,' Jayant admits after the 2009 general election, but before the 2012 state election verdict, 'even in the Assembly elections next time, there's a possibility of it growing further. However, he adds presciently, 'See, on the ground, the Congress doesn't really have a presence. It hasn't had a presence for a long time, in terms of workers.' 'Even now, I don't think one day in three months makes much of a difference,' he says, referring to Rahul Gandhi's publicized appearances in the state – at colleges thronged by young girls and at Dalit homes, seen eating with poor families. 'Of course, I'm not criticizing what Rahul is doing. He has quite a task ahead.'

Chaudhary predicts, 'The 2009 result isn't showing some sort of long-term trend. In Uttar Pradesh, ultimately, the dynamics are always evolving.'

In the present economy-driven India, Vir Sanghvi and Shekhar Gupta assert that UP's right-wing Hindu fervor has cooled down, that no one cares much about the Ram Mandir-Babri Masjid issue anymore. 'Muslim memories of Narasimha Rao have faded. With Rahul Gandhi, they see the Congress returning to the Nehru-Gandhi legacy,' Sanghvi says, although he too, agrees with Jayant's view that the Congress lacks real local leadership in the Uttar Pradesh heartland.

Aditi Phadnis, another senior journalist, thinks the Congress has a tough time in Uttar Pradesh because small parties – like Jayant Chaudhary's RLD and also others such as the Peace Party, the Indian Justice Party and the splinter Muslim parties – 'nibble away' at the Congress party's share of votes in the state.

Gupta, Sanghvi, Phadnis, and Chaudury all turned out to be correct, in a way, in their tentative predictions for 2012 – the Congress, without local leadership, made no impact in the UP state elections. The BJP too with its half-baked message (the aged Advani was seen leading an anti-corruption *yatra* reminiscent of his earlier communal Ayodhya Yatra) lost vote share. The Samajwadi Party, with its sudden, new promises of education, and laptops to school children and its local organizational spread, won.

The Congress totaled just twenty-eight seats, only six seats more than it had won in the 2007 state elections. The Samajwadi Party, which had seemed to self-destruct during the 2009 general elections, won with a clear margin. Refueled by internal changes, it emerged with a stunning 224 seats out of a total of 403 seats in the state, more than double the number it had won in 2007.

The 2012 UP state results are now being read as a precursor to the 2014 general election, just as the 2009 general election results were seen as a precursor to 2012.

Despite all the commentary, however, before any UP election, no one dares to really hazard a guess as to which way UP will swing. 'You can never say about UP,' Jayant reasons lightly, an old hand already, 'every month you'll find there's a political shift, something is shaking up.'

***

Today, Jayant's challenge is to steer his party in the face of two major elections: the Uttar Pradesh state Assembly elections in 2012 and the General elections soon after in 2014. Jayant is pragmatic, calm, and strangely cheerful, about his options. First of all, he says, they're trying to recruit strong candidates to stand from the RLD.

'A lot of people who left the party at various points are people we're going to try and get back. I'm also going to get young faces to contest, it makes a difference,' he chuckles; imagining fresh faces amongst all the grandfatherly members of his party. The RLD will have a membership drive starting in December this year, but Jayant is unsure of what it will bring. 'The sad bit is, people who feel they want to contest; they typically make up their mind when the elections are a little closer. They watch the pre-election dynamics unfold to guess which party has the best chances. They hop from party to party opportunistically. When the BSP came to power, we lost an MLA, we lost an MP. And, in fact, one MLA of ours, he contested an MP election from the BSP! So it's very localized, very seat-specific,' he laughs. 'The decisions about candidature, you can't have any trends.'

Jayant takes things lightly, laughs easily, perhaps knowing that a sense of humour is vital in a tiny party with a questionable future. Meanwhile, the RLD continues Charan Singh's style of 'agitation' politics, making its presence felt by leading marches, organizing *dharnas* (peaceful demonstrations) and delivering speeches on land acquisition and other agrarian issues. In 2009, the RLD, in alliance with the SP, organized a huge rally on sugarcane prices and blockaded Parliament for two whole days. Thousands of farmers, with Mulayam Singh Yadav and Ajit Singh at their helm and TV cameras in tow, walked from Old Delhi to Parliament. The next day, the Congress announced it would raise the minimum sugarcane support price for farmers. 'That was huge,' Jayant says optimistically.

'People remember these things.' In his own election in Mathura, Jayant took up the cause of a goat-rearing community that wanted Scheduled Caste/Scheduled Tribe status. Jayant and his workers broke barriers, got *lathi*-charged by the local police and walked to protest at the District Office.

After he got elected, Jayant organized a march protesting the condition of the roads in his constituency. With a motley group of supporters, he stormed several districts, making speeches and raising questions about the Rajiv Gandhi Sadak Yojna (Road Fund). In keeping with his own grandfather's tradition, Chaudhary spoke out in favour of stricter land acquisition laws. Most recently, Jayant led a Badlav Yatra, a 'march for change', through twenty-one districts in eastern Uttar Pradesh. The march agitated at high pitch against the corruption and the lack of employment and education under the BSP government's rule of the state.

Some say that the way for a small party to increase its clout would be to cut itself a smaller piece of the state to rule over. Jayant animatedly endorses the idea of four new states in Uttar

Pradesh. It is like the 'largest nation in the world, too big to manage, too big to be developed,' he says. Chaudhary's view is sometimes endorsed by other parties – the BSP and the Congress – who talk of roughly three possible states: Harit Pradesh in Western UP, Bundelkhand in south-central UP, and Purvanchal in eastern UP. If Uttar Pradesh were to split three-way, Harit Pradesh, which has a large number of Jat farmers, would be the domain of the RLD. The party would turn from a small fish in a big state, to a big fish in a small pond. Jayant jumps at the idea, though the 'split' seems unlikely – for the additional administrative costs it would add and for demands from other states it would spawn.

The most likely option for the RLD, realistically, is always a pre-election alliance with a larger party. Jayant makes no bones about what decides an alliance. 'It's not about ideology or faith,' he says straight up, 'it's about the number of seats an alliance gives you.' While the RLD and Ajit Singh have been particularly shameless in picking allies (the SP, the BSP, the BJP, and the Congress have all been partners once), every party today, the Congress most conspicuously, can be accused of having strange, ideologically different allies.

In the run up to 2012, there were already rumours that the RLD was leaning towards the Congress. Apparently, Ajit Singh didn't want Jayant to be left with the burden of managing a small party; reporters speculated that his father wanted him secure as a young MP in the Congress. The two parties were said to in negotiations on seats, on a future Ministerial position for Ajit Singh in the Cabinet and on Jayant's future.

Yet, with elections approaching, and negotiations still in limbo, in early 2011, the RLD took more immediate steps. Ajit Singh announced that the RLD would form a 'Small Party Coalition' in tandem with the Peace Party, the Indian Justice Party, the Bharatiya Samaj Party, the Janwadi Party and the Itehad-e-Millat Council – all little-known parties who have put up candidates in the past, but never actually won any seats. This shoal of small parties called themselves the Lok Kranti

Morcha. As head of the largest party within it, Ajit Singh was named Chairman of the Morcha.

However, alliances were bartered up to the last minute. As it turned out, in end 2011, the 'flip-flop' politician, Ajit Singh, ditched the Morcha and ended up making a deal with the Congress – the Congress and the RLD decided to split seats in the upcoming state elections and, as part of the deal, Ajit Singh bagged a position in the Union Cabinet as Civil Aviation Minister. In the 2012 state assembly elections, however, neither the Congress nor the RLD fared well – both finished more or less where they had been in the last 2007 elections.

***

Despite the vagaries ahead, Jayant Chaudhary looks upon the future – his party's and his own – with optimism. Talking of his father, Ajit Singh's experience, Jayant says, 'he's seen a lot of highs. I've not seen those highs. I feel that's why I'm more aggressive and positive. To him, the RLD doesn't seem perhaps like much. For me, starting out, looking to build the organization, it's fun.'

Jayant seems happy with where he is, for now. He relished the unpredictability and the eventual breakthrough of his first election in Mathura; he enjoys organizing party marches and demonstrations. He's inspired by the intellectual stimulation of Parliamentary debate and he admires, in particular, the Congress Minister for environment, Jairam Ramesh. The outcome may not be certain, but Jayant Chaudhury seems determined to enjoy his ride in the tidal wave of Uttar Pradesh politics.

Notes

1 Shekhar Gupta, 'Tearing Down Narasimha Rao,' *Indian Express*, 28 November 2009

2 Shekhar Gupta, 'Hindu Rate of Growth,' *Indian Express*, 9 May 2009

The Observer

Having come from the fiery Shiv Sena to the Congress, Rane has had the chance to watch leaders of different stripes up close. Rane reflects on what made Bal Thackeray larger than life.

NILESH RANE
Indian National Congress (INC)
Ratnagiri-Sindhudurg Constituency, Maharashtra
Born on 17 March 1981
28 years of age at first election
Last victory margin of 46,750 votes

'Delhi is still new to us,' Nilesh Rane says, fidgety, tapping his feet. 'We have no relatives, no friends in Delhi. Delhi politics, the politicians, how the Delhi network works... But I am getting there, starting to get to know people.' In the small living room of Nilesh Rane's ministerial residence in the capital, a couple of young men casually hang out, organizers and friends from Ratnagiri-Sindhudurg, Nilesh's constituency on the Konkan Coast of Maharashtra. There's a pent up energy in the room. Its evening and the street outside the neat row of bungalows on North Avenue is much too quiet for the guys from Mumbai.

Nilesh sits on the couch. He is short and stout like his father, former Shiv Sena politican Narayan Rane, but fitter, tightly packed together.

The Ranes have their own network of 4,500 kilometers on the Konkan Coast. When the Shiv Sena lost Narayan Rane, Nilesh shrugs, they lost the Konkan altogether. 'A person like Narayan Rane, you have to fight the election in his name because he has a name in the district, among the people,' Nilesh continues offhandedly. 'When we shifted to the Congress four, five years ago, right from the *Guardian* Minister to the *Gram Panchayat*, all the people who were there in Sindhudurg district particularly, they all shifted to the Congress with us,' he says.

Nilesh has worked the Konkan coast with his father, taking up youth issues and employment, getting to know people, since he was seventeen. On the Coast, Nilesh walks out of his house and everyone from the *taluka* (district) President down to every single party worker is a friend. Nilesh is used to being at the centre of things on his home turf, so being a newcomer in Delhi, on the outskirts of action in the Congress Party is annoying for the young, restless MP.

As the streets get even quieter outside, Nilesh watches the door from to time. Meanwhile, he shares the family's history in Maharashtra politics.

***

Narayan Rane is said to have started in a local 'gang' in Chembur. When he was fourteen years old, he joined the Shiv Sena, enamoured by the Sena's leader Bal Thackeray (or Bala Saheb as he's known to everyone around him). Over the next four decades, Rane worked to build the Sena's network in the Konkan region. But with Bala Saheb getting older, tension was brewing in the Shiv Sena. On 2 July 2005, after a fall out with Bala Saheb's son Uddhav, Rane announced he was leaving the Sena (a few months later, in an explosive turn of events, Thackeray's nephew Raj, also quit the Sena to start his own party).

Within just two weeks of their departure from the Sena, the Ranes announced that they would be joining the Congress. In a quick turnaround, father and son formally joined the party on 20 July 2005.

'My father Rane Saheb met Sonia Madam (Congress President, Sonia Gandhi). I think Madam spoke very well. I was not there inside, but my father was happy,' Nilesh narrates. 'Madam said that we welcome you and you'll always be welcome and you'll always be treated as a member of this party. So, for someone of her stature to say something like this, to be a part of this... for her to identify and make it a point to meet one man coming out of one party from a state like Maharashtra,' Nilesh muses appreciatively, 'that shows the alertness of the party and the leader.'

'My father really felt very nice. I mean, we all felt very nice,' Nilesh says. 'It is something that we always see, leaders have these qualities.' The younger Rane adds with a touch of emotion, 'Once you are in this line, once you are in politics, you want to know how your leader is from inside? You know, what kind of a leader are you going to follow?'

'You see,' he says, musing over this observation with satisfaction, 'already we saw that small alertness, small things you want to do for people.' Sonia Gandhi struck the Ranes as an alert, able leader. Her swiftness in getting in touch with them days after they quit the Sena, her graciousness, warmed them. After wandering out from under Bala Saheb's large umbrella into a brief, tenuous relationship with Uddhav Thackeray, they felt safe once again under Madam's watchful guard in the Congress.

In the late 2005 assembly elections, the Shiv Sena was defeated in Narayan Rane's constituency Malwan, in Maharashtra. It was a landmark win for Rane who gained 63,000 votes, as compared to 34,000 in the previous 2004 election. The Konkan Coast, with its mango and cashew orchards and great tourism potential, had voted for upward mobility by choosing Rane over the Sena, media reported. The 'sylvan and literate' population of Malwan, the *Indian Express* opined, voted for the 'helpful home boy' image of Narayan Rane.[1] Upon winning, Rane himself declared, 'The Konkani people have voted for development. They have taught the Sena a lesson that you can't fool all the people all the time with emotional promises.' With the 2005 win, the Ranes proved their power to turn the tide of elections on the Konkan Coast.

In the State election of 2008 in Maharashtra, the Congress and the National Congress Party (NCP) combine came to power and Vilas Rao Deshmukh became Chief Minister (CM). But following his admistration's failure over the Mumbai terror attacks in November the same year, Deshmukh soon stepped down. Finance Minister Pranab Mukherjee flew down from Delhi to speak with the Maharashtra Congress and to pick a new CM. Narayan Rane had his eye on the position, but instead the Congress chose Ashok Chavan, who had Deshmukh's and NCP President Sharad Pawar's support. Feeling sidelined by the Congress, Narayan Rane vented his frustration on national TV, declaring Chavan to be 'unqualified.' The older Rane ranted that he had no faith in Sonia Gandhi or the Congress. Rane's supporters protested around the Chief Minister's residence. Following his father, Nilesh promptly quit his post of General Secretary of the Youth Congress in Maharashtra, declaring to the media that he was 'disillusioned' with Congress MP Rahul Gandhi.

Narayan Rane was suspended from the Congress. However, a few weeks later, he was forgiven and cajoled into rejoining. 'See today if you ask me after may be twenty-five years, would you like to be the Chief Minister, I would say 'yes.' Who doesn't want to be CM?' Nilesh says loyally, in defence of his father's stand. 'But it's about what the party high command decides, it's not about what an individual decides,' Nilesh adds, reconciliatory.

To seal his return to the party, Narayan Rane was made Maharashtra Revenue Minister and Nilesh got the ticket from Sindhudurg-Ratnagiri in the 2009 general election. The episode, in some ways, added to the senior Rane's standing; it established his volatility, his indomitability – he'd thrown a fit and he'd been pampered and brought around.

'Things are good. I mean the party has adjusted to us very well. We have adjusted to the party very well,' Nilesh sums up, putting the whole episode in the past. 'It's a good experience and we have settled down now.'

***

On his former party, the Shiv Sena, Nilesh shares, 'It's not the same as it looks from the outside, things have changed.' Nilesh speaks with distaste about Uddhav Thackeray, about the new Shiv Sainiks who 'have no idea what the party's about', about the old Shiv Sainiks who are 'lost'; he even dismisses Raj Thackeray for flaming false hopes of 'revival'. But when Nilesh talks about Bal Thackeray, a strand of wistfulness still enters his voice. 'I mean Bala Saheb will still have respect in my heart and will always have… Because of him we are what we are…,' he stops.

Nilesh recalls the atmosphere of the early years of the Shiv Sena. 'All the *andolans* (movements) that took place in Mumbai and the Konkan region, we were obviously a part of that.' A huge amount of energy was generated in the Sena and unleashed through the Sena's movements. 'And, basically, the word of Bala Saheb Thackeray,' Nilesh reminisces, 'you know, when we thought sitting in one corner of Shivaji Park, you know, when we thought he was making sense...' Once again, he stops, at a loss for words.

'First of all there were Bala Saheb's speeches,' Nilesh says, trying to explain the culture of the early Sena. The Dussehra *Mewada* is the annual speech Bal Thackeray has been giving to thousands of party workers in Shivaji Park in Mumbai since 1966 when he launched the Sena. 'It was complete madness,' Nilesh shakes his head, describing how people came together to be energized by their leader, to soak in his words. 'I have seen days when people were crazy about Bala Saheb Thackeray.'

When Bal Thackeray spoke, thousands and thousands filled the park. A sea of people faced the tall, skinny man on stage, his body relaxed, standing at ease in front of a mike. Bala Saheb didn't raise his voice, intone high or low with drama. He didn't speak forcefully and pause, for applause, like politicians tend to do. Bala Saheb spoke as if he were telling a story to a few close friends. The audience of thousands was, at times, electrically silent, hung between words. At times, there were ripples of approval or giggles. All of a sudden, the hall would erupt with laughter as Bala Saheb arrived at his punch line. Other Shiv Sena leaders, sitting on the stage behind Bala Saheb, slumped in their chairs, would chuckle, shaking. Even when they weren't laughing, you could see them leaning forward, their chins in their hand, shuddering with anticipation. Bala Saheb had the dry timing of a comedian. Yet, Nilesh points out, when he spoke, or wrote in his columns in the Shiv Sena news weekly, *Saamna*, he came across as grittily real and empathetic.

In the Sena, under Bala Saheb's tutelage, charged up by his words, Nilesh recalls, they were part of a symphony of thousands, all fearless in his shadow. 'If a person like me has to tell you what Bala Saheb was...,' Nilesh says, at a loss for words again.

***

'Aside from a four or five year long term, it was never in power, so it was always in the Opposition,' Nilesh says of the early Shiv Sena. 'And you know, the role of the Opposition is to fight for whatever they stand for against the government,' he explains, looking at the Sena with some distance now. 'So when Bala Saheb used to run it, it had a very aggressive face.'

There were rallies, protests and shut-downs against South Indians taking away Marathi jobs and against North Indians for the same; Shiv Sainiks stormed the streets. The Marathi *manoos* (the Sena's term for native Maharashtrians) theme, the idea that Maharashtrian Marathi-speaking people had a unique hold on Mumbai and Maharashtra above other Indians, was fiery. It seemed to hold, back then, the promise of revolution, of improving Maharashtrian lives. To the Sena and its followers, it seemed worth the fight to throw out all the North Indian taxi and rickshaw drivers, and all the other 'outsiders', and keep Mumbai for themselves.

The problems, as Nilesh sees it, started as Bal Thackeray got older and succession happened in the Sena.

'See, Balasaheb was very direct,' he says, comparing the Thackerays, 'he created the Shiv Sainiks. Bala Saheb's word in the party was the final word… See, Uddhav Thackeray can never be him, nor can Raj Thackeray.' Uddhav, Bala Saheb's introverted, educated son had, till then, been a wildlife photographer, aloof from politics.

'He doesn't have that… he doesn't have that,' Rane explains, becoming exasperated. 'I don't know how much he understands politics, but it doesn't matter now.' 'See, Uddhav Thackeray, he never used to pick up anybody's call. Like if you tried to contact Uddhav Thackeray…. you won't be able to,' Nilesh says. 'But I heard from other media people that nowadays he picks up everybody's phone,' Nilesh shrugs dismissively.

More than the issues he endorsed, it appears Uddhav wasn't able to win people over, to give them their due. He was removed from the Sena in its early, tough years, and when he joined the Party later, he wasn't able to establish a connect with the older guard. The younger Thackeray just wasn't able to listen, cajole, lead, accommodate and play, essentially, the requisite politics.

In the rare speeches Uddhav Thackeray gives, he stands in front of a poster of himself – a tall, lanky figure. Even when he's trying to be forceful, he sounds placating and he looks at the audience worriedly, not sure they're convinced. Khaki-clad security men stand behind him, their eyes darting about, scanning the audience, largely uninterested in what's being said. The experience – with the big grandiose poster, the security men – couldn't be more different from an original Bal Thackeray rally.

When Uddhav was given control of the Sena and Bala Saheb's nephew Raj Thackeray stormed out in 2005, he dealt the party a blow. Raj had watched Bal Thackeray operate closely for years. He launched his own party – the Maharashtra Navnirman Sena (MNS), a revivalist version of the Shiv Sena.

'Raj Thackeray *ne to,* he has divided all the Marathi votes... People see Bala Saheb in Raj Thackeray now,' Nilesh points out, 'People think, *theek hai*, Bala Saheb has become old now, so he will take care of us.' Nilesh expands, 'See people are emotional, you know, Marathi people, or Gujarati people, or any people, they are emotional people. They look for leaders who'll take care of them for so many years, like Bala Saheb took care of Marathi people. Now, they might think Raj Thackeray will take care of Marathi people; see, these are all emotions.' Taking 'care', as Nilesh talks about it, seems more a figurative notion; it involves speaking out, reassurance and cultural solidarity, rather than material progress.

When Raj Thackeray speaks, at the many rallies he holds, the similarity to his uncle is apparent. The audience laughs periodically. Behind him, there are people seated on the dias giggling. No security. But Raj speaks with a lot more force than Bal Thackeray ever had to employ. His voice is louder, his questions and answers, and pauses, more dramatic. His face is intent. The performance is a good one, but rehearsed. It isn't the wry-dry, easy delivery of his uncle.

'People compare Bala Saheb with Raj Thackeray, but I don't know for what,' Nilesh mutters. Having watched Bal Thackeray intimately, he feels no emotional connect with Raj.

'He looks like him, style *uskey jaisa hain*, Bala Saheb *jaisey baat kar raha* (he has the same style, the same manner of talking), his movements are like him, his way of doing politics is like him...But he is not Bala Saheb.'

***

How have the Ranes adjusted to the Congress, to working with Sonia Gandhi, after all this? 'See, Bala Saheb and Madam,' Nilesh says, immediately, 'we don't compare the two.' The Ranes – father Narayan and son Nilesh – were under Bala Saheb's wing right from childhood; they grew in politics under him, were fired up by him, were molded by him. However, when they joined 'Madam', she accepted them as full-blown mature politicians.

The Ranes brought with them Assembly seats in the Konkan Coast, the potential of a couple of Lok Sabha seats. Traditionally, the Konkan Coast had been a weak spot for the Congress in Maharastra, a state where its grip in other areas had also been eroded by the Sena and Sharad Pawar's breakaway party, the Nationalist Coalition Party (NCP). In the Sena, Bal Thackeray had been like a family patron to the Ranes, a leader with a god-fatherly aura. But now, with the Congress Party, the Ranes entered a polite, mutually beneficial alliance.

'With the Shiv Sena, I never had a post, I never wanted a post. You didn't need a post,' Nilesh says. When he joined the Congress, however, he was given an official post. 'I was called, Observer, Ratnagiri District.' Shortly after, he was given a ticket to stand for elections from Ratnagiri. It wouldn't have happened so early in the Shiv Sena, Nilesh ponders with satisfaction.

Narayan Rane and Nilesh cranked all their old networks along the Konkan coast. Ratnagiri, so long stuck with the Shiv Sena, turned to the Congress. Suresh Prabhu, a former banker and a long time Konkan MP (he'd also been Minister of Industry in the Vajpayee government) fought opposite Nilesh from the Shiv Sena. In fact, up until this election, the Ranes had been managing Prabhu's campaigns in Ratnagiri. 'Prabhu Saheb didn't have party workers of his own, so this time when he looked around him, there was no one there,' Nilesh smiles.

'He lost touch with his constituency,' he says of Prabhu, 'He stopped coming there. That's how you lose touch.' He thought he'd become 'a very big leader,' having been in Vajpayee's cabinet, Rane postulates. Nilesh, on the other hand, knew the entire system, bottom to top. Perhaps, because of the organizational, protest-oriented culture of the Shiv Sena, he'd learnt to build bonds. He knew people, he'd run career counseling programs among the youth, had made his own networks on the Coast. 'The relation is such, that's the reason they work for you,' he explains. 'That's what went wrong with Suresh Prabhu – for a taluka President, he was just a Member of Parliament... Now, for the same *taluka* President, I wasn't just a party associate, I was a friend.'

A whole lot of dirt was flung about during the election. Uddhav Thackeray said Nilesh Rane was a *goonda* (hooligan), with a bevy of criminal cases against him ('a small, car accident case,' Nilesh clarifies, true to style). The Shiv Sena further alleged that Narayan Rane and his son had illegally given out land for mining in one of the *talukas*. When the Ranes agitated against this, Uddhav Thackeray held a counter protest, calling the Ranes *murgi chor* (literally, 'chicken thieves'). Narayan Rane retaliated by accusing Uddhav of selling election tickets to candidates. 'They don't know how to convince people,' Nilesh says, firmly casting aside the mud-slinging. And he was proved right – in that election, also his first, Nilesh Rane won Ratnagiri by a comfortable margin.

'See, regional parties will always target things. You will see that in other states also.' Now ensconced in the Congress, Nilesh analyses 'regional' parties with skepticism. He rues the plight of the regional party – they tend to 'think about the next election, but issues take time to build. People are tired of listening, you know, *isse yeh nahi hoga because yeh Hindu nahi hai* (he won't be able to do this because he's not a Hindu) etc...,' Nilesh says, in sync with his new party's secularist motto. 'They want development now and they believe in their hearts and minds that the Congress Party is the only party that will think about development... It's not like we are making schools for Hindus or Muslims. It's not like that. See, once you are development oriented,' he says, warming to his theme, 'naturally, you do good for all people.'

Nilesh Rane adopts the Congress totems easily – development and secularism. When I ask him about development within his own constituency, he says he's been busy with his father's assembly campaign, then talks of the mango and cashew plantations in the Konkan, how he wants to encourage food processing and tourism and real estate development. He discusses a scheme to convince villagers in the Konkan Coast to exchange their plots of land for ones closer to city centres so that there is 'access to better civic services.' (I can't decide if the scheme is a state government ploy to free up Konkan land for re-sale or an actually beneficial program.)

Rane finally comments on Rahul Gandhi, the star of the Congress Party. 'You know what Rahul Gandhi is,' Nilesh muses, 'he wants to understand his country, that's why he goes to the remotest of areas, something his father Rajiv Gandhi couldn't do before he became Prime Minister. Rahul Gandhi could have thought, 'I want to become a Minister.' He could have become a Minister anytime, but he didn't. He wanted to travel all over India, to reach out to the last person. He gives support to people like us... because a *neta* should rule a country which he has had a look at,' Rane says, appreciatively. 'That is what party workers like us see – what is the leader looking at?'

In the end, I sense Nilesh Rane adapts quickly and doesn't hold fast to any particular ideology. He's observed different buckets of leaders, and postulates on their qualities with ease – Bal Thackeray's oratory skill, Sonia Gandhi's diplomatic sensibility, Rahul Gandhi's common-man oriented hitch-hiker approach. 'I don't talk that much. I like to listen to people because that is what helps me to judge people. *Ki yaar, ke yeh aadmi kaisa hoga*? (To think, what must this person be like?)...,' Rane says. 'I like to listen to leaders, to different personalities and people. I like to listen to someone like (industrialist) Laxmi Mittal. I like to watch the qualities of these people, who are different in people eyes.'

More than the fire of ideology, more than the allure of Marathi pride or development, Nilesh seems a keen observer of power. He has an eye for political style and tactic. Having gone from the experience of the Shiv Sena *andolans* as a child, through periods of uncertainty, to his current position in the Congress, Rane has come to learn how power is built, what sustains it, what undermines it.

***

In the pot-holed political landscape of Maharashtra, Nilesh and Narayan Rane take care to cultivate their own power and retain some independence from the Congress. In 2008, they started their own newspaper called *Prahar* – having observed the Sena's weekly paper *Saamna* and Bal Thackeray's way of writing columns to keep in touch with his electorate. For *Prahar,* Narayan Rane writes columns as Advising Editor; Nilesh and his brother are Directors. Today, the paper already has a circulation of almost 100,000 readers.

Nilesh has recently been in the news for, among other things, commissioning a commercial Hindi film on Chhatrapati Shivaji, the iconic Maratha warrior.

With this, it appears he has trumped the Sena once again; Bal Thackeray's daughter-in-law Smita Thackeray being a film producer, Nilesh will be the first to bring Shivaji to Bollywood.

As we wind down, I can't help but ask Nilesh Rane how, having observed so many different leaders, he see himself, how he envisions his own future as a leader.

'See, I don't see myself as a leader at such an early age. If I think I am the leader of the masses or leader of such... I don't believe in all that,' Nilesh scoffs, quick to catch on. '*Bas, kaam hona chahiye* (Your work's got to speak).'

Notes

1 Rakshit Sonawane and Abhiram Gadyalpatil, 'Konkan was Sena's Bihar,' *Indian Express*, 23 November 2005

The Man With The Blues

Milind always talks as much about the blues and music as he does about politics. As a politician from South Mumbai, he manages to retain an urban, eclectic set of values.

MILIND DEORA
Indian National Congress (INC)
South Mumbai Constituency, Maharashtra
Born on 4 December 1976
27 years of age at first election
Last victory margin of 112, 682 votes

At *Q'BA*, a bar and performance space, on Malcha Marg in Delhi, Milind Deora plays a guitar solo in Little Walter's blues song *You Better Watch Yourself* on stage. He's bent over as he plays; he barely looks up, except to nod at the band's other guitarist.

Tonight, Milind is jamming with Soul Mate, a band from the northeast, Meghalaya. The lead singer, with wispy black hair and a thin line of red lipstick, has plastic flowers and a paper butterfly hanging off her mike. She sings Sam Cooke's civil rights song barefoot.

At Milind's intermittent gigs, at Q'BA and at Turquoise Cottage in Vasant Vihar, there's a mix of friends and politicians – friends from Mumbai, the Venezuelan ambassador, Congress MP Sachin Pilot and his wife Sara, Congress MP Jitin Prasada's wife Neha, Nationalist Congress (NCP) MP Agatha Sangma, Biju Janata Dal (BJD) MP Jai Panda and his wife Jaggi, Congress MP and author Shashi Tharoor and his wife Sunanda, and also Tathagata Satapathy, BJD MP from Orissa and a close friend of Milind's – all looking relaxed in jeans.

Later in the night, everyone dances, or at least bops in their chairs; the table and chairs are this way and that.

At the very end, as the place is shutting down, one or two of Milind's close friends and the band hang out. Milind tells stories about his favorite blues players – about playing with his idol, blues musician Buddy Guy when he came to Mumbai, and about finding himself in a conversation about Buddy Guy's jazz bar in Chicago, Checkerboard Lounge, with President Obama when he came to India.

***

The first time I meet Milind, I end up waiting for an hour; I ask for 'Mr Deora' so the man in his office assumes I'm there to see Milind's father, Murli Deora. Everyone in the office calls Milind by his first name. 'Ah, Milind,' the man says and phones him as soon as he realizes the mistake.

Milind sails in and slips into his chair. He's in a loose suit and has an effortlessly casual air about him.

Milind is Member of Parliament from South Mumbai, an urban, disparate constituency. 'A lot of friends I know stay in Delhi and go to their constituency in XYZ place. There they're wearing a *kurta-pyjama*, and saying *Namaste*, and all that, and in Delhi, they're sort of T-shirt, jeans, chilled out. But, I don't have that luxury in South Mumbai,' Milind explains, talking about what it's like to be an urban politician.

'I'm never, in a way, not interacting with constituents. If I go out to a bar and I shake hands with someone, it's a constituent. For most MPs, the guy they shake hands with in a bar is just someone in the city they live in and they'll take a train the next morning to their constituency. I'm playing at Jazz by the Bay in Mumbai, the 150 people watching me there, they're voters also.'

'One could say it's annoying, but at the same time, it's a good thing,' Milind muses, sitting back. 'It allows you to be who you are and I believe these are things you can't be contrived about. It's annoying because you don't have that distinction between personal space and public space, but it's a good thing because I wouldn't want to be two different people.'

Milind speaks easily, without editing his words too much.

'I mean, I'm very comfortable with who I am; I could go for a program in jeans and straight from there, go to a party...or vice versa. I don't think it's a luxury; most MPs I know say it sounds horrible,' he says, reflecting on his persona. 'But, I think it keeps you in check. I don't have a complex about my guitar and my music. Okay, with my constituents, I have to have this image of a serious politician and later I can have this guitar image. It's the same both ways. If you find it frivolous: tough luck.'

***

Milind always talks as much about music as he does about politics. 'It's like, I actually can't not talk about music. I can have endless conversations about music,' he says.

His mother sent Milind and his brother, Mukul, to guitar lessons when they were twelve, Milind tells me. He learned a couple of songs and dropped the classes. Later, in 1992, when he was sixteen and listening to Nirvana, Guns n Roses and Jimi Hendrix, he picked up the guitar again. Milind bought a book of guitar cheats to play Guns n Roses. 'I associated it with the lifestyle of Guns n Roses,' he says, with the same unapologetic, renegade attitude. 'It became much more than just a guitar to me. I picked it up on my own.'

Later, Milind moved from rock and roll towards blues music. In college in Boston, USA, Milind says, a friend made him listen to Stevie Ray Vaughn, a Texan musician, who was 'like a bridge between rock and the blues.' From Stevie Ray Vaughn, he started listening to Buddy Guy, Muddy Waters, and the old Delta Blues records of Robert Johnson and slowly picked up how to play the blues guitar.

Blues music evolved through black slaves living in America singing their spirituals. 'When they began to learn English, they added a chord or two and they kept repeating that chord,' Milind explains. The blues sprang up in plantations on the muddy Mississippi delta in the 1930s and 40s, in black tailor shops and barber shops, behind closed doors, in the segregated South, when black people weren't allowed into white areas.

The first time he listened to blues music, Milind says, it had sounded too 'simple,' too plain. 'You learn to like the blues. It's like a drink. I didn't realize it's meant to be that way. I didn't even realize the influence of blues music. I had no one to tutor me about what this was about.'

'I was drawn to it,' he says, thinking out loud, 'because I think everyone is looking for something they want to believe in, some religion or something, some higher form of faith, or spirituality, and I found that in the blues. From an early age, I found that in rock music in that sense. I never thought of rock as just music or a guitar chord only, I always thought of it as – it's my little universe. For me, when I'm alone in a room, playing the blues, I'm connected to these artists. We're sharing notes – what happened to you, what's happened to me.'

A lot of blues music is about homelessness, loneliness, about constantly leaving and, of course, about women. Rock, which was born out of the blues in the 1960s and 1970s, is similarly about the alienation and restlessness of the young. Rock, and later the quieter, humbler blues, gave Milind an alternative, removed world.

'You know, you deal with the blues by singing it, listening to it, playing it. At the same time, it's a community,' he muses, describing what drew him to the blues. 'I don't like to fit in. I find it very uncomfortable to fit in. I've always found anything that's mainstream, I don't like it, instantly. So when things are going very well, I'm worried.'

'Mukul and I both always wanted to be musicians really, I think, in our heart of hearts,' Milind mulls. Mukul, Milind's brother, is now a musician and a music and film producer. 'I was always jealous of the fact that when I was studying in Boston, a lot of my friends were at the Berkeley College of Music in that city. I know if I applied I would have gotten in there,' Milind says, still a little wistful. Instead, his parents – like most Indian parents would – had encouraged him to study business. 'I always felt bad that I wasn't able to go there and wasn't encouraged to study music.'

***

After he finished his degree at Boston University – Milind eventually studied Business – he moved back to Mumbai and started working in the family plastics business. At the same time, he became involved with a non-profit organisation called SPARSH, started by his father. SPARSH organized hardware and IT, job-oriented training in high schools. 'And in the government-aided schools, not in the posh schools, because South Mumbai is a posh constituency, relatively,' Milind points out.

Murli Deora. Milind's father, is a Congress politician; until very recently, he was the Oil and Natural Gas Minister and then the Corporate Affairs Minister in the United Progressive Alliance (UPA) Cabinet. He came into politics 'very gradually,' Milind says of his father, becoming a Municipal Councilor first, then Mayor of Mumbai, then fighting for a Lok Sabha seat. The elder Deora has been close to the Gandhi family, and his political career has zigzagged with theirs – he lost the Lok Sabha elections three times when they weren't in power (in 1980, 1996, and 1998) and won four times.

He always had a business 'to fall back on,' when he wasn't elected, Milind says. He's often said, 'You have to have some business, something to do. You shouldn't be sitting around, with nothing to do, when you're not in power.' His parents, particularly his mother, never wanted Milind to enter politics. They had a family business and she'd always advised him to work in the business and do social work that interested him. The demands, the publicity, the highs and lows that come with politics, she felt, didn't make for a stable life. Till the very last moment, before he got his ticket, his mother was nervous. 'Are you sure you want do this?' she kept asking him.

Through his NGO, Milind had come to interact with local political leaders – government school trustees, who were also local politicians, and party workers. That was around December 2003, Milind narrates, when the Bharatiya Janata Party (BJP) was in power. State elections had just happened in four states. The Congress Party, which had been in power in all four states lost three out of the four to the BJP, and retained only Delhi. The BJP had been on a high. 'Mr Vajpayee had decided that they'll call the General Election early because there was a feel good factor and all that. And they decided to have the General Election in April.'

That was the time, 2003 to 2004, when the BJP's vocal, aggressive leaders had seemed to stand out against the sleepy, old, extinguished faces in the Congress. The BJP had launched the impressive 'India Shining' campaign.

'I remember South Mumbai was a constituency where anyone you met at a restaurant or out, they were all totally into the BJP – 'the BJP is great; they're the only party that appeals to us; Congress doesn't have any leaders that appeal to us; the economy's booming blah blah blah,' Milind recollects their words. 'All my friends said there's no way you can win; the BJP is so powerful, India Shining, all that. But if the campaign had any impact, it made it in South Mumbai's Peddar Road, Altamount Road, and Marine Drive. Another section was totally ignored.'

'Contrary to a lot of people who said the Congress is going to do badly, because of my exposure to a different section of society through SPARSH, I was convinced that people are not happy with what's going on. This section is still struggling, not just to get a computer education in a school, but to earn a livelihood and feed their family. This gave me a strong sense of conviction to actually say that, no, there's still a strong opportunity politically. It's not all that rosy for the BJP here.'

When elections came around, the Congress Party needed a candidate. Milind's father was already Rajya Sabha MP by then and couldn't fight. Eventually, Milind got a ticket and, despite his mother's fretting to the end, stood in the 2004 elections. He pulled through against the BJP's Jayawantiben Mehta, his father's old rival (whom his father had defeated in two elections and who in turn, had defeated the senior Deora in the previous election) by a slim margin of about 10,000 votes.

***

In late 2009, in his office at his father's residence in Delhi, Milind talks to me about urban development and the Jawaharlal Nehru National Urban Renewal Mission (JNNURM). 'I firmly believe,' Milind says, 'that for a long time in India, we've given a huge emphasis to agricultural, rural economy and we should; but the rate at which the country is urbanizing, you can't ignore the issue of urban development.'

There are thousands of cities mushrooming chaotically around India, and the JNNURM is an effort to regulate, and allocate funds for, urban development. JNNURM has gotten some appreciation for its vision – to encourage urban planning, to make municipal bodies accounts transparent online, to withdraw urban land ceiling acts. It's also gotten flack for being ramshackle in its approach – it encourages cities to take big loans, it recommends privatization of water and other public services without guidelines, and doesn't offer much real assistance in urban planning to cities without planning experience.

'It's the first urban initiative in a long time, twenty years, since Rajiv Gandhi set up the Urbanization Commission. And it's the first of its kind to attempt creating a uniform approach towards urban development around India,' Milind says. However, he doesn't embrace privatization in water, and other public services unreservedly. 'The whole notion of government being bad – In the last year or so, we've seen that public sector banks and Public Sector Units (PSUs) are better managed than private banks. Also, a private company is not going to go in unless there's a profit motive behind it,' Milind ponders. But in case the government does privatize a service people can't pay for, he says, the government has to make sure it shells out the amount to the private player.

Apart from his continued work in SPARSH on computer education in government schools, Milind talks about fund-raising for government hospitals and about his recent events in Mumbai – he last took Bollywood star Salman Khan to a juvenile detention center just outside his constituency.

When I next meet Milind, in late 2011, he's been handed a major new responsibility. Murli Deora formally resigned as Minister for Corporate Affairs in July 2011. A week later, Milind was appointed Minister of State in the Ministry of Telecom and IT. Sachin Pilot, a good friend, is also Junior Minister in the same Ministry; Kapil Sibal is currently the Cabinet Minister for Telecom and IT.

***

When he came to Parliament in Delhi for the first time, at just twenty-seven, Milind reminisces with a laugh, 'The first day, I was wearing a short-sleeve shirt, tucked in, trousers, and these evil-eye beads. I was this kid, with an interest in the social sector.'

In Parliament, he observed the various kinds of dress, language, background and experience MPs came with, Milind shares, and realized how representative politics actually is. Parliament was fantastic and, at the same time, overwhelming. 'Parliament may have been too big a platform to start out with. Now, looking back, maybe I should have started with local elections.'

'I had worked in an NGO and that's what I thought politics was about,' Milind shares. 'I was into development and politics just seemed like a natural progression.'

Unlike other politicians, Milind says, 'I didn't know how to identify people's community and caste by their names. I didn't know how to address them properly.' He had come from an urban constituency, had an urban upbringing, gone to college abroad. Working in government schools, surrounded by slums and skyscrapers in Bombay, he knew enough about economic disparity, but he had never encountered the strong social stratifications of Indian society.

Only two years in did Milind begin to realize the importance of community, of caste, religion and region. He couldn't, he says, for instance, walk into an area and just talk about the work on water he's done there. 'People are often more interested in the assurances you give them, related to their religion and community, than in the water coming out of their taps,' Milind muses. He's learnt to give subtle deference to people's social identity, in Parliament and in his constituency, though the posturing and pretence that it involves still makes him uncomfortable.

'It's only now that I've attained political maturity,' Milind says candidly, after two elections, at the age of thirty-four. 'When I talk to Sachin (Pilot), he tells me he always knew about caste alliances in politics and so on. But I didn't. I wasn't raised like that. I've learned.'

In 2008, during his first term as MP, Milind got married to Pooja Shetty, whom he'd been dating for some time. Pooja, the daughter of film producer Manmohan Shetty, runs her own production company Walk Water Media and shares Milind's love for music.

A few weeks after their wedding in November, at the Oberoi hotel, the terror attacks on the Taj and the Oberoi hotels in South Mumbai took place. In the aftermath of the attacks, people were dissatisfied with the government's response. 'What people wanted was some leadership and a voice of reassurance,' Milind points out. On the night of and in the days following the attacks, Milind roamed the city. The very next morning, he was on national television to talk about what was happening. He let people know – 'I hear you and we're doing something about it.'

'I was in touch with people. I let them know what they should do, what they shouldn't do.' In the moment of panic, just that was enough. 'People appreciated I was out there,' Milind says.

Milind was re-elected in 2009 in an election that generated speculation: The de-limitation of the South Mumbai constituency brought in a new electorate of mill workers; analysts commented, 'South Mumbai will go to the person who carries the morning walkers on Marine Drive and the Mill workers of Parel with the same ease'.[1] In 2009 also, the banker Meera Sanyal, fighting as an independent candidate, and the ophthalmic surgeon Mona Shah, fighting from the Professionals Party of India, threatened to split liberal votes.

However, Milind won by a ten-fold margin over 2004, nearly 113,000 votes. (A candidate from Raj Thackeray's Maharashtra Navnirman Sena was the first runner up, with the Shiv Sena candidate a close second. Sanyal and Shah came fourth and fifth.) By then, the Deora family had sold their plastics business – Milind's father, Murli, his brother, Mukul, and Milind himself all had a diminishing interest in it.

Last year, on 12 July 2011, Milind was sworn in as Minister of State in the Ministry of Telecom and IT. The next day, on 13 July, there were bomb explosions in Dadar, Javeri Bazaar and the Opera House in Mumbai. Milind got a call from Home Minister P. Chidambaram and flew with him from Delhi to Mumbai the night of the blasts. This time, Milind admits, people were angrier. 'They said, you all just come here, but nothing happens.' Still, when the anger dies down, Milind says, people do appreciate you're out there, reassuring them and doing your best.

From a clueless twenty-something in jeans entering Parliament for the first time, Milind has come some distance. His interests and his own eclectic urban values haven't changed: Milind talks about (Mahatma) Gandhi's creative politics and his ability to unite people, about Robert Kennedy's courage in backing the black civil rights movements in America, and about reading the biographies of Eric Clapton and Slash –

the Guns n Roses guitar player – about how much they gave through music, all in the same breath. However, over seven years in politics, Milind has become alive to the other realities around him.

***

Now when I meet him, Milind talks about the Ministry. He has to spend increasingly more time in Delhi, which involves a big shift for him. Within the Ministry, he's handling telecommunications (his fellow Minister, Sachin Pilot handles Posts and IT). 'I'm trying to re-energize the Ministry's focus towards protecting the consumer,' Milind says, a few weeks into the job. He's trying to make provisions to better respond to customer grievances with telecom operators, to protect consumer privacy and consumer health. For consumer health, he's trying to build capacity in the government to test imported handsets for radiation. 'A lot of it depends on you,' Milind says, explaining how he took on these particular projects. 'It's your instinct; you decide what to do.'

The move into the Ministry will leave Milind less time for playing concerts, something he sounds slightly jittery about.

***

'Have you ever thought of playing at your campaigns?' I ask Milind, imagining his political and music personas mix. I imagine him playing the guitar to political lyrics, perhaps inspiring a whole mass of people in a new kind of political action.

'No,' Milind says flatly, realistic in response to my question, 'that's a bit far-fetched.'

Notes

1 Liz Mathew, 'Marrying Marine Drive and the Mills,' *The Mint*, 19 April 2009

SIDHANT MOHAPATRA

KALIKESH SINGH DEO

The Prince And The Actor

Former Oriya star, Mohapatra, talks about dialogue, and responds emotionally. From the royal family of Orissa, Deo talks about development and industrialization. Both share approaches to the problems of tribals and Naxals in a remote, rocky state.

SIDHANT MOHAPATRA
Biju Janata Dal (BJD)
Behrampur Constituency, Orissa
Born on 4 May 1966
43 years of age at first election
Last victory margin of 66,566 votes

KALIKESH SINGH DEO
Biju Janata Dal (BJD)
Bolangir Constituency, Orissa
Born on 26 May 1974
37 years of age at first election
Last victory margin of 90,835 votes

Sidhant Mohapatra is called the 'chocolate boy' of Oriya cinema. He's also seen as the *Badshah* or emperor, of Ollywood (as the Oriya film industry is known); the *Badshah* moniker is a reference to Bollywood superstar Shah Rukh Khan. At other times, Sidhant is referred to simply as *Munnabhai*, after Sanjay Dutt's lovable character in *Munnabhai Zindabad*. After acting in over 150 movies in Oriya cinema, at forty-three, Sidhant is a superstar in Orissa, with the accumulated aura of Shah Rukh and Dutt.

Sidhant has an MBA from Delhi's Faculty of Management Studies (FMS) and was preparing to take his IAS exams (both his parents are doctors), when a cousin came to his house with a producer and insisted Sidhant accept an acting offer. In 1990, at the age of twenty-three, Sidhant blazed into Oriya cinema with the lead role in the melodramatic romance, *Shradhanjali* (offering.)

In the two decades since, Sidhant has made over 150 Oriya films; about eight movies a year, nearly a movie a month. Sidhant's repertoire includes love stories, tear-jerker family dramas and stunt-filled action flicks.

Sidhant's now in his early forties, his chocolate good looks burnished, roughened around the edges, and softened with age.

Mukhya Mantri (chief minister) was the last film Sidhant acted in before he got elected to the Lok Sabha. He played a local rickshaw-puller who becomes Chief Minister in a case of mistaken identity. His character becomes popular as a beloved ruler who fights corruption and makes things better for his people.

Ironically, just a few months after the film released, Mohapatra was called on by the Biju Janata Dal (BJD) Revenue Minister's son and asked if he wanted to join the party. Mohapatra formally joined the BJD on 13 March 2009, received his ticket for Behrampur on 3 April and, two weeks later, easily defeated his Congress party rival and veteran politician Chandrashekhar.

When I meet him a few months later, he's in Delhi for Parliament, trying to figure out how Parliament runs, puzzling through Question Hour. 'It's not a very normal language,' Sidhant says, 'I'm listening to everything, I'm watching. So many types of questions. When do I have to raise this question? When do I have to ask that question?' Suddenly script-less, the erstwhile actor is now trying to figure out his role in Parliament.

The switch to politics wasn't unusual. Hugely successful actors, especially in regional cinema, regularly come into state politics. The first major actor-turned-politician in the country was Tamil superstar MG Ramachandran, who became Chief Minister of Tamil Nadu in 1977. MGR played Robin Hood-like characters, who stood up for the poor – He was elected Chief Minister three times in a row. MGR once won an election even when he was laid up in hospital and hadn't actually been able to campaign. In Andhra Pradesh, NT Rama Rao, who played well-meaning gods – Krishna, Ram, Bheem – in fabulously popular Telugu movies, was also elected Chief Minister three times through the 1980s. And Jayalalitha, the current Chief Minister of Tamil Nadu, used to be a popular actress in Hindi and Tamil cinema.

So, it came as no surprise that Sidhant Mohapatra was a big success on the campaign trail. He'd travel in an open jeep, smiling and waving at his fans. He didn't have to say much – 'everyone shouted *Munnabhai Zindabad* (Long Live *Munnabhai*!),' he quips. 'Day and night, day and night, people have touched me. I told them, just you give your blessings, I don't need your votes, and people have blessed me. Today, I'm here. People have shown their love,' Sidhant narrates, with the tenor of an actor.

***

Even in his new role as politician, Sidhant still itches to make movies. He's taken permission to continue acting from the BJD President, the Orissa Chief Minister Naveen Patnaik, he tells me. Patnaik told Sidhant knew how much people loved him and encouraged him to continue his film career. Sidhant hopes to make at least a couple of movies a year.

His voice becomes conspiratorial as he mentions his next film, *Swayamsiddha (*Personal Principles*)*. 'My character is a Naxal Area Commander,' Sidhant says quietly, with excitement and trepidation.

The Naxals or Maoists, as they're alternatively called because of their affinity to communist ideas, are radical, militant groups that operate in the backward and forested corridors of the southern and eastern states of India – Andhra Pradesh, Bengal, Bihar, and of course, Orissa, among them.

In Orissa, Naxalism is said to have spread as a result of the harassment of tribal people by local authorities, the prevention of tribal access to forests and their displacement owing to large industrial projects in the region. Tribals account for twenty-two per cent of Orissa's population, but development and access to education, health and even food amongst them is abysmally low. Declared 'terrorists' by the Central Government, Naxalites are a subject of hot national debate. In 2004, the Naxals looted the police armoury near Orissa's Koraput forests, and ever since, have been hiding out in the forests, locked in opposition with the state police.

In February 2009, the central government announced plans for coordinated operations in all affected states, but no solution or two-way dialogue has ever borne much result (each time, both sides allege that the other side didn't make a sincere effort and undercut the agreement).

When I ask Sidhant more about *Swayamsiddha*, he introduces me to the film's director, Sudhanshu Sahoo. One Sunday afternoon, Sahoo passionately narrates the story of the movie over the phone.

'Five years ago, I had the idea. I wanted to make a film on the Naxals.' Sahoo pauses, then adds, '*Kya chahte hai? Sochne ki baat hain*. (What do they want? That's something to think about).'

Swayamsiddha tells the story of the Naxal movement through three characters – a journalist, a Naxal commander, and a young woman.

The journalist, played by Oriya actor Sunil, is the narrator – he's researching Naxal history and he becomes the conduit between the Naxalites and the government. Through him, Sahoo explains, 'You see the debate within the government. Like, right now, some people are planning this Operation Green Hunt (the name of the central government's effort to use the army and paramilitary forces to hunt down Naxalites), and other people are saying: No.' While sympathizing with the Naxal plight, the journalist is against their violence.

Sidhant's Naxal Area Commander (NAC) is a fierce character – cynical about change and justice, fed up of persecution by the local administration, he perceives violence as the only option.

Sahoo reasons, 'There's no peace in guns. But the government hasn't solved anything either, hasn't tried to understand what problems the poor have. In the Maoist areas, they've made a few houses, one or two small, concrete structures,' he adds. 'There's nothing else.'

A young village girl, the third pivotal character in the movie, represents the common people, the tribals at the periphery of the movement. Her family is falsely accused in a case and harassed by the local police. 'The police don't cooperate with the public in these areas,' Sahoo informs me. So the girl turns to the Naxals for help and joins their movement. '*Woh system key khilaf ho jati hai* (She turns against the system). She wants revenge and justice,' narrates Sahoo passionately.

The young woman in the movie, however, becomes disillusioned when she doesn't get either justice or a better life with the Naxals. 'People have died on both sides. What did I get?' she asks.

She tries to convince Sidhant's character, the Area Commander, to leave the cause with her, but he refuses. The story ends with the girl returning to 'mainstream' life, her future a question mark.

'What does she do after joining the mainstream?' I ask Sahoo.

'The government has no rehabilitation programs or anything worth showing. She leaves the movement – we just ended the movie there,' he retorts glumly.

For Mohapatra, *Swayamsiddha* is relevant on two main counts. It asks what Naxals are really fighting for, suggesting that more than a communist revolution, the tribals of Orissa want a sensitive police and state administration. They need freedom from violence and rape, from the daily bullying by state officials and the police. The tribals also want land promised to them and freedom to continue their way of life. At the same time, they want access to the basics: schools, education, and health care. They want that they be included in the nation's development.

This leads to the next question the film raises. What is the government doing to address Naxal issues, to give them incentives to lay down their arms? Sahoo finds no answers here; he insists that there is no real government effort in this regard.

The film doesn't, in the end, offer any solutions, Sahoo and Mohapatra conclude, but it raises awareness and a forum for debate on the ongoing crisis.

***

Swayamsiddha was shot in Naxal-dominated areas – the Koraput forests of Orissa and Lakhimpur in Chattisgarh. The crew felt ill at ease walking through miles of absolutely empty forest land. The risk and danger seemed palpable; everyone was on edge. Sahoo says he made sure he was always the last to leave the sets.

'Once, while shooting, a group of Naxalites come to us,' the director narrates. The crew froze. The Naxals had guns hidden under their clothes, and demanded to know what was going on. But once they were told, they quietly left. 'Their fight is with the government,' Sahoo tells me. 'Not with anyone else.'

'Have you met and spoken with Naxalites in real, political life?' I ask Sidhant.

'They don't have any special identity that says, 'I am a Naxalite.' They don't have a badge, or a uniform, or a turban, or anything,' Sidhant Mohapatra states, annoyed at the question, at this overblown image of the militant revolutionary. 'Who are the Naxalites? Common people only... any common man can be a Naxalite.' Though not every tribal in the village is a Naxalite, he clarifies, many common people turn to Naxalism from time to time. The police and local government tend to brand all tribals as Naxalites and this pushes even more common people towards Naxalism for protection.

We need a new approach, Sidhant suggests, and military action against the Naxals doesn't strike him as the right response. 'There will be lots of casualties, which I don't want. I have seen the poverty, I have seen the pain in their [the common people's] eyes,' he says sentimentally.

And yet there are no solutions, only a stalemate. Mohapatra believes in dialogue, and tries to listen and make sense of the problems in his constituency, Behrampur.

People come to him with cases of police violence, with land issues and water problems. For the first time, the MP says, he is dealing not just with the people's adulation but with their demands.

'You need to have patience,' Sidhant says. 'If you have patience, nothing is impossible.'

Water is a big problem in Behrampur. Mohapatra has been working on rain water harvesting and trying to figure out other ways to bring water into the region. The national highway, connecting Behrampur to other parts of the state, will soon be completed, he says, after almost ten years of waiting. 'I thought that if I want to do something in my constituency, then first I have to clear the roads, open the communication.' Local people had stalled the project. Mohapatra brokered the problem with them, speaking personally about what the highway would mean for them. 'I made my people understand that they need to sacrifice some ponds, some land, for this project. That this would, in the end, benefit them.'

***

On 6 April 2010, about a month after I'd first met Sidhant Mohapatra, 76 Central Reserve Police Force (CRPF) personnel were ambushed and killed by about 1,000 Naxals in the Dantewada forests of Chattisgarh.

This incident enraged the country. Even the more liberal media advocated the unleashing of the Air Force to carpet-bomb Naxals in the Chattisgarh forests.

It was a tense time, particularly for Sidhant Mohapatra, who, usually open about his empathy for the tribal Naxals, fell silent. I called to ask him about the government response to the incident; he was tightlipped. 'We don't want to disclose more. We have instructions to keep our plans confidential.'

A year later, the Supreme Court's Mander Report released its findings. The report wrote about 'acute hunger and starvation' in the Dantewada district.[1] Naxals in the area press on the tribals for food and protection, it said, and national security forces passing through the villages grab their grain and cattle. Instead of providing support, the state wantonly jails many ordinary tribals as Naxal sympathizers and government-backed para-militaries like the *Salwa Judum* further terrorize tribals. There's 'an undeclared civil war' against the poorest people in the country, the Mander Report concluded.

Recently, newspapers reported that Special Police Officers (SPOs) in Dantewada had burnt 300 homes, killed a few men and molested some tribal women. A few days later, these SPOs attacked truck drivers that were bringing food from the District Administration to villages.[2]

Although the Dantewada ambush happened in Chattisgarh, it left an impact on the discussion and action around Naxalism throughout the country. Today, public consensus has started to move towards recognizing the complexity of the Naxalite situation, rather than retaliating with more violence.

Mohapatra talks about the state government's plans to increase road communication to Naxal areas and to give forest land over to tribals. He adds with the emotional intelligence of an actor, 'We have to go there and talk with all these people without fear. We have to take them into our confidence.'

For Sidhant Mohapatra, this simple approach, whatever difficulties it brings in implementation, still seems the only way forward.

***

Kalikesh Deo is terribly good looking. He could be an actor too (one of his brothers is, in fact, at acting school and trying to break into Bollywood). When I meet him, Kalikesh is in a well-cut white *kurta* with rolled up sleeves and a sleeveless charcoal north-west fleece – effortlessly stylish.

Kalikesh Singh Deo is a Biju Janata Dal (BJD) MP from Bolangir, Orissa; he's also from the former royal family of Orissa. Kalikesh dated Raima Sen, the Bollywood actress, who also comes from royal lineage, for a while, everyone loves to remember. He eventually married Meghna Rana, who grew up in Nepal but went to school at Welham's in India; they've just had a baby boy. A big, new pram lies in the porch of the house.

Kalikesh's air is informal and well-mannered. His office, though simple, has a note of style – a classic, old wooden desk and chair, in an otherwise bare room with standard steel shelves and newly whitewashed walls.

Kalikesh went to boarding school – the Doon school in Dehradun – and studied economics at St. Stephen's College, Delhi University. Deo then worked in financial services in India, before leaving for the United States for a job with the then enormous power company, Enron. Deo rose quickly while at Enron and managed entire businesses in Latin America. The experience of corporate America was eye-opening, he says – young managers were given a great amount of freedom, the atmosphere was casual, he'd play golf over the weekends with the company's CEO. By the time he left, however, Deo admits he begin to see some unusual practices – the hiving off of assets, which would lead to Enron's eventual downfall.

As a teenager, Kalikesh, along with his parents, would travel through villages in the Bolangir district of Orissa, watch them as they stopped in villages and interacted with people; very early, Kalikesh decided he wanted to be a politician. His grandfather, R.N. Singh Deo, the last real Maharaja of Patna-Bolangir, had transitioned into democratic politics in 1948 after the merger of the country's royal states with the new Government of India. The senior Deo was Chief Minister of Orissa in 1967 and then, later, joined the Opposition. Kalikesh's father, A.U. Singh Deo, is also a politician as well as a hotelier. He is currently a Member of the Legislative Assembly (MLA) in the state government of Orissa.

Kalikesh tells me about how his father, A.U. Singh Deo, tried to jump the palace gates before his first election, when he was twenty-seven years old. He had been a very reluctant politician; he'd wanted to develop hotels in Orissa. But he was pressured by Kalikesh's grandmother and quickly made to stand. Many of the elections he fought, A.U. Singh Deo lost – to other members of the Deo family or to Congress party candidates, when there were waves of Congress support. In time, Kalikesh's father built hotels, which had been his first interest.

Kalikesh chats very easily about all the Deo family drama, perhaps because there's been so much of it. Kalikesh's branch of the family fights elections from the Biju Janata Dal (BJD), his uncle's branch of the family fights from the Bhartiya Janata Party (BJP). During elections, different parts of the family campaign opposite each other for votes in constituencies that were once part of the royal kingdom.

The story is not unusual for a royal family. Still, the Deo family is particularly knotty. In the last general election in 2009, Kalikesh stood opposite his cousin's wife, his sister-in-law, Sangeeta Deo, in Bolangir. Meanwhile, in Patnagarh, Sangeeta Deo's husband, Kanak Singh Deo, fought against his own brother's wife, Prakriti Singh Deo. The entire family was on the campaign trail, cutting up votes.

Kalikesh's father too had fought earlier against his nephew's wife, Sangeeta Deo, and lost. 'My father had refused to fight the 1989 election, because my uncle was fighting,' Kalikesh explains. 'But in 1991, when we thought my father would win hands down, he lost because my cousin fought and the family split votes.' Since then, there's been no love lost between the two branches of the family. In 2009, Kalikesh defeated his sister-in-law, Sangeeta Deo. The Congress candidate came second and three-time MP Sangeeta Deo stood third. 'My sister-in-law was MP for three terms, so they know what she did and they decided to give me a chance,' Kalikesh shrugs.

The conversation turns to Rahul Gandhi's rally in Kalahandi, Orissa, to the tribal population of Orissa, to development in tribal areas, and the spread of Naxalism. In August 2010, the Congress Party's Rahul Gandhi visited Kalahandi and congratulated the Dongria Kondh tribe for stopping the bauxite mine being made by the conglomerate, Vedanta. The mining project had been cleared by the Biju Janata Dal state government, but was stalled by the central government. On the foothills of the Niyamgiri mountain, which the tribe considers sacred and which they'd been fighting for, Rahul Gandhi promised the tribe that he would be their 'soldier' in Delhi. After Gandhi's speech, it is assumed that it will be near-impossible for the company to get the central government to reverse its decision on the project.

'The entire statement about tribals, and being a soldier to tribals, in Kalahandi, that move should backfire,' Kalikesh analyzes Gandhi's stand. 'Because it actually stopped a project which would have brought a lot of money into the system and done a lot of work in Kalahandi.'

One school of thought argues that tribals should be allowed to continue their way of life, maintain their original livelihoods on their land, and that the pace of mining, the appropriation and development of tribal land, should be slowed down. Since tribals have been displaced from their lands by mining projects, the reasoning goes, they've become more impoverished.

Kalikesh, however, doesn't agree with this school of thought. He has a more development and industry-oriented approach. He supports a kind of trickle-down theory, assisted by government-backed social development.

'There has to be a balance between a way of life for local inhabitants and mining activities, which do lead to employment and, you know, growth. Let's face facts: revenue comes in from industrial activity, whether it's for people who get jobs in that area, or people who are indirectly employed, contract workers, hotels, *paan-wallas*, taxi-*wallas* etc, or for governments,' Kalikesh explains, using macro-economic logic. 'Now, Orissa is a fiscal surplus state from a position where it was almost bankrupt in 1998 and 1999. That money is being used to set up tribal schools for girls, to build *aanganwadi* (primary states) centres, so you need the money; you need to have a balance.'

'To make development sustainable, you have to have a driver in an area. It could be a big industrial project, or it could be a big education project that actually generates revenue. In Kalahandi district, the mine was the driver,' says Kalikesh. 'They've spent about 10,000 crore. A lot of the contracts are being done by the local people.'

Kalikesh's macro-economic logic may be sound in theory. However, tribals, with their unique language and skills, aren't really able to get contracts, or participate in industrial activity. They tend to get displaced from their land and sidelined by such projects. Orissa has become richer as a state – state revenue has swollen, state debt decreased – but that hasn't translated into much for its tribals by way of good schools, homes and livelihoods.

In tribal areas, as Sidhant Mohapatra and Sudhanshu Sahoo point out, there are still no government services, nothing more than a few, unused concrete rooms in the name of development.

Movements against the mine reason that until tribal children are fully integrated into modern life with education and development, tribal land should not be taken away and mined.

(Kalikesh, however, tells me that the mining at Niyamgiri wouldn't have destroyed the mountain. The decision to halt mining, he insists, was a political move for the Congress.)

Deo analyzes further that there is nothing unusual about tribal aspirations. 'To my experience, even tribals today, even though they have a different way of life, and different priorities, a lot of them want to join the mainstream. Just because they are tribal, doesn't mean they should live off the forest and feed on 500 rupees in a year on forest produce. A lot of them want to get their children educated, get access to proper healthcare facilities, get jobs… I find this to be their primary driving force. It could be different in other areas, but, certainly, in Bolangir, there is a desire to join mainstream India and to participate in that process of growth.'

Tribals may want to join the mainstream, but as Mohapatra and Sahoo show in their movie, it's not easy for them in remote, under-developed villages with a hostile administration, to find a window into 'mainstream' life. Even close to major capitals, government schools in India barely function – teachers are absent, the administration negligent. So, in the periphery, in remote tribal areas, government-backed education and healthcare services are rare.

'I think there is a necessity to give a lot more to the people who are displaced, a lot more stake to the people who are of that local area,' Kalikesh admits.

Kalikesh has, in his own constituency, been trying to create new livelihoods. Bolangir is a remote area, which doesn't draw much investment. Deo has built roads and bridges to connect major economic centers.

Kalikesh is trying to bring in a 2,000 MW power plant, which will create about 5,000 jobs. The contract mentions that 90 per cent of the jobs will be local.Deo has got the Xavier's Institute of Management (XIM) to set up a rural management degree campus in Bolangir. An infrastructure company (IL &

FS) is going to build and run a 2,000 seat English-medium CBSE school, where apparently 30 per cent of its students will get a free education. They're also starting a vocational training center that will, to start with, train workers for the construction and the garment textile industry. Kalikesh explains the terms of the PPP with the company, 'They'll only get subsidized when they get a letter of appointment from employers.'

Deo is also trying to get clothing companies like shirt brand Pro Vogue and others, to set up small garment workshops in Bolangir. However, bringing in investment and jobs to Bolangir isn't easy, Kalikesh admits, because the area is remote, the terrain is hilly. 'It can't be a very major project because, even now, it's difficult, communication is difficult. There's no airport nearby, there's no ships there...'

Deo and Mohapatra shed light on a state poised between two struggles – for the right to land by local, indigenous tribes and for industrial projects by a state that wants to boost its revenues. Deo is conscientious but practical. He looks to the future, to industry to bring revenue into the state to, eventually, support spending for social welfare. He uses macro-economic measures for long-term growth, which will make everybody better off in the end. Mohapatra, on the other hand, is more emotional. He brings up the picture on the ground. He points to near-starvation tribes, to decades of neglect by government and to abuse by local administration. He doesn't say much about the mining projects, but asks for a fresh perspective.

Both paint glimpses of a difficult landscape, very remote from the world we can imagine.

Notes

1 Seema Chishti, 'Mander Report sees tribals caught in undeclared civil war,' *Indian Express*, 1 May 2011

2 Aman Sethi, 'SPOs assault truck owner for delivering rations to burnt village,' *The Hindu*, 24 March 2011

The Good Son

Hooda made sure women in his constituency were able to come to vote after he read an article that said they weren't being allowed.[1] He's a favorite among women in Haryana, young and old.

DEEPENDER SINGH HOODA

Indian National Congress (INC)
Rohtak Constituency, Haryana
Born on 4 January 1978
26 years of age at first election
Last victory margin of 4,45,736 votes

September 2009, a few weeks before the Haryana State Assembly Elections, Chief Minister Bhupinder Singh Hooda's house is crowded. Congress party workers from the state, in white kurtas or saris and sneakers, file through the gate, line the driveway and fill the big *shamiana* (tent) in the garden.

The Congress party has given the incumbent CM Hooda a fairly free hand to choose candidates and manage the Haryana elections. Candidates who'll fight elections in the state are

going to be announced in a few days. People linger, waiting for a nomination, an appointment, a word from the CM.

In the midst of all this, Deepender Hooda, the Member of Parliament (MP) from Rohtak, Haryana, and CM Bhupinder Hooda's son, speaks with me in his small, organized office at the back of the house. Deepender's phone vibrates throughout the interview. '*Haan*, Captaan Saab, *abhi aaya* (Yes, Captaan Saab, I'm on my way),' Deepender says into it. He's wanted outside to meet people.

As we walk out of his office into the garden full of Congress workers, I ask Deepender if he's also involved in choosing candidates for the elections. 'No,' he replies immediately, reddening, 'that's all my father.'

Many Haryana politicians' sons are infamous for toting guns, blazing through nightclubs and throwing their fathers' names around. The leader of the opposition in Haryana, the Congress' main rival, O.P. Chautala's sons, Ajay and Abhay Chautala are rumored to be ruffians and fixers; they're believed to be part of a call girl racket operating out of a dodgy hotel in the state. They've been accused of fixing cricket matches for big money.

In the Congress as well, high profile Haryana minister Venod Sharma's son has been embroiled in scandal. Manu Sharma was convicted in 2006 for murdering Jessica Lall, a former model who was mixing drinks at a bar in Delhi. Manu Sharma shot Jessica when she refused to serve him a drink after last orders; he fled the scene and buried the gun. The Sharmas paid off witnesses to manipulate the trial and Sharma was acquitted. Later, after a storm of public and media pressure, he was re-tried and convicted.

Deepender Hooda is a far cry from the spoilt, lawless stereotype. He's studious: Deepender has a Bachelors degree in Technology from Haryana and a Masters in Business Administration from the Kelley School in Indiana in the United States (Hooda later worked for a Dallas, Texas based company for a couple of years). Now, as an MP, he participates in Aspen Institute organized debates in Delhi and writes editorial columns in the *Indian Express* from time to time.

Deepender is conscientious: he travels around Rohtak with a light entourage of just two station wagons. People mill around his car at traffic lights; they wait for him in clusters on the road. Deepender stops the car everywhere and engages them. Other politicians sons travel with a posse of armed cars, four commandos ahead and four commandos behind, Congress workers tell me; 'MP *saab* travels like an *aam aadmi* (Our MP travels like a common man)', they say fawning over Deepender. Other party's sons, when they come, they say, even their own party MLAs are scared of approaching them, forget about regular people.

In the middle of one of his meetings at a village in Rohtak, a cranky old man interrupts Deepender with a rant and everyone tries to get him to shut up. '*Baba, Main Sunoonga* (Baba, I'll listen)', Deepender says, letting the old man finish his rant and responding to him. He, ultimately, wins him over.

Apart from old people, women of all ages seem to like Deepender. He's fit, fair, and sweet-looking and he hums with an eager, nervous energy. He was considered a heart throb among young girls before he got married, one of his assistants shares as we drive through Haryana; old women look upon him like their son; he still gets about a hundred *rakhis* every year from women who consider him their brother.

Deepender's wife Sweta describes him as 'gentle' and 'emotional' – unexpected words for the standard Haryana husband, known to exemplify machismo. Sweta, the granddaughter of Nathu Ram Mirdha, the Jat politician from Haryana, and Deepender married in February 2010. Sweta is opinionated, independent and goal-oriented. Apart from her background, she defies all my expectations of a political wife. Sweta studied Accounting and Business Statistics at Rajasthan University because she wanted 'a thorough grounding' in finance. She then did an MBA from the University of San Francisco, again with a focus on finance. After her MBA, she worked in the US, as her husband did, and spent over eight years in California in mergers and acquisitions.

Sweta's sister, Jyoti Mirdha, is now an MP from their grandfather's constituency, Nagaur, in Rajasthan. Jyoti introduced Sweta to Deepender when she moved back to India from San Francisco. Sweta had always said, 'I'm not going to marry a politician' and 'I'm not going to get married in Haryana.' Deepender was an MP from Haryana, disqualified on both counts, but he managed to win her over. Deepender 'wasn't jaded by politics,' Sweta says, 'he was sensitive, he had a lot of him intact.' She was also thirty-two when they married, so she felt she'd done enough by then to shape her own life and identity.

Apart from the odd visit, Sweta isn't involved in her husband's constituency. She has, so far, refused to be an accessory to his politics. 'I'm the last person at every political dinner,' she tells me, wearily. She's taken on a freelance research project with the World Bank and has been studying water issues, conservation and delivery in Rajasthan, her home state. (I rattle out some names on water conservation I know and quickly realize she's read extensively, and met everyone possible, on the subject.) When she's not in Rajasthan, Sweta works out of home. As a result, their apartment in central Delhi is another ode to her perfectionism – sofas covered in matched floral chintz, lots of silver photo frames with pictures of the couple, and Darjeeling tea served with healthy home-made cookies.

'I can't relate much to wifey type conversations,' Sweta says decisively, 'I need a productive environment.' It's really after meeting Sweta Hooda that I conclude: the fact that Deepender chose to marry such an outspoken, strong-willed woman means his sensitivity, his open-mindedness couldn't be skin deep.

Deepender's good reputation seems to prevail with everyone. Even journalist Aditi Phadnis, who has been following father Bhupinder Singh Hooda's politics, grants that his son is 'not a chap who throws his weight around.'

The younger Hooda is careful to maintain his identity – that of the sincere, conscientious boy. It's his cornerstone and it's important to him. Hooda's campaign videos show him earnestly touching the feet of elders, old men and women, and diligently making speeches. Deepender won his first election by two lakh thirty-one thousand votes and his next election in 2009 by double the margin – four lakh forty-six thousand votes. 'The first time I won because of family, but this time people voted for me,' he says with pride.

In Rohtak, as his car drives through a village, Deepender looks constantly out of the window. An old man with a moustache sits outside his house with his wife, blankly watching the MP's convoy go by. As his car passes, Deepender looks the old man straight in the eye, as if recognizing him, and raises his hands up in a *namaste*. The man's face cracks into a smile; he stands up, beaming, and salutes back, watching the car till it's out of sight.

***

Though he 'doesn't throw his weight around,' all said and done, Deepender can't separate himself from his father's politics. The rewards and the pitfalls of being the Haryana Chief Minister's son are constantly with him. If Deepender gets something done, people say it's because his father is Chief Minister. If he doesn't, as Deepender says, they say, 'How can you not get this done? Your father is Chief Minister!'

As soon as you cross over from Delhi into Rohtak, huge billboards with Bhupinder Singh Hooda and Deepender Hooda's photographs soar over the highway to greet you.

In February this year, Deepender travelled around Rohtak to invite people to a meeting that his father was hosting to announce a new economic package for Haryana. Deepender announced the meeting and was also empowered to fulfill various demands as a run up the to the meeting: grants for roads, water works, stadiums, pipelines, cowsheds, and other projects from the Chief Minister's fund. In various villages, Deepender promised Rs 40 lakh for a stadium, Rs 50 lakh for roads and drainage, Rs 4 lakh for a basketball court, Rs 30 lakh to make retaining walls of village water bodies, Rs 20 lakh for cow sheds and so on. It's unlikely he would've gotten this mileage if he weren't his father's son.

Because he's traveling in the Chief Minister's area (the CM's assembly seat Garhi-Kiloi falls within Deepender's Lok Sabha constituency), some of the CM's close associates travel with Deepender. One called 'Professor' Virender Singh is the CM's proxy in his constituency. The Professor has an old-fashioned style, with a flair for dialogue. He gives speeches in Haryanvi and says things like '*Ab dekhon, apno gaon mein bachhon ke gal lal lal ho rahe bilkul tamatar jaisey.* (Now [during the Congress government], look at how in our village all the kids' cheeks have become bright red like tomatoes.)'

Apart from the Professor, Deepender's own friend and associate, Vishesh Singh, whom he met in College, travels with him. A part time business consultant, Vishesh has a passion for technology and consumer research. For each village Deepender visits, Vishesh pulls out the relevant data.

A big *shamiana* is up for each meeting. People tie a big pink *safa* (turban) on Deepender's head to honor him. The Professor opens with a speech welcoming the young MP to each village as '*hamara ladla beta* (our beloved son)'. Deepender addresses each village as '*apno gaon* (my village)'. 'I'm so happy to be at my village. Last time I came to my village…,' he says. Vishesh carries sheets with data on the village for Deepender to refer to – when exactly Deepender last visited the village, what promises he made, what development work has actually happened since then and what the village's current demands are. In the middle of his emotional speeches, Deepender methodically drops references to what project was promised and what work was done after he visited the village last (electrification or roads, for instance), then he lists out his new promises.

Whatever commitments Deepender makes in the villages, Vishesh says, he anxiously follows up in Chandigarh, Haryana's administrative capital. Being the Chief Minister's son is a major advantage in moving things along; it ensures a quick response time in the state capital. Still, as a Congress MP in a Congress state, given how eager and anxious he is, Deepender may have managed to get things done just out of follow ups and pushiness, even if he weren't the CM's son. It's the larger projects where the Chief Minister's support has been un-expendable: after his election in 2004, Deepender wanted to make Rohtak an education hub. In just his first term, he managed to get six national and state institutes sanctioned – the Indian Institute of Management (IIM), an institute modeled on the All India Institute of Medical Sciences, a state level fashion institute, and a Footwear Design Institute (FDDI), as well as Colleges for the Arts. A big chunk of Rohtak falls under the National Capital Region (NCR) so Deepender would have been able to attract some institutes, anyhow. However, it's said that Rohtak would not have managed so many important institutions, so fast, had it not been the CM's son's constituency.

And yet, being the CM's son also comes with baggage.

Aditi Phadnis, the political editor of the *Business Standard*, has been following Haryana politics and Bhupinder Hooda for decades. 'Hooda came to power in the Congress, because, to his credit, he could unite everybody,' Phadnis says. The Hooda government has also been praised for putting in place a progressive Land Acquisition policy after the land boom in Haryana, with payments of annuities to farmers (the Haryana land policy is now being used as a benchmark for all of India).

But, Phadnis observes, politics in the state has become slanted towards Jats – Jats are a fairly well to do agricultural caste in Haryana. The Hoodas themselves are Jats and Jats are a big chunk of the Hooda family voters. (The Chautalas, the Congress' main opposition in Haryana, are also Jat and vie with the Hoodas for Jat votes.) Jats are only twenty per cent of the Haryana population, but, in most constituencies, the concentration of Jats is higher than that of any other community. In Deepender's constituency, Rohtak, too, the concentration of Jats is highest in all but one of the nine assembly seats.

'Everything is Jat in Haryana,' Phadnis says. Most Haryana politicians– not just the senior Hooda – tip-toe around local Jat leaders and Jat sentiments. However, the state government's pampering the Jats, Phadnis feels, has tilted the balance of power between communities too far. Jats, already dominant in Haryana, have become bolder.

Last year, in Mirchpur, Haryana, a group of Jats set fire to Dalit huts in Hissar district, killing a father and daughter. The fight, it turned out, had started over a dog barking at a Jat boy and escalated. The Chief Minister's silence on the case and the string of incidents that followed gave the impression that the state government was being soft on Jats again. (A year later, in August 2011,the Delhi High Court released its verdict on the case (of the 100 Jat men arrested, the court exonerated 85, held 15 and charged only 3 with criminal conspiracy). By then, the *Times of India* reported that most of the Dalit community, petrified of retaliation, had moved out of Mirchpur.[2] The *Indian Express* reported that among the Dalits who'd stayed in Mirchpur, some were still scared, while others hoped things would return to normal quickly.[3]

Mirchpur doesn't fall within Deepender's constituency, Rohtak, so the entire incident actually has nothing to do with him. Phadnis agrees, 'There's no evidence of his son having much say in his father's politics.' However, other people I meet – young journalists, bloggers and students – press me to ask the younger Hooda about the Mirchpur violence, about the leniency shown towards Khap Panchayats. They direct the questions they'd like to ask the Chief Minister to Deepender.

Khap Panchayats are 'councils' of elderly men, which act like a social police and claim to uphold social order. Today, Khaps take issue with same-*gotra* or same-clan marriages (and, sometimes, other social causes like drinking and smoking). Khaps in Haryana have been in the news for instigating the murders, suicides, and banishment of couples who marry within their *gotras*. However, their hold on the Jat vote is such that most Haryana politicians bow to them.

'Do you think Khap Panchayats should be banned?' I ask Deepender on the phone.

Deepender answers carefully, 'They've been here for the longest time. Lately, they've outraged a lot of us, but they have positive roles too. You cannot ban anyone or anybody. That's not what our constitution says. But, their agenda needs to be modernized…,' he trails off.

'Have you tried to talk with them about changing their violent agenda?'

'I've not; I've not interacted with them on these matters,' Deepender admits, probably reeling at the thought of such a thankless venture.

In the car on the ride from Delhi to Rohtak, I ask Deepender again about the rise in caste violence, the Mirchpur incident and Khaps. He, in turn, tries to explain that he has other, more winnable battles to fight.

In addition to the Khaps, there are other caste based institutions on the ground, Deepender explains. There are *numberdars* for each caste, 'a British or Mughal system' that still carries on. Each caste in the village appoints a *numberdar*, one family from among them who are chosen to voice the demands of their community. As an MP, Deepender gets demands from *numberdars* of all castes, which he takes into account.

'Caste remains a factor on the ground,' he sighs. But apart from caste, he points out, there's the acute problem of female foeticide and infanticide which occurs across castes in Haryana. It tends to get less attention than caste because it holds little political advantage – it doesn't sway community votes one way or another.

On the Mirchpur incident, 'the state government did file 100 FIRs,' Deepender says. He adds, however,

'Mirchpur does not fall in my constituency, so it's a state government matter.'

Education and development, Deepender emphasizes, are the way out of Haryana's social problems. The Haryana government started a stipend for lower caste students because dropout rates among them were sixty per cent, he says. Stipends of Rs 200 to Rs 500 a month reduced the drop-out rate among lower caste kids to ten per cent; today, in Haryana, Deepender says, the overall drop-out rate is a mere seven per cent, whereas in Rajasthan it's as high as seventy per cent.

Deepender talks about the multi-lane highway he's been able to facilitate to attract industry to Rohtak, about the new small and medium-sized factories being set up here. The MP has been trying to green-light land and licenses for investment in Rohtak. He points at factories on either side of the road as we pass, new-looking steel and concrete blocks. These, he says, were not here two years ago. 'You go inside these factories you'll see a Jat boy, a Scheduled Caste boy, a Brahmin boy, all working together.'

'There's a tendency to have a regressive political debate in Haryana. We can't talk about reservations, caste percentage of reservations forever; we have to shift to a progressive political debate.' Looking out of the window at the steel sheds, he says, 'You see what I'm saying? That's where I want to take the debate. I want to steer the discussion, even our discussion, in the other direction.'

***

'When President Obama came to India in 2010, they announced 50,000 new jobs. But in India, we were focusing on this and that, other issues,' Deepender tells me. (During the Obama visit, American news channels had talked only of jobs, while Indian channels had speculated mainly on Obama's thoughts on Pakistan.) 'The Prime Minister should talk about how many jobs have been created. Our policy and political debate should be centered around job creation.'

'Deepender is obsessed with national statistics and with CSO (Central Statistical Organization) data on employment. He thinks the data's not good enough,' Mihir Sharma of the *Indian Express*, who's interacted with Deepender for his columns, tells me. 'It's unusual,' Sharma tells me, outside the *Express* office, 'It's cool in a way that he's so concerned about this stuff.'

The excitement on relevant data infects everyone around Deepender Hooda. Vishesh talks excitedly about a 'tool' he's designed to capture data on Deepender's constituency. The software holds together data on each of the about 500 villages in Rohtak, updated with information from Deepender's visits and from state government records. At a click, for every village, it shows the development projects sanctioned by Deepender in past years and which of these have been completed. It shows the male to female ratio and also the number of children. Recently, they've included data from the education department – how many children are going to school in the villages, the overall school dropout ratio.

Sweta Hooda tells me she believes every MP should have 'a clear agenda' towards 'nation building,' 'something that you're genuinely passionate about.' 'In too many young politicians what stands out is a lack of clear agenda,' she says. Jyoti, her sister, for instance, studied medicine and has a take on the national health system. Sweta, though she's not a politician, is intent on building an agenda on water. Deepender is passionate about creating jobs; he's intent on improving employment data and making it an integral part of national statistics. Sweta doesn't mince words. 'I, for example, think he could play a very important role in the debate to form national policies but he spends a lot of time on the ground, and gives due time to everyone who comes his way.'

In December 2010, at the plenary session of the All India Congress (AICC), Deepender also gave a well thought speech on unemployment and statistics – in a country with a large young population, he said, job creation should be the most important economic indicator – ahead of Gross Domestic Product(GDP) growth or inflation. By 2018, he pointed out, eighty per cent of India's current population will be of working age and a 100 million new jobs – the total number of jobs in America – would be needed. When the budget is presented, let the government tell us how many jobs were created in the last year and the last quarter, Deepender said, let us judge our government on that.

***

As Deepender takes on bigger responsibilities, it'll be interesting to watch what stands he takes. In Haryana, as in many parts of India, the conversation often still stops at caste. As he deals with incidences of caste violence, it'll be interesting to see how the conscientious young politician reacts – what he says, whether he chooses to speak or to remain silent. It'll also be interesting to see Deepender share data on job creation and employment, on drop-out rates in schools.

In politics, where the conversation tends to remain stagnant and allusive, it'll be particularly interesting, in every aspect, to see him bring about a real change in the parameters of discussion – what should and what shouldn't be talked about.

Notes

1 Sunetra Choudhary, *Braking News* (New Delhi: Hachette India, 2011)
2 Joel Joseph, 'Mirchpur Still Under Shadow of Jat Violence,' *The Times of India*, 15 March 2011
3 Ruhi Bhasin, 'In Mirchpur, Scars Remain but Hope Floats,' *Indian Express*, 26 September 2011

The Man In A Hurry

Thakur rushes across Himachal Pradesh, not returning home for a month at a time. At just twelve, he changed his last name, hoping to have a separate identity from his Chief Minister father.

ANURAG THAKUR

Bharatiya Janata Party (BJP)
Hamirpur Constituency, Himachal Pradesh
Born on 24 October 1974
33 years of age at first election
Last victory margin of 72,732 votes

Anurag Thakur almost sleepwalks into the Chief Minister's suite on the mezzanine of Himachal House, New Delhi. His eyes are red and bleary as he picks up the intercom and mutters '*Ek* cup *chai aur.*' (One more cup of tea).

Anurag is Member of Parliament (MP) of Hamirpur in Himachal Pradesh, the son of the state's Chief Minister, Prem Kumar Dhumal. Thakur also serves as President of the Bhartiya Janata Yuva Morcha (BJYM), the youth arm of the BJP.

Anurag sinks into a plush sofa. He's in dark jeans, a T-shirt and a black jacket; luckily, the suite is heavily air-conditioned. With a trimmed goatee and ruffled hair, Thakur looks less like a politician and more like a snazzy, young businessman. Next to him, two cell phones buzz constantly.

'You cannot keep your phone off for a long time or you'll start getting negative comments like "Oh! Your phone is switched off!"' Anurag complains, as he monitors his two phones. He hates and loves, is addicted to, their constant buzzing.

'See, I cater to 1.6 million people, so even if one per cent calls me, that's 16,000 calls a day. If I take about 0.1 per cent, it should be about 1,600 calls. Who's going to manage that?' he asks.

'People call with their problems, the delay with water and road connections, the many other village and district issues. That's the common people and then you have to stay connected with party people as well. Anyone can call you and you have to look after them, because you are the elected leader. Even if you get five hundred calls a day, you have to make five to seven hundred calls to get their work done,' Anurag sighs, puffy-eyed.

Five hundred incoming calls a day would be thirty-six calls an hour, a call every two minutes. One of Anurag's phones buzzes again and he gives it a baleful look.

The current Parliament session started in Delhi some days ago, but Anurag couldn't make it in time. The morning I meet him, he's just arrived in the capital after weeks of touring Himachal.

'I started around four o'clock on the twenty-first of last month. That's four in the morning. I went first to Ponta Sahib (the Gurdwara town in Himachal),' Thakur explains. At Ponta Sahib, the Himalayan Youth Sports Club, which organizes tournaments for young players, was hosting an event. Anurag was specially invited and spoke to a crowd of more than five thousand people.

On the way to the village where the function was ('the remotest area of Himachal', he says), Thakur stopped to meet his party people at four different places. At each halt about three hundred people had gathered. 'So when you get out of your car, meet them, listen to their problems, it takes about one to one and a half hours.'

'From there,' Anurag continues, 'I went to a place called Vikas Nagar in Uttarakhand. Then I came back and visited another remote area, a small village, where I met people at almost midnight. They had been waiting since 8.30 p.m. for me.'

The next day, Thakur continues breathlessly, he took a four and a half hour flight to Una in southern Himachal Pradesh. Then, after four hours of sleep, he left for a place called Santoshgarh. *Prashasan Janta Ke Dwar*, a campaign called 'Government at the People's Door, was in progress there. The District Commissioner of Police (DCP), the Superintendant of Police (SP) and the Sub-divisional District Magistrate (SDM) – all the important administrative officers – met and tried to solve problems there and then: pending issues of development, land demarcation, unsolved police cases, medical aid required and so on. About five hundred people came to the meeting and Anurag tried to meet everyone possible.

'*Woh karne ke bad*,' Thakur sighs, 'I went to see those families *jinke log* bus accident *mein mar gaye the.* (After this, I met the families of those who had died in the bus accident from Santoshgarh to Dera).' Anurag distributed cheques to this bereaved group.

From there, he drove two and a half hours back to Hamirpur to attend the wedding of the Vice President of the Akhil Bharatiya Vidyarthi Parishad (ABVP), the BJP's student wing. After the wedding, he drove back to Una for yet another night meeting.

'What kind of meetings take place at night in Una?' I ask.

'Political meetings, workers from the constituency, they get together and tell me their problems, the issues they want raised in Parliament with the Central Government,' Thakur explains. 'Take, for instance, the Post and Telegraph Department. These guys, they deliver posts within a circle of, say, twelve miles. They don't have cycles or scooters or whatever. They have to walk from village to village. They don't get pensions, they don't get perks as do other government organizations, so they wanted me to raise that with the Ministry. Another issue would be the trains which go from Una to Ambala and all over,' he continues. 'These trains have a total distance journey of six to seven hours. But they don't even have a single toilet. I mean, there are so many issues, some related to agriculturalists and all, the local price rise, the unavailability of sugar.'

Anurag is a proficient networker; on the way to Delhi, he squeezed in another political wedding – that of a BJP ex-District President's son, in Nankhal.

'I visited my wife only yesterday, after thirty full days,' Thakur sighs. 'I have a son, he is five years old. He was awake at 11.30 last night just to see me.' But Anurag Thakur isn't really complaining – I get the feeling that he loves the pace of political life, thrives on the constant jostling and networking, the hyper-active meetings that happen at all hours of day and night.

***

Anurag attended the Dayanand Model School and then the Doaba College, both in Jhalandar, Punjab where his uncle lived; his father was in Himachal Pradesh, building his political career. Through school, Anurag was an avid cricket player.

'He wanted me to go to the Sainik School,' Anurag mumbles, talking about the chief minister, 'I used to run away from my house and play cricket.' Anurag defied his father and became excellent at cricket.

Anurag also changed his name when he was thirteen. 'I thought, I will do something in the field of cricket, play for country, and I won't be known as so-and-so's son. Today, my father writes his name as Prem Kumar Dhumal and I write my name as Anurag Thakur,' Anurag tells me, revealing a brooding and obsessively independent streak.

'I was captain of the Punjab under-sixteen and under-nineteen teams, as well as the northern teams. We won the Ranji trophy, the All-India championships,' Anurag continues. 'I was hard core into cricket.'

Cricket also paved the way for Anurag's political innings. In 1999, some time after he'd stopped playing and joined the family export business, Thakur was made the President of the Himachal Cricket Association (HCA).

Through his work in the HCA, Thakur tells me with some pride, acquired a reputation in Himachal – As HCA President, he raised the state Cricket Association's budget from twenty lakh rupees to thirty crores. He built an international level cricket stadium in Dharmshala with a budget of fifty crores. In 2003, the Congress came to power and tried hard to take over the HCA, Thakur says, but he fought the party in court for five years and won.

For all his individualism, Thakur does admit that it helped tremendously for him to stand election from Hamirpur, where his father had been MP three times over. In 2007, when Dhumal became Chief Minister, Anurag fought the Hamirpur by-poll and won. 'Twenty years of work had been put in the constituency by my father, so the base was there for me,' Anurag says candidly.

Anurag's relationship with his father still appears fractured, but they've gotten closer since Anurag entered politics. 'We hardly meet in the year. He is busy with his own work and I am busy with mine,' Thakur says of Dhumal. 'It has always been a very formal relationship,' he adds haltingly, referring to the years of schooling he spent away from home. 'Before getting into politics, he was more distant, like a father figure I'd listen to – whatever he said that's the way it had to be. Now, he has taken an initiative and we are much closer.' Anurag pauses, then murmurs, like a young man still seeking his father's love and attention, 'But I still keep mostly to myself.'

***

Prem Kumar Dhumal started his career as a clerk in the Life Insurance Corporation (LIC) in Jalandhar, Punjab. He enrolled in evening college classes, and became first Student President, then Union Leader at Punjab University. Dhumal started a small business and eventually steered into full-time politics, standing for his first election in 1984 under the BJP. This was the year Prime Minister Indira Gandhi was assassinated, and with the wave of sympathy for the Congress, Dhumal lost. But this only motivated him further. Anurag explains, 'After that election, my father didn't stay back in Delhi. The very next day, he left for his village and worked with his people at the grass-root level for the next three years.' 'He is a real politician,' he concludes, with real admiration.

Anurag is as focused as his father, it appears; he too throws himself into whatever he's doing. When he was playing cricket, all he thought about was cricket. When he managed the family export business, he worked fourteen hour days. Now that Thakur is an MP, he travels all over Himachal Pradesh, constantly meeting people and relentlessly organizing party initiatives.

And yet, Anurag insists, politics has mellowed him, taken off some of the edginess he possessed when he was younger. He feels it's a part of maturing, of accepting what can and sometimes cannot be done. '*Kisi ne bol diya ki aap us din kyun nahi aye jis din bus giri thi? Aapko us din aana chahiye tha.* (Somebody said, why didn't you come the same day the bus fell off the cliff? You should've come).' 'I was in Mumbai that day, how could I have come?' says Anurag, '*Kuch log apney aap ko budwane ke liye bol denge.* (I guess, some people say things to make themselves seem more important).'

***

Anurag's two cell phones continue to buzz; he calls the intercom. Tea finally arrives, from somewhere in Himachal house. The exhausted MP stretches his legs out and looks suddenly more alert. I steer the interview now towards what Anurag has on his political agenda.

'There are so many issues,' Thakur says thoughtfully. He talks about power generation and alternate power sources, then about Naxalism and the lack of development in parts of the country. He mentions his concern over the lack of water in the dams of Himachal Pradesh, the special industrial package that's been earmarked for the region. He then switches topics, says he'll always continue to promote sports in his state.

'Khali was to meet me in the evening,' Anurag says, with a worried smile. 'Khali's leaving for America today. I was in Parliament, so I said "I'll see you in the evening." But I might be busy.' Anurag is referring to Khali 'the Great'. The seven foot tall, four-hundred pound wrestler from Himachal Pradesh.

Born to a family of labourers, Khali was a police officer who made it to the World Wrestling Federation (WWF) in the United States. In one of his first matches in the WWF, he defeated the Federation's fighting phenomenon, the Undertaker.

Khali had taken a break from wrestling in 2008 and is now finally returning for a match. Anurag appears upset that he won't be able to personally wish Khali luck.

I'm amazed that before leaving for the US, Khali should be trying to meet Anurag Thakur and that the MP is trying equally hard to meet the wrestler. But then, if Khali invited Anurag to a match as his lucky mascot, I can imagine Thakur flying, driving, going by train, doing just about anything, to be there for the Himachal sportsman.

More than the issues he takes up, this is what makes Anurag Thakur stand out – his relentless activity, his hyper-responsiveness, his willingness to constantly engage and be there for people, at the expense of all personal time.

***

In the last couple of years, Thakur has been especially active with new responsibilities.

He's spoken extensively in Parliament – on the Himachal Development Board, on the delay in setting up Central Universities in Himachal Pradesh, on the Employment Guarantee Act (NREGA), on the Right to Education, on the Rail Budget. In 2009, Mail Today rated Thakur the best parliamentarian among young BJP MPs.

He's been socializing with political colleagues across all parties. He attended the wedding of Biju Janata Dal MP Kalikesh Deo's brother in Jaipur. He talks about chatting with Congress's Deepender Hooda in Central Hall after the Haryana elections (Central Hall is where everyone catches up between Parliament sessions). They discussed, he tells me, how the Congress had suffered a smaller a majority in Haryana for the same reason the BJP lost in 2004: because their campaigns were overconfident. ('*No. 1 Haryana*' was the Congress tagline; '*India Shining*' was the BJP campaign in 2004.)

In mid-2010, Anurag organized two Indian Premier League (IPL) matches in the Dharamshala stadium he'd had built. People feared the matches would get rained out, but Thakur held an elaborate *puja* (prayer) to make sure it didn't rain that day. Thakur was then on TV with the Dalai Lama and Preity Zinta among others to promote the match. His phone rang several times during the show and each time, Thakur anxiously scuttled on and off screen to answer it.

No rain fell and the IPL matches were big successes. On the day of the second match, in a TV interview, Anurag, sitting on the steps of the Dharamshala stadium, dapper in a suit and tie, looked tired but very relieved and happy.

Weeks after the matches, BJP President Nitin Gadkari announced that Anurag Thakur would head the party's youth wing, the *Bhartiya Janata Yuva Morcha*. The role is especially significant because it mirrors Rahul Gandhi's position in the Youth Congress. It speaks of bigger things to come.

In early 2011, Thakur organized an *Ekta Yatra* (National Unity March) from Kolkata to Kashmir. The March was meant to press the Congress government to 'solve the Kashmir problem' and was meant to end with Thakur and the Morcha hoisting the Indian flag in Kashmir on Republic Day. The *Yatra* got a fair bit of media coverage, but didn't become a national rallying point. It did, however, give Anurag the chance to talk about Kashmir, to poke at the Jammu & Kashmir Chief Minister Omar Abdullah, to criticize Jawaharlal Nehru for his historical weakness on Kashmir and to talk about the plight of the Kashmiri pundits. It gave the BJP the chance to hoist the national flag with fanfare. It gave the BJP Yuva Morcha workers, from Himachal and all over North India, the chance to march. It gave the BJP high command – Arun Jaitley, Sushma Swaraj and Anant Kumar – the chance to fly to Kashmir, to have a scuffle with the police, and to try to get arrested.

Their plane, Sushma Swaraj explained later, was met by police at Srinagar airport. They refused to follow the order to turn back, insisted on getting out; all three of them sat down on the tarmac in protest. They were, eventually, told they'd be arrested; they were piled into cars and dropped outside the Kashmir border where their party workers from Punjab picked them up. The media also met them there and they issued statements on how the Congress and Kashmir state government was preventing them from flying the national flag. The *Ekta Yatra* ended with Thakur going to jail, getting released and finally hoisting the flag at Kathua, Kashmir.

At a time when the BJP was rudderless, Anurag's *Yatra* gave everyone an issue to talk about, something to do. (That was a few months before Anna Hazare swept Delhi and made corruption the only issue worth discussing.)

Since then, through 2011, Thakur made himself heard. He's spoken on a host of issues: he condemned Sharad Pawar's slap, he wrote a letter to the Broadcasting Minister Ambika Soni saying Big Boss 2 was leading to the 'moral degradation of children', and he spoke about the Congress' leniency towards terrorism, its inability to execute the death sentence against Afzal Guru, the prime convicted in the Parliament bombing, for ten years. Still, the young MP hasn't yet carved a definitive identity; he seems to be wavering between floating a saffron campaign, talking about corruption, and picking on security issues.

With the Uttar Pradesh election coming up, in late 2011, touring UP, Thakur, dressed in a *kurta* not a suit now, took his party's line against FDI; he said it would be harmful for Indian traders and would lead to a loss of jobs. Meanwhile, on his UP tour, Rahul Gandhi talked about how FDI would be good because it would give the farmers more bargaining power.

In the coming months, Thakur will campaign as the BJP's young poster boy in UP, opposite the Congress' Rahul Gandhi. In the general elections, he'll shape the BJP youth agenda, juxtaposed by Rahul Gandhi in the Youth Congress. As Rahul projects himself as the 'common man's soldier', it'll be interesting to watch what approach Thakur takes, what image he cuts for himself.

ECONOMIC IDEAS OF DR. RAM MANOHAR LOHIA

Contents

Preface

Today in the first decade of 21st Century when socialism is defensive and capitalism is basically inequalitarian in character, India needs an alternative model of economic development suited to its political economy to alleviate poverty and provide full employment to every working population of India. Dr. Ram Manohar Lohia was the first Indian thinker who devoted his life in search of such an alternative model. He considered both capitalism and communism irrelevant in a developing economy like India. As such a deep analysis of multifacets of Dr. Lohia's ideas and personality is urgently needed.

Dr. Lohia was not a formal economist in strict sense of the term. He studied Political Science and submitted his thesis on 'Salt and Satyagraha' to Berlin University in Germany for the award of Ph.D. degree. It shows the impact of Mahatma Gandhi on his mental set-up. When Mahatma Gandhi remarked that the God of poor is bread, he danced in the hostel while a student in Berlin University. It shows his keen desire to synthesise socialism with Gandhism in Indian context. He indulged himself in politics and entered into national freedom movement. He remained a chronic bachelor throughout his life.

Dr. Lohia was a studious reader and prolific writer. He studied the social, economic, political and cultural aspects of Indian political economy in-depth and interpreted these all aspects in a fresh way. In this way he was the most original thinker in the fifties and sixties of 20th Century. It is why his socio-economic ideas are still relevant in the Indian context and has wide impact on the current socio-economic and political scenario. His forecast that people may not hear him in life time but they will hear him after his death; has come true. I believe that the search for alternative model of economic development in Indian context is possible only through Dr. Lohia's thought. This anthology of sixteen articles is an humble attempt towards this direction.

Delhi

ANIL KUMAR THAKUR
SHRI NIWAS PANDEY

List of Contributors

A.K. Gupta, Professor, Department of Commerce, JMDPL Mahila College, Madhubani

Abhas Saurabh, Research Associate, Research Institute for Rural Development, Hajipur, Vaishali, Bihar.

Ashwini Kant Jha, Head, Department of Economics, P.G. Centre, (W.C), Saharsa.

Banarsi Yadav, University Department of Economics, L.N. Mithila University, Darbhanga (Bihar).

Bharat Bhushan, Lecturer in Economics, T.S. College, Hisua, Distt: Nawada, Bihar.

Bharti Kumari, Research Associate, Research Institute for Rural Development, Hajipur, Vaishali, Bihar.

Bhavna Jha, Dept. of M.A.M. College, Naugahia.

Bijay Kumar Prasad, Department of L.S.W., M.U., Bodh-Gaya.

Binod Prasad, Lecturer, Department of Commerce, Gaya College, Gaya, (M.U.).

Birendra Kumar Jha, Reader and Head of Department of Economics, D.B.K.N. College, Narhan (Samastipur, Bihar).

Chandrika Prasad, Lecturer in Economics, Nalanda College, Biharsharif, Nalanda.

Dayanidhi Pd. Roy, A.N.D. College, Shahpurpatory, L.N.M.U., Darbhanga.

Hari Narayan Pd. Singh, Lecturer, Deptt. of Economics, Kisan College, Sohsarai, Nalanda (M.U.).

Indurani Kesharwani, Lecturer in Economics, A.S. College, Deoghar.

M. Masood Alam, UGC Research Fellow, University Department of Rural Economics and Co-operation, T.M. Bhagalpur University, Bhagalpur.

N. Sharma, Principal, A.S. College, Deoghar.

P.K. Roy, Lecturer in Pol. Sc., A.S. College, Deoghar.

Ram Bharat Thakur, Professor of Economics, R.B. College, Dalsingsarai (Samastipur).

Ravi Shankar Bhakta, Post Doctoral Fellow, B.R.A. Bihar University, Muzaffarpur.

Sarita Kumari, Lecturer in Economics, SMD College, Punpun.

Shambhu Deo Mishra, Research Associate, Agro-Economic Research Centre for Bihar and Jharkhand.

Shambhu Sah, Reader, Department of L.S.W., A.S. College, Deoghar.

Shrmishtha Priti, Lecturer in Economics, Dr. J.N. Mishra College, Muzaffarpur.

Sunil Kumar, Professors Colony, Alalpatti, Benta, Darbhanga, Bihar.

Upendra Sharma, Reader and H.O.D., Economics, Kisan College, Sohsara, Nalanda (Bihar).

Introduction

Dr. Ram Manohar Lohia (1910-1967), the hero of Quit India Movement; a thinker whose heart was Gandhi and mind was socialist, a champion of individual freedom, a great visionary and founder of non-Marxian path of socialist development in India had multi-facets personality and is credited with contributing several new ideas both during freedom struggle and post-independence era.

Dr. Lohia's contributions are both in ideas and practice and relevant in may respects even today. His ideological analysis of economics after Marx; his circular movement of history substituting Marxian analysis of dialectical movement through class struggle; the twinity of capitalism and imperialism and irrelevance of western capitalism and communism in Indian context, original analysis of the concept of third world, mixing of socialism with Gandhism and a model of non-Marxist socialist path of development are still relevant in many respects. Dr. Lohia's advocacy for decentralization of political and economic powers through four-pillar State or Chaukhabha Rajya; Price Policy, economic disparity in the proportion of one to ten, balanced development of agriculture and industry; equity with prosperity and original analysis of Caste *vs.* Class and slogan of non-congressism to break the monolithic citadel of the then Congress rule made him the most powerful and popular leader of masses during sixties. He did not compromise on principle and believed in the seven facets of revolution for which even went to the extent of breaking socialist movement in India several times. He was a crusader of social equity. His substitution theory commonly called reservation policy for women, backwards, minorities and dalits has changed the socio-political scenario of India and acclerated the path of social transformation of the country. His saying that people may not listen him during his life time but they will listen him after this death, has come true. His advocacy of intermediate technology justifies small is beautiful.

This book is an humble attempt to depict the multi-facet personality of Dr. Lohia both in ideology and as a crusader against all kinds of injustices and a constant and consistent fighter for individual and national freedom. In total there are sixteen articles dealing with almost all aspects of Dr. Lohia as a man and his works.

Mr. **N. Sharma and P.K. Roy** deal with a brief life-sketch and his contributions to economic thought with emphasis upon small unit technology and decentralised economy; Mr. **Ram Bharat Thakur and A.K. Gupta** examines ideas of Dr. Lohia in the context of globalisation of Indian economy, Mr. **Dayanidhi Pd. Roy** examines Lohia's concept of agriculture development and concludes that they are relevant even today.

Mr. **Upendra Sharma** while dealing with economic ideas of Dr. Ram Manohar Lohia touches all aspects in brief but nicely analyses. Mr. **Sunil Kumar** analyses Dr. Lohia's concept of industrialisations and includes that his contribution of the concept of intermediate technology and advocacy for small and cottage industries will remain always relevant is the context of Indian economy.

Ashwini Kant Jha and Bhavna Jha dwell upon socialist approach of Dr. Lohia and highlight on the development of Socialist movement in India and Dr. Lohia's contribution. Mr. **Bimendra Kumar Jha and Shambu Sah** deal with Lohia's vision for India's economic development and concludes that Lohia was nearer to Gandhi than Nehru in his vision for economic development of India. Mr. **Bharat Bhushan** while dealing with economic ideas of Dr. Ram Manohar Lohia conclude that his economic ideas are still beneficial to socio-economic transformation of the country.

Mr. **Abhas Saurab and Bharti Kumari** analysing Dr. Lohia observes that Dr. Lohia was both Socialist and individualist. **Sarita Kumari** discussing the economic ideas of Dr. Lohia concludes that he fought constantly against the

Socio-Economic injustices in the society while Mr. **Hari Narayan Pd. Singh and Binod Prasad** deal with all theoretical framework of Dr. Lohia's thought, Mr. **Banarasi Yadava's** emphasis is upon the social justice aspect.

Dr. **Shrmishtha Priti and Indu Rani Keshherwani** briliantly formulates Dr. Lohia's non-Marxist socialist path of development and concludes his model of development superior to capitalist and Marxian model of devevlopment, **Shambhu Deo Mishra and M. Masood Alam** deals with relevance of Dr. Ram Manohar Lohia for Indian economy, **Chandrika Prasad** opens a new door of governance, democracy and development in Bihar and advocates to remove some of the limitations of the political system so that reformist and distribution become a reality. **Ravi Shankar Bhakta and Bijay Kumar Prasad** deal with economic agenda to become a reality, economic philosophy of Dr. Lohia on price policy, surplus labour, capitalist development and observes them in the present context also.

ANIL KUMAR THAKUR
SHRI NIWAS PANDEY

1

Dr. Rammanohar Lohia's Economic Thoughts: A Brief Description

N. Sharma and P.K. Roy

Dr. Rammanohar Lohia is one of the greatest leaders of modern India. He ruled over the hearts and minds of many, the records of recent times would bear sufficient testimony to that. He inspired many to act when the going was rough, to rally when the rout seemed total, to get back repeatedly to the path of struggle, suffering and sacrifice. He even made the humble and the lowly scale heights that until then were the exclusive preserve of the privileged few. (V. Grover 1996) In the evolution of the socialist movement of India, Dr. Rammanohar Lohia occupied very important place. His contribution to the socialist movement was outstanding. He was the first socialist thinker in India who denied to have his mental horizon limited by the ideas borrowed from the Soviet Union or from the west. His socialism was a product of the India Soil. He was fully aware of the situation that the socialism of text-books was beyond the understanding of the common man in India, as he is shrouded in superstitions, obsolete customs, poverty and ignorance. Therefore, Dr. Lohia dreamt such types of socialism which would be free from all type of exploitation—social, political and economic.

Dr. Lohia was of firm belief that political philosophy has no meaning if it did not take into consideration the interest of the people and their problems. Hence, he took into consideration the complex socio-economic problems of India and on these grounds framed his political ideas distinctly. He discarded many of the outdated concept of Hegel, Marx and Lenin, because he knew that the Indian mass needed a simple and understandable form of socialism. So Lohian brand of socialism was so simple that even an illiterate labourer or farmer could understanding its meaning without any mental strain.

Dr. Rammanohar Lohia, a great leader of 20th century, saw the first ray of the sun on 23rd March 1910 at Akbarpur in Faizabad District (U.P.) in a Vaishya Family. His ancestors had acquired the surname of 'Lohia' for their dealing in the business of Lohia (Hardware). His father, Hiralal was a nationalist and from his father Lohia inherited the feelings of Nationalism, love and affection for the poor and needy. The environment in which Lohia spent his childhood was free from caste feelings. Even as a child, Lohia took keen interest in helping the poor, the needy and downtrodden and the weaker section when they were exploited.

Lohia completed his primary education at his native place Akbarpur, passed Matriculation in 1925 from Marwari Vidyalaya, Bombay, Intermediate in 1927 from the Kashi Vishwavidyalaya, Banaras and B.A. in 1929 from Vidyasagar College, Calcutta. He did his Ph.D. from Berlin in 1932. Since his very childhood Lohia took active part in public life. In 1920 on the death of Lokmanya Tilak, Lohia at the age of 10 years, took initiative in organizing a strike in school. His major passion was to free India from the foreigner's rule. He, therefore, became a freedom fighter at a very early age and played a magnificent role in organizing the Quit India Movement in 1942.

After the achievement of Independence Lohia took active part in organizing many movements which he thought were beneficial for the Country. He struggled throughout his life for human freedom. He went to Goa and fought for the establishment of democracy in Nepal. He not only defeated the western imperialism but also Vehemently opposed the forceful entry of Soviet Union troops into Hungri in 1956 and Chinese troops into Tibbet (A.P. Kamal, 2003). Though he was a political opponent of Nehru, he had love for him and had no hestitation to accept that Nehru was a veteran politician and the Congress had great need of his. While Gandhi was a dream for him, Netaji Shubhash was a brave leader in his eyes. He after independence, fought for many years to establish non-Congress governments in the states. His long cherished political desire could be fulfilled in 1967 when there was non-Congress government in eight states of Indian Union. He was an eloquent speaker, a great freedom fighter, a brave soldier of democracy and socialism, a courageous critic and independent ideologist, thinker and above all a great humanist. He left this earthly world for heavenly abode in the year 1967. (A.P. Kamal, 2003) After his death the socialist movement got divided into many factions.

Dr. Lohia's contributions to economic thoughts and action came out of this single-minded preoccupation with the need to free the individual from the shackles that chained him all-around.

Dr. Lohia had very clear views about women, farmers and the backwards. He used to say that women were suppressed, farmers were compelled to remain poor and illiterate and people of backward class were exploited. They were compelled to work as slaves for upper class. Therefore, Lohia had great worry for these three sections of the society. Dr Lohia was of the view that unless they are not uplifted the country will not progress. His socialism gives priority to the upliftment of these three classes.

Women are backbones of the society. It was his firm conviction that women without education can not be rational, and capability to taking right decision can never be developed in them. Economic dependency is a vital reason of women's backwardness. Lohia wanted that women should read. They should be self-dependent. So he wanted to have such a society which should be free from women's suppression and women may use their rights freely. What our politicians are doing today for empowering women, Lohia did that 50 years ago. Thus, he was a farsighted politician.

Lohia had great affection for farmers. He was deeply shocked at the miserable economic conditions of the farmers. Their poverty was a fundamental cause for the downfall of farmers. He wanted to make the farmers literate. He thought that literacy could save them from all sorts of exploitations. So he emphasized on education of farmers, their standard of living and the level of thinking.

Gandhi, the Congress and Lohia had anxiety for backward class. After independence backwards had been misutilized for their votes by the so-called politicians who represented backward class. Lohia was dead against this. According to Lohia "upliftment of backward means to provide them such economy in which they can play their roles in the reconstruction of the nation doing hard labour and raise their standard of living themselves" (A.P. Kamal, 2003). This was the fundamental 'Mantra' of Lohian socialism. He wanted such a revolution in which labour class may improve and individuals should be awarded on the basis of deeds (Karma). Thus, Lohia wanted to give the society a healthy social vision.

Creation of "Land Army" was a unique contribution of Lohia. The objective of 'Land Army' was not to fight the battle but putting pressure on the government to frame such policies which can create employment for labourers and development process may be intensified. He was against the European Model of development. He knew that the benefit of this model would be reaped by the people of upper strata. This development process will be misutilized by bureaucrats, businessmen and brokers and common man will get neither work nor benefit. To get work from them a section of broker will emerge who will earn substantial profit by exploiting labourers. This is what happened in Nehruvian model.

Broker-culture grew in place of Labour-culture. What Lohia had forcasted 50 years ago that is happening today. The government at the center as well as in the state should follow Lohia's philosophy to end this culture.

Dr. Lohia, being the follower of Mahatma Gandhi, was a supporter of 'Khadi Udyog'. According to Dr. Lohia Khadi is a source of self-employment in village. The slogan 'work to each' can be achieved with the improvement of Khadi. Khadi will provide employment to all those who want to work with hands. It will create self-confidence. This country cannot create employment in abundance, so employment will be searched in the works done by hands. Today Khadi has taken the form of an established business and has spread, from cosmopolitans to remote villages. Dr. Lohia, like Gandhijee used to see the progress of villages in Khadhi Udyog.

Dr. Lohia wanted the all round development of the Country. Development linked with the direct participation of common men of the nation was his dream. He wanted the development of towns and villages simultaneously. Development should be at par and its advantage should reach the last man dwelling in the remote villages just like the literate persons of cosmopolitan city. The dream of Gandhijee and Dr. Lohia about village Swaraj was quite similar. Gandhijee wanted to see the last man of the village happy. He wanted to develop such economy in which the tears may not roll down from the eyes of the poorest of poor. Dr. Lohia was also of the view that the government should see the village and town impartially.

The idea of achieving both equality and prosperity is socialism. According to Dr. Lohia, where there is poverty, absolute poverty, the only means to achieve prosperity is equality. Equality by itself is a very good thing, but considering the present poverty of India I want to emphasize to you all our prosperity can also be achieved through equality, because the more we minimise our luxuries, extravagance from our annual income and utilize them on improving agriculture and industry, the more prosperous we shall become. Therefore, when I have talked of achieving these two ideals of equality and prosperity, I would also like to say especially of our country that equality is a means to achieve prosperity. (Extract from Lohia's lecture entitled "India's Path to Socialism")

Dr. Lohia in his presidential Address at Panchmarhi in 1952 bared the kinship between techniques of production both under communism and capitalism and claimed that these are irrelevant to two-thirds of the world, which was underdeveloped and had high density of population, inadequacy of capital and large unemployment. Dr. Lohia brought out the most glaring fact that communism borrowed from capitalism its conventional production techniques; it only sought to change relationship among the forces of production. Such a process, Dr. Lohia emphasized was completely unsuited to the conditions prevailing in India. He, therefore, pleaded for a small unit technology and the corresponding decentralized economy which is not to be confused with the Gandhian Economy based on village self-sufficiency. Dr. Lohia's insistance was on research and innovation to invest a new small unit machine run on electricity or diesel that could be taken to the remotest villages of India so as to fulfil the twin claims of providing jobs to the rural population and of augmenting production. Dr. Lohia claimed that such a small unit technology would be able to overcome the difficulties created by inadequacy of capital, and the technique being labour intensive, it would also eliminate to a great extent the concealed rural unemployment. Dr. Lohia was greatly influenced by Gandhi, but he was not a slavish follower of the Mahatma. He wanted the implementation of the principles of decentralization in all aspects but rejected the Gandhian concept that at the technical level India's ills can be solved by the use of Charkha. He was in favour of innovative technology for fields as well as workshops. He admired the non-violent resistance forged by Gandhi and rejected armed revolution.

Dr. Lohia's economic thoughts are still relevant today. Even after six decades of independence Indian economy is suffering from gender disparity, farmer's suicide, dalits' oppression, poverty, unemployment, ignorance and superstition. These problems have become chronic. After independence our politicians followed the European Model of Development which later on was termed Nehruvian Model. Consequently big industries were set-up and such industries were called the temples of modern India. Our leaders, politicians and think-tank began to seek the remedies of the ills of Indian economy in the Nehruvian Model of development. The result is before us. This model failed miserably in solving the problems of the economy. Again our think-tank, politicians and bureaucrates by implementing the policy of globalization are committing mistakes. A lopsided development has emerged. The gap between rural and urban has widened which Dr. Lohia wanted to bridge out through equality of development. Therefore, Dr. Lohia had suggested the use of small unit of technology. Dr. Lohia and Gandhiji were forgotten and their economic thoughts were not brought in practice. Had their thoughts been implemented, the economy would have become free from all maladies affecting the economy of India. Remedies lie in the economic thoughts of Dr. Lohia. His thoughts are much relevant and all the ills of the society can be removed by adopting Dr. Lohia's economic thoughts.

Economic Philosophy has no meaning, if it does not take into consideration the people and their problems. Our present policy of Economic Reforms does not take into consideration the mass and their problems, so the problems will remain. Dr. Lohia took into consideration complex socio-economic problems of India and on these grounds enunciated his economic ideas. Dr. Lohia can be distinguished from other political leaders for his dynamic and uninhibited to the various problems. Freedom in thought and experimentation was that he cherished most. That is Lohia's most valuable contribution to the socialists in India. (V. Grover, 1996)

References

Grover, Verinder, Editor, Rammanohar Lohia; "Political Thinkers of Modern India", Deep and Deep Publications, F-159, Rajouri Garden, New Delhi, p. 675.

Kamal, A.P. (2003), Dr. Rammanohar Lohia (Hindi Version), Raja Pocket Books, 330/1, Booradi, Delhi.

"Economics After Marx" in Marx and Socialism (Hyderabad: Navhind Pub., 1963)

Lok Sabha Debates, R.M. Lohia, III Series, Vol. XXIX, 1964.

Rammanohar Lohia (1963), Marx, Gandhi and Socialism.

2

Globalisation and Economic Ideas of Dr. Ram Manohar Lohia

RAM BHARAT THAKUR AND A.K. GUPTA

In this paper an attempt has been made to discuss the globalisation with its negative effects on the Indian economy which can be changed into positive effects with the help of economic ideas of Dr. Lohia.

I. UNEMPLOYMENT FROM GLOBALISATION AND SMALL-TOOL TECHNOLOGY PRINCIPLE OF DR. LOHIA

The result of 60th Round of the National Sample Survey on Employment and Unemployment reported in the Economic Survey, 2005-06 show that the unemployment rate between 1993-94 and 2004 for males increased from 5.6 per cent to 9 per cent in rural areas and from 6.7 per cent to 8.1 per cent in urban areas, and for females it increased from 5.6 per cent to 9.3 per cent in rural areas and 10.5 per cent to 11.7 per cent in urban areas.

Dr. Lohia propounded his theory of the small tool technology for the increase in the employment in his famous Presidential Address at Panchmarhi, Lohia pleaded the case of small-unit machine in the following words:

"This machine shall be available to hamlet and town as much as to city; it may be made for all work or as many kinds as possible; it shall be built on the principle of immediacy in operation and output; it shall not require a large capital investment. This machine will not only solve the economic problem of the underdeveloped world; it will also enable a new exploration and achievement of the general aims of society."

2. INDIAN AGRARIAN CRISIS AND DR. LOHIA'S APPROACH TO AGRICULTURAL DEVELOPMENT

The annual rate of irrigation expansion in India has come down from 2.3 per cent during 1978-81 and 1988-91 to 1.60 per cent during 1988-91 and 2000-03. This has been followed by a marked decline on the net sown area from 142.41 million hectares in 1988-91 to 138.42 million hectares in 2000-03. The annual consumption of fertilizer has declined from 17.2 million tonnes during 1998-01 to 16.75 million tonnes during 2001-04. Over the same period, the average annual use of electricity in agriculture has gone down from 91 to 85 million Kwh. Thus, the annual compound growth rate of agricultural Gross Domestic Product has gone down from 3.70 per cent during 1978-81 and 1988-91 to 2.37 per cent during 1988-91 and 2002-05.

Agriculture is the backbone of the Indian economy and without bringing about radical and structural change in this sector; it would be inconceivable to think of rapid economic development of the country. Lohia considered the inequitable distribution of land as the most important factor contributing to the poverty in the masses. He was always alert and alive to the basic problems of the people and thought it expedient to strike at the root of the problem. He suggested the creation of Land Army or *Anna Sena* for reclamation of land and irrigation purposes mainly on the basis of small irrigation schemes through tanks and wells.

3. INFLATION AND DR. LOHIA'S PRICE POLICY

Inflation had touched 6.58 per cent for the week ended

January 27, 2007 and Finance Minister P. Chidambaram had expressed concern over the rising price line. It is possible to achieve high growth rates with low inflation, as China has demonstrated. But inflation of the sort, we are seeing now in India, is politically unacceptable, ironically because globalisation has reduced inflationary expectations to well below 10 per cent. The long-term consequences of inflation are severe, particularly on the poor.

Dr. Lohia criticised the Price Policy of the government and suggested a definite principle to guide it in future on a regular basis. Dr. Lohia wanted to a relationship between the agricultural and the industrial prices and farmers must get prices that cover their cost and a minimum standard. He emphasised the point that price differential between the harvest season and off-season should not vary beyond 16 per cent. There should be some sort of equilibrium between agricultural and industrial prices.

4. CAPITALISM AND DR. LOHIA'S SOCIALIST SOCIETY

According to Human Development Report (2003), the poorest 20 per cent earn 8 per cent of total income whereas the richest 20 per cent earn 46 per cent of total income, creating a wider gap between the rich and the poor.

Dr. Lohia speaking on the no-confidence motion in Lok Sabha on the 16th March, 1965, suggested the following measures for transforming a feudal and capitalist-society into a socialist one.

(a) Uniform primary schools for all children whether he is a son of the President of India or a son of a sweeper.

(b) There should be only third class in the railway and other classes should be abolished.

(c) There should be ceiling on expenditure over Rs. 1000. Nobody should be allowed to spend more than Rs. 1000 per month.

(d) English language should be abolished. If English language continues, socialism can not be brought about.

(e) All the cultivable land must get water without any kind of water rate.

In this way, Dr. Lohia discarded the capitalist as well as communist path of development. He pointed that both capitalism and communism were equally irrelevant and he propound a theory of equal-irrelevance.

5. INDIAN PLANNING AND LOHIA'S CHAKHAMBHA RAJ

Indian plans have multiple objectives and emphasised growth as well as social justice. But since Second Five Year Plan, the primary attention came to be developed to growth centered planning.

For this Lohia suggested that the economic planning should be decentralised and it should be implemented through Chakhambha Raj, i.e. Village, District, State and Centre. He wanted democratic decentralised planning and this principle was enunciated and elaborated by him in "The Four Pillar State." He was firm in his conviction that unless all the powers and resources are decentralised, there can not be uplift of the rural masses, rather than poverty, misery and unemployment bound to increase and accentuate.

6. WORLD ECONOMIC CRISIS AND DR. LOHIA'S SEVEN REVOLUTION'S THEORY

Post-cold-war world has become uni-polar world characterised by American Dominance and hegemony as manifested in war against Afghanistan and Iraq. In the era of globalisation and liberalisation economic interest of nations has become core national interest. America due to its strong economy and paramount military might has been vigorously pursuing its national interest by subjugating, intimidating any annihilating and power which try to challenge its hegemony. Nation across the globe has facing menacing challenges of terrorism and Islamic fundamentalism.

Dr. Lohia maintained that so long as there is injustice in the world, so long as the return to labour is so unequal between the white one-third of the world and the coloured two-thirds, neither can armament be abolished nor permanent peace established on this earth. He considered civil disobedience and non-violent resistance as the sovereign remedy of the 20th century and felt that the seven revolutions can be realised only through this method.

Thus, India can be a developed country by 2020 with the help of economic ideas of Dr. Lohia, making negative factor of globalisation into positive factor in one hand and on the other hand it may fulfil the call of "Faster and More Inclusive Growth" in the 11th Five Year Plan (2007-12).

References

Singh, R.B. (1986), "India's Economic Development and Lohia's Thought" Pratipalesh Prakashan, Delhi.

Poddar, D.D. and Jha, Sureshwar (2003), "Dr. Ram Manohar Lohia: Victitwa Aur Vichar" (Hindi), Dr. Ram Manohar Lohiya Smark Samiti, Darbhanga (Bihar).

Thakur, R.B. (2005), "Bhumandalikaran: Dr. Lohia Ke Arthik Chintan", *Chouthakhambha*, Vol. 27, New Delhi.

Kelkar, Indumati (1996), "Ram Manohar Lohia", National Book Trust, India, New Delhi.

Shared, Onkar (1985), "Arthshastra: Marx Se Aage: Dr. Ram Manohar Lohia", Lok Bharati Prakashan, Allahabad.

Bose, Prasenjit (2006), "Liberalisation with a Human Face", *Economic and Political Weekly*, Vol. XLI, No. 23, June 10-16.

Lohia, Ram Manohar (1964), "Jatipratha", Ram Manohar Lohia Samata Vidaylay Nayas, Hyderabad.

3

Lohia's Concept of Agriculture Development

DAYANIDHI PD. ROY

Indian peasants have not only played a glorious role in the country's struggle against foreign domination but also produced many socialist leaders and workers, and formed the backbone of the socialist movement in this country. Indian socialists have also all along been conscious of their responsibility to peasants.

Dr. Ram Manohar Lohia was undoubtedly the most original thinker, and perhaps, the only one, produced in India during the last 12 decades. He was a man of action who paid a heavy price for the courage of his conviction, having been arrested and jailed on innumerable occasions by the Britain's government, United States, Portugal, Nepal and India. He was also a political seer whose foresight into events always put him in situation of being at least twenty years ahead of his time. Perhaps it is this prophet in him which once made him say: 'People will listen to me, perhaps, after I am dead. But they will certainly listen to me (Singh)'.

Lohia was one of the best pioneers of Gandhian tradition throughout his life, he was out and out Gandhian.

Youth of Country were greatly influenced by Lohia as a great socialist, one of the top freedom fighters and the hero of the Quit India Movement, a relentless fighter against all injustices any where in the world.

Lohia has definitely played a leading role in the day-to-day struggle for the abolition of landlordism and the liquidation of claims and privileges of intermediaries.

He stands for the solidarity of peasants and industrial workers in their endeavour to build a new society free from exploitation of man by man, classes and peoples. He opposed to the forced collectivisation of land, the subordination of agricultural economy to industrial economy and the idea of aconomic development at the cost of peasants. He favoured equal treatment of needs and requirements of peasants and workers, and are pledged to develop national economy in a way equally beneficial to both.

Lohia was of the view that the role of agriculture in the national economy is very significant. Its development and rejuvenation has assumed paramount importance on accounts of various socio-economic-political factors. Social structure can not be changed without effecting radical change in the agrarian system. Apart from social values, political and economic considerations are also inseparably associated with agricultural operations and agrarian system. The agriculture policies and consequent developments have many dimensions e.g. what has been the role of agriculture in the process of economic development and changes that take place in the economic structure? What are the degree and nature of transformation of the agricultural system as a result of the process of industrialisation? The mutual relationship between these vital sectors of the economy is of much academic as well as practical significance. Did agriculture get the priority under different plans which it strategically deserved? Was it recognised as a vital sector in the national economy? If so, were the steps necessary for its reorganisation and radical transformation taken either by the Planning Commission under various Plans or by the respective states? These are vital issues which are to be touched upon and Lohia's scheme has to be studied and analysed in this context.

It is a well admitted fact that agriculture is the backbone of the Indian economy and without bringing about radical and structural change in this sector. It would be inconceivable to think of rapid industrialisation of country. It is also a fact that policy of piecemeal industrialisation may succeed only for the time being as far as the transformation of the economy from the agraian to the industrial one is concerned, it is rather unthinkable in the long-run.

In the light of the observations made by Ashok Mehta, the doyen of the Indian socialists, Lohia's approach to agricultural development can be judged in a better way. Mehta asserted that our basic problem is productivity. In most countries productivity differs sharply from sector to sector but wondered whether differences are as sharp and acute as they were in India. Over 70 per cent of the population is engaged in agriculture and the country does not produce enough to feed 50 per cent of the people.

Agriculture is incapable of creating surplus sufficient enough to feed the process of industrialisation. Unless self-sufficiency on food front is achieved, the whole scheme of industrialisation is doomed to fail in due course. Lohia was the greatest exponent of the intergrated approach of economic development. Unless the process of economic development is integrated, all piece-meal measures are bound to end in a fiasco.

Lohia considered the inequitable distribution of land as the most important factor contributing to the abysmal poverty of the masses. He was always alert and alive to the basic problems of the people and thought it expedient to strike at the root of the problems. He suggested the creation of Land Army or Anna Sena for reclamation of land for irrigational purposes mainly on the basis of small irrigation schemes through tanks and wells.

Lohia, while discussing the problem and scope of land reclamation with Gandhi, pointed out to Nehru that at least 17-18 crore acres of land is such which can be brought under cultivation. Out of this 3.4 crore acres of land are such on which cultivation can be started without incurring extra expenditure. Kitchen-garden or roof-farming may not be the solution of this problem (Lok Sabha, Vol. I).

Lohia discarded the Capitalist as well as Communist path of development. He was of the view that democratic socialism will abolish large inequalities of ownership and tenancy rights, clear the jungle of land tenures, and in each state to resettle revenue on a uniform, equitable principle that small may get substantial relief. Efforts will also be made to replace revenue, whenever possible, by a graded agricultural income tax.

The ejectment of tenants will immediately be stopped and steps will be taken for the redistribution of land and the consolidation of fragmented holdings. The land will belong to the tiller: the intermediaries between him and state will be abolished; and no one who does not personally participate in the processes of cultivation will be allowed to possess land. Efforts will be made to ensure as soon as possible that no cultivating family has less than an economic holding, and that no family will be allowed to possess land more than three times the size of an economic holding.

Farm workers will be freed from their burden of debt, which is usually the cause of their serfdom, and the maintenance of even a vestige of serfdom will be made a penal offence. They will be provided independent means of livelihood. For this purpose rural industries and decentralised process even of large-scale industries will be located in villages, works of public utilities will be organised in villages and new lands will be reclaimed through state efforts and the food army. They will be settled on them as well as on lands taken over according to the schemes of the redistribution of land and the liquidation of absentee ownership of the land. Constant efforts will be made to so reorganise the economy and social relations as to bring income of the agricultural workers to the level of the national minimum wages and to provide them with facilities for cultural advancement and for the enjoyment of civic amenities of life.

For Lohia, land reform was not only aimed at increased production rather equality and social justice was more important. This view is further corroborated by Peter Dorner. If the land reform is an essential condition for economic development, the question to be asked about a country's development is, therefore, (a) what has been happening to poverty? (b) What has been happening to unemployment, and (c) what has been happening to inequality ? If all three of these have declined from high level, then beyond doubt this has been a period of development for the country concerned. If even any one of these central problems has been growing worse, it would be strange to call the results development even if per capita income is doubled (Dorner, 1972).

No peasant family can thrive if its holding is below 5 acres but the holding of 59 per cent of the peasant families in the Indian Union are below 5 acres. In this respect the policies adopted by the government have to be examined on the following criteria (Sen, 1955):

(a) The agrarian economy should provide an opportunity for the development of the farmer's personality.
(b) There should be no scope for exploitation of one class by another.
(c) There should be maximum efficiency of production.
(d) The scheme of reform should be within the realm of practicability.

He advocated redistribution of land among the landless labourers and agrarian reform in all aspects. Zamindari abolition had nothing to do with the agrarian problem. Land reform in its traditional sense has taken place over years primarily in response to the demand for greater equality or justice. But what is new is the attention which is now being given to the development implications and to its possible contribution to improved agriculture productivity and expand employment. If it is to contribute significantly to these objectives, it will clearly be necessary for it to be taken in conjunction with a variety of supporting institutional improvements including better credit provision, marketing facilities and extension and advisory services (Dorner, 1972).

Lohia was supporter of the idea of co-operative farming to increase the production of agricultural sector and also for better and fuller utilisation of the agriculture tools and implements available to the farmers. Moreover, on the basis of co-operative farming modern method of farm operation will be feasible for the small farmers who, left to themselves; are incapable of doing the same on account of various limitations.

Co-operation shall be basic principle of the new village economy. Co-operative farming will be encouraged and multi-purpose co-operative societies will be organised for marketing, irrigation, the supply of better seeds, manures, implements, etc. as well as for the processing of agriculture products. Rural credit and industries will also be organised on co-operative lines. Newly reclaimed lands will not be distributed on the principle of peasant proprietorship, but will be cultivated cooperatively by those settled on them. Settlers of these reclaimed lands will not be entitled to claim them as their personal property, but will have right to use them in perpetuity for the purpose of cultivation in cooperation, to manage the farm on well known democratic principle, and to share its yield on the basis of their contribution of labour in production.

The State will help the tillers in solving many of the difficulties that face them today. These would include the provision of better manure, seeds, implements, better marketing facilities, cheaper finance, technical assistance and research. It will also be responsible for the reclamation of cultivable wastelands, the prevention of soil erosion, the development of irrigation, the taming of rivers and the proper maintenance of major roads, bunds and the drainage of rain water; special attention will be paid to the promotion of small irrigation projects. In all these matters the volunteers and food army will play a vital role, canalising individual efforts into communal endeavour. The state will also be responsible for the planning of production and the maintenance of prices of agriculture goods. It will also be responsible for the provision of free medical care to the people through a system of nationalised medical service and rural hospitals as well as for the provision of free education and other civic amenities of life necessary for decent cultured life.

Lohia found the Indian peasantry in a deplorable condition where poverty had stayed; improvements had stopped; farmers were ejected and where artificiality has been created due to delay in abolishing wicked laws about ownership. To Lohia, for improving the condition of agriculture and rural institution, the decisive factor of Indian economy, teeming millions and poor equipment must be taken account of. In India where an agriculture worker works around 1.5 acres of land, any scheme to rationalise it on the basis of the communist or the capitalist variety would be an utter failure.

Lohia wanted that the agricultural problem of India must be considered from the angle of its depressed personnel. They were: (1) Agriculture labourers, (2) Share croppers, and (3) Old tillers of economic holding. For them, Lohia also suggested such programmes as: (1) improving agricultural wage, (2) legal and actual fixation of the sharecroppers share at the minimum of 2/3rds of the produce, and (3) abolition of rent on uneconomic holding (Mehrotra, 1978).

As a first step towards land reform, Lohia wanted a drastic change in agrarian land ownership. Even a few days before independence, Lohia suggested that the declaration of independence should at the same time be accompanied with the issue by the Government of a proclamation abolishing landlordism. Unless this is done the man in the street would not feel that India is entering the temple of freedom (*The Patriot,* 1947).

He criticised the price policy of the government and suggested definite principle to guide it in future on a regular basis. He raised the issue of trade in food grain and its prices.

For controlling the price fluctuations, Lohia wanted certain directive principles to be followed :

1. The sale price of essential manufactured commodities should under no circumstances exceed one and half times of their cost of production which means that the taxes and profit must be kept within limits.
2. Fluctuations in the prices of food grains should not exceed 16 per cent between two harvests.

3. A relationship of justice and parity must exist between the agriculture and the industrial prices and farmers must get prices that cover their cost and a minimum standard.

By advocating the fluctuations of prices within certain limits Lohia wanted to save both the consumers and the agricultural producers from the clutches of profit-makers, hoarders, etc. Lohia pointed out, "we are all consumers and in our capacity as consumers we are thoroughly unprotected because there is nothing to protect as against the exploitation of high price." (*Mankind*, 1955).

The farmers are not benefited from increased prices of foodstuff, because the price at the time of harvest is low.

He emphasised the point that price differential between the harvest season and off-season should not vary beyond 16 per cent (Lok Sabha Mein Lohia, Vol. I). There should be some sort of equilibrium between agricultural and industrial prices.

This price policy is intended to bring about stability in agricultural and industrial production and will be able to prevent the exploitation of producers as well as of consumers. Scope of black marketing, hoarding and profiteering will be eliminated by this national price policy. This policy alone can abolish the price loot by the traders and the Government. He cited example in support of his policy. For a commodity available at Re. 1 in the market, cost of production is nearly 40% while the rest are other charges included in the price (*Ibid.*, 1-15).

He asserts that there is sufficient evidence to show that the price parity between agricultural and manufacture as it prevailed in 1961-62 was not conducive to development of agriculture and that the small movement in favour of agriculture which occurred between 1960-62 and 1970 was desirable. There are other developments also which argue for a change in parity in favour of agriculture. According to all cannons of justice and fair play, the procurement price of agricultural produce should be based on principle of parity between agricultural and non-agricultural prices. *Inter-alia*, the principle serves to strike a balance between the prices paid and prices received by farmers. The view is also shared by Mao-Tse-Tung when he said:

"The root cause of the failure to increase agricultural production in some countries is that the State's policy towards the peasants is questionable. The peasant's burden of taxation is too heavy while the price of agricultural product is very low and that of industrial goods very high. While developing industry, especially heavy industry, we must, at the same time give agriculture a certain status by adopting-correct policies for agricultural taxation and for pricing industrial and agricultural products." (Mao-Tse-Tung, 1966-71)

The policy followed by the government is obvious from the facts that the benefits of higher prices is denied to the Indian farmers which was being given to the farmers in Canada and America. This is justified on the specious pleas that the living standard in India was much lower than the international standard. It is further asserted that the price to be paid to the Indian farmers must be related to the country's economy.

There are cases of increasing poverty and misery of the masses even when there has been a period of growth of the economy. In India also this paradoxical situation is true.

As a result of this lopsided policy, the wealth is not increasing at a satisfactory rate. Unless this section of the people is well-off, the wealth of the nation will not increase. I am not explaining this only for the sake of justice but with a view to increasing the production of the country (Lok Sabha mein Lohia, Vol. V).

Lohia advocated the concept of small tool technology for India as it could not be developed on the basis of western technology. This view has been widely shared by the Gandhites and Western thinkers like Gunnar Myrdal and others.

Western technology today has a labour-saving bias. In India and a number of others underdeveloped countries, the basic ratios between the available stock of capital and existing supply of labour are far more favourable than they are or perhaps were in the industrially advanced countries. The underdeveloped countries must evolve a method of production suited to their own resource endowments.

Indiscriminate adoption of advanced western technology in these countries will almost certainly produce more unemployment than is either safe or good for them. The economists have thought in terms of maximisation of production. Gandhi stressed the importance of providing maximum number of people with productive work. Our real malady is not distribution but laziness. He thought nothing was more corroding than enforced idleness (Ray, 1970).

Backward regions suffer from variety of tangible (material) and intangible (culture and educational) handicaps. A plan for dispersal of centres of growth seems to be called for. One effect of regionally balanced development would be to reduce the contrast between overgrown urban centres and impoverished villages. Agro-industry and intermediate technology seem to indicate a new pattern of industrial growth (Ray, 1970)).

Lohia pointed out that only 6 lakhs of houses out of 80 lakhs might have got electric connection and rest of the house are still in darkness (Lok Sabha Mein Lohia, Vol. V). This is yet another instance of the egalitarian approach of Lohia who refused to be charmed by the deceptive figures supplied by the governments. The real yardstick of the plan expenditure should be what proportion of expenditure has incurred for the uplift and betterment of Harijan, Adivasi and people of backward castes and classes. There are cases of increasing poverty and misery of the masses even when there has been a period of growth of the economy. In India also this paradoxical situation is true.

He advised peasants to be engaged in voluntary constructive cooperative efforts in building a new village. Band of land volunteers (Bhumi Sevaks) are to be raised in the village to dig wells, tanks, compost pits and drains, reclaim water logged areas, construct roads, bunds, fences, etc. It is this which will make them realise of their own experience the virtue of joint efforts for happiness and walfare. So our task in villages is manifold. It is organisational, educative, constructive as well as combative. All these tasks require our careful attention and devoted service. We cannot, therefore, afford to be purely constructive or purely militant, but will have to coordinate construction and struggle in the service of the toiling masses and cause of socialism.

Lohia speaking on the no confidence motion in Lok-Sabha on the 16th March 1965 suggested the following measures for transforming a feudal and capitalist society into a socialist one (Lok Sabha Mein Lohia, Vol. I).

(a) Uniform primary schools for all children whether he is a son of the President of India or a son of a sweeper.
(b) There should be only third class in the railway and other classes should be abolished.
(c) There should be cealing on expenditure over Rs. 1,000. No body should be allowed to spend more than Rs. 1,000 per month.
(d) English language should be abolished. If English language continues socialism can not be brought about. If it is claimed, it is a total lie, it may be a fraud, hence English should be abolished.
(e) All the cultivable land must get water without any kind of water rate, socialism is impossible to be achieved without this minimum provision.

Lohia was greatly influenced by Gandhian economic thought and naturally he was a vehement critic of indiscriminate industrialisation and urbanisation. Mahatma Gandhi was the strongest opponent of the multiplication of wants and production of commodities by the cities which could be produced by the villages efficiently. Multiplication of wants, extensive use of machinery, urbanisation and industrialisation all these according to him, were interconnected and added to the pauperisation of villages and degradation of human personality, emergence of mass unemployment or its continuance and exploitation of the weak by strong both within the nation and internationally (Rao, 1970).

With Satyagraha as the means and socialisms as the objective to be achieved, Gandhi offered an alternative to the class war and proletarian dictatorship that communists and scientific socialists have professed as the only means for the achievement of what they called socialism.

Lohia was ardent advocate of decentralised socialist State, the village panchayat elected on the basis of universal franchise, will be the chief organ of the State authority in the village or the zone concerned. Most of the aforesaid functions and responsibilities of the State will be performed by, or in consultation with, and on the recommendation of village panchayats, looking after the affairs of the general interest to the community in the field of economic, social, civic and cultural life of rural India. It will be their responsibility to prepare a crop plan for their village to send it to the higher organs of the Planning Commission, and ultimately to work for the realisation of the target fixed by the Planning Commission. They will have the right to represent the village community in all matters affecting village polity and economy, and will be the main local agency for executing schemes of rural development and welfare. Their relations with higher organs of the State will be determined on principles of decentralised democracy.

References

Dr. R.B. Singh, Preface, *India's Economic Development and Lohia's Thought,* Samata Prakashan Dilshad Garden, Delhi.

Lok Sabha Mein Lohia, Vol. 1, p. 82.

Dornor, Peter (1972), *Land Reforms and Economic Development,* Penguin Book, p. 15.

Sen, Bhowani (1955), India Land System and Land Reforms, PPH, Delhi, p. 2.

Dornor, Peter, *Land Reforms and Economic Development, op. cit.,* pp. 11-12.

Mehrotra, N.C., Lohia: A study, Atma Ram and Sons, Delhi, 1978, p. 158.

The Patriot (1947), Delhi, July 14.

Mankind, November (1955), p. 384.

Lok Sabha mein Lohia, Vol. 1, pp. 82, 86.

Mao-Tse-Tung (1966-71), Unrehearsed talk and letters, edited by Stuart, Schram, p. 64.

Lok Sabha mein Lohia, op. cit., Vol. V, p. 12.

Roy, Shivnarain, (ed.) Gandhi (1970), India and the World, Nachiketo Publications Ltd., Bombay, Datta, Amian, Aspects of Gandhian Economic Thought.

Lok Sabha mein Lohia, Vol. V, p. 17.

Rao, V.K.R.V. (1970), The Gandhian Alternative to Western Socialism, Bhartiya Vidya Bhawan, Bombay, Vol. 7, pp. 10-11.

Economic Ideas of Dr. Ram Manohar Lohia

UPENDRA SHARMA

INTRODUCTION

Economic ideas of Dr. Ram Manohar Lohia are embedded in his political philosophy and it is very difficult to separate them completely. Sometimes, they overlap each other. Due to this problem, it is very natural that readers may view some of his economic ideas as his political thought and *vice-versa*. In spite of this, a sincere effort has been made in this paper to put his economic ideas as separately as possible and any criss-cross is simply regretted and may kindly be excused. Unless we touch the border line of his political philosophy, we cannot fully understand and appreciate the economic ideas of Dr. Lohia. In fact, there is not a water-tight compartment between his economic ideas and his political philosophy.

INDIVIDUAL FREEDOM

Like most of the classical economists such as Adam

Smith, J.B. Say and J.S. Mill, Dr. Lohia advocates Individual Freedom. He holds that men are by nature equal and free. His mind was tremendously influenced by the German Philosophers and Scholars—namely Kant, Hegel, Karl Marx and others. He agrees to Kantian view point that the individual is rational and has will of his own. Like Kant and Laski, he considers Liberty and equality as the necessary attributes of the individual. Lohia in the preface to his monumental book 'Marx, Gandhi and Socialism', has mentioned seven revolutions, through which a better society can be established which will result in the progress of both individual and the society. His seventh revolution aims at protecting privacy against encroachment by the collective. He regrets to see the modern trend in which the individual has been steadily losing his sovereignty to organisation. Laski and Russel have also expressed similar views. According to Lohia, the individual welfare and happiness, education and health, also his leisure and much of his life and thought are subject to planning of various kinds. "This planning is rigorous in lands of communism but a growing element of organisational compulsion is present everywhere."

Lohia further argues that there are certain spheres of life which should be free from the control of State, Government, organisations and groups. Rights of privacy in the sphere of house keeping, entertainment, marriage should be maintained. An individual should have full freedom for choosing any profession and membership of any political party. State or Government or political party should not interfere with the private life of individual. Every individual should have right to lead his life according to his choice upto a certain limit. Lohia fears this right may be misused by the individual. But when one's right is recognised and if that is misused then what should be done. In this connection Lohia says let the individual suffer. Lohia surpasses Mill, when he firmly opines that every man or woman should have even the right to commit suicide. No body has right to interfere with this personal matter of individual, his choice of committing suicide. Mill allows interference in purely personal matter when one is about to commit suicide or insists on doing something whose dangerous nature is not known to him. It will never be an attack upon one's liberty if individual is prevented from committing suicide. Mill justifies such intervention on the ground that the individual at the time of committing suicide does not know his own true interest; society knows it better and so can legitimately restrain him. The notion of individual freedom as advocated by Lohia is criticised on the ground that his argument is rather dangerous and it may create anarchy in the society. Lohia has divided freedom into two parts—the first is connected with non-property matter and second one is connected with property. He advocates full freedom to individuals in non-property matters. He asserts, "Rights of pirvacy and freedom must be recognised in all those spheres which are not directly connected with property." It shows that Dr. Lohia also accepts certain degree of interference in property matters but even in property matters Lohia never approves of complete State control as is prevalent in the communist system. He wants to restrain state interference only in those spheres which are directly connected with property.

Lohia is a staunch supporter of liberty for backward people which Mill refuses to grant. Lohia wants to give preferential treatment to backward people for a certain period. In this connection, he surpasses Mill who proves to be a bit conservative in his approach to liberty.

PLANNING

Lohia does not outrightly oppose State planning. He says that State Planning always aims at doing good. But he does not like such a planning which is rooted in compulsion and curtails much of the individual freedom. Lohia fears that State Planning may encroach on the individual privacy.

Lohia points out the defect of the then Congress in matter of planning. The Congress had not planned things well. It is protecting the capitalist. It is like a person in whirlpool reaching out its hands in whatever direction it can without success. He observes, "Thus, while classless society is declared as its goal, the Congress in practice aligns itself with Landlords and Capitalists." The pattern of big fish devouring small fries is prevailing under the Congress regime. Poverty, increasing population, unemployment lawlessness, corruption, deceit, arson and loot have become the normal features of the society. As a result, there is frustration everywhere. To quote Lohia, "owing to the planlessness and the initial blunders of the Congress, the country is at a standstill with an ever-increasing population; this means retrogression. Production is declining, poverty is on the increase, and there is disillusionment and distrust all round."

GENDER DIFFERENCE

In Lohia's view, there is no distinction between men and women. Men and women both should be equally placed in the society. Like Plato, Indian saints and other thinkers, Lohia also advocates equality between men and women. He observes "women will be given equal status with men in all matters—political, social and economic. In the sphere of education women will receive preferential treatment to enable them to overcome existing disparities with men." Through legislation and through propaganda and education, all social customs and practices that go against the principles of equality of women with men will be ended. Lohia holds the view that women have always been neglected in the society. Their status is very low. They are backward in all respects. Therefore, it is necessary to bring them on equal footing with men. He further says that women can be equated with men only by preferential opportunity rather than equal opportunity. Lohia opines that "equal opportunity would not solve the problem of inequality between the sexes. When a group of people is held down by debility, physical or cultural, the only way to bring it up to equality with others is through conferment of preferential opportunity. An Indian woman is a bond maid at the mercy of her parents till her marriage and after marriage a slave to her husband. Lohia wants this to be done away by giving preferential treatment to the fair sex. Like men, participation of women in the socialist movement is equally necessary, as Lohia says—"A socialist movement without the active participation of women is like a wedding without the bride."

SOLUTION TO FOOD PROBLEM—GHERA DALO ANDOLAN (GHERAO)

Lohia has suggested Ghera Dalo Andolan for the solution of food problems during the time of famine. The socialist party believes in the method of Ghera Dalo Andolan which makes an appeal to the Government either to—"give bread." to hungry people or "send them to jail." According to Lohia, "under the Ghera Dalo Andolan hungry people should gherao the Government's offices, Government's godowns, godowns of big traders and hoarders upto the time they get food or they get themselves arrested." Such movements were launched at Deoriya in U.P. and Daltonganj in Bihar and people got success in the year, 1958. This Ghera Dalo Andolan should be strictly peaceful and non-violent in Gandhian way. Lohia has suggested two other movements for solving food problem. First, the socialist party should launch Anna Banto or distribute food movement. Under this movement, hungry masses should peacefully seize godowns, weigh foodgrains, maintain an account of the total food grains and then distribute foodgrains among themselves. Later on, when they become capable of paying, they return the taken food grains plus one-fourth more or pay in cash. But Lohia says this movement is possible only when the people are strong and police weak.

Secondly, without weighing and maintaining account of food grains, hungry masses should distribute foodgrains among themselves but this should be performed peacefully and non-violently. In this connection, Lohia warns people that "godowns of retailers or commission taking goledars should not be seized. Such type of movement was prevalent in Germany."

Ghera Dalo Andolan, Anna Banto and Anna Banto Movement without keeping records of foodgrains—all these three movements suggested by Lohia for solving food problem during famine are sound in theory but impracticable, unmanageable and undesirable in practice. These will create chaos and anarchy in the society, and the problem may be further complicated.

IMPERIALISM AND COLONIALISM

Lohia was against imperialism and colonialism. According to him all forms of colonialism are shame to mankind and serious impediment to growth of equal world. Political rule of an occupation army and of one nation over another must go. All colonial states of the world must be set free. "Socialist internationalism must stand behind all struggles against colonialism and render all possible assistance to freedom fighters."

INTERNATIONAL TRADE AND AID AND ASSISTANCE TO UNDER DEVELOPED COUNTRIES

Lohia favours international trade but he warns that such trade should not be a one-way traffic rather it should be a two-way traffic. According to Lohia aid to underdeveloped countries must come through a World Development Authority to which every nation contributes according to its ability from which every nation receives according to its need. He further points out that "until such an authority comes into being, international socialism may attempt to set-up model projects through a capital collected from all such organistions and men as would listen to its appeal." Even within a nation, the more fortunate persons are called upon to assist the less fortunate ones, so in the international world, the more favoured ones should assist the less advanced. Backward nations should be helped to acquire the economic apparatus by which they can raise themselves. Our fight should be against hunger, disease and illiteracy. Economic inequality is the main source of discord and war in the world. In order to remove the economic disparities, a World Development Authority should be established. Like Lohia, Radhakrishnan also supports the concept of World Economic Development Programme. Foreign aid in its present form is not only humiliating and dangerous to the receiving countries but can never be adequate to meet their needs and requirements. Such aid definitely, corrupts the backward countries. Such a one sided giving and taking is one-way traffic and is erroneous in conception and harmful in consequences. Technological skills and economic aid should be voluntarily exchanged between rich and the retarded states through World Development Authority. And this mutual exchange should result in approximation not in imposition. This concept of two way traffic in the field of International Trade, Aid and Assistance is sound in theory but difficult in practice so long as distinction between Big and Small exists in the International field.

THE CONCEPT OF FOUR-PILLAR STATE AND DECENTRALISATION OF ECONOMIC AND POLITICAL POWERS

Lohia belives in decentralisation of economic and political powers. For giving a solution to the malady of Indian administration, he gives the concept of Four-Pillar state which is based on the principle of division of powers. According to him Four-Pillar State constitutes four limbs of the State. They are the village, the district, the province and the centre with sovereign powers. All these four limbs of the State will organically function. They will work interdependently. Sovereign powers must not reside alone in the centre and the federating units but also with district and villages which are the primary political institutions where a group of men and women work for the interest of the whole community. Thus Lohia considers that the greatest defect of Indian administration is the concentration of economic and political powers either in the centre or in the federating units. He suggests that there should be decentralisation of political and economic powers in the four limbs of the Four-Pillar State. Unless this is done, democratic institutions can not flourish and active participation of people in administration can not be a reality. Concentration of economic power gives rise to inequality and is a characteristic feature of capitalism where the economic power remains concentrated in the hands of a few.

DEMOCRACY AND DEMOCRATIC INSTITUTIONS

Lohia considers democracy and democratic institutions very important for any nation. He says that democracy and socialism are the two sides of the same coin. "Democracy in all circumstances shall be the sheet-anchor of the ideas and programmes of the socialism. Democracy means the inevitable answerability of elected assembly. It also means the recognition and respect of limited personality of individual, party, Government and the State–four categories which together constitute the agencies of political action."

Thus Lohia is fully convinced that it is only through democracy that freedom of thought can be best maintained. At the same time, he believes if democracy is organised on the principles of socialism, both freedom of mind and economic security to the individual can be attained. The enjoyment of individual liberty can not take a concrete form unless the state assures economic security or equality to the individual. Nobel laureate Prof. Amartya Sen later testified it through practical examples of famines that took place in many countries. Countries with democratic system saved countless lives whereas people in large number died in other system of Governance.

SOCIALISM, CAPITALISM AND COMMUNISM

Lohia is an exponent of socialism. He believes in the system of socialism. He is a born critic of capitalism and communism. He criticises capitalism and communism on the ground that both the systems have failed to prepare the soil for the germination of the seeds of liberty and equality evenly. Therefore, Lohia prefers the system of socialism which believes in the equal growth of liberty and equality both.

According to him "if socialism is to be defined in two words then they are equality and prosperity. I do not know if this definition has been given earlier at any time. If so, I could call it the best definition given so far."

Lohia says real freedom is not possible in capitalism and communism because capitalism breeds inequalities on the one hand and communism kills the spirit of individual freedom on the other. Therefore, both the systems are inimical to the true spirit of democracy which signifies liberty and equality both. Lohia, Russell, Laski and Nehru want to establish a democratic socialist society which will constantly move on the axis of liberty and equality. Liberty thus implies equality. Liberty and equality are not in conflict nor even separate, but are different facets of the same ideal. Lohia opines : "Freedom and bread are inseparable, at least in Asia, and neither communism nor capitalism can supply these two articles to us. I would suggest that Asia can be saved from communism only if it is saved from capitalism and feudalism."

Therefore, to Lohia and Laski, equality is the primary condition of attaining freedom or justice. No one can dare to believe that it can be obtained under the capitalist system which practices privileges and distinctions. The real point that they wish to place in their discussion of liberty is that in the present hierarchically organised economic and political order, opportunities for creative self-expression are denied to all but small group of men. Liberty in the sense of free play of the relative impulses of men and a high degree of individual diversity is incompatible with the present system of property, for its result is a concentration of power in a few hands which makes for the political personalising of the average citizen ineffective. Inequality is an inherent characteristic of capitalist society, while a Socialist Society will necessarily be an equal society. Both Lohia and Laski argue that economic inequality is the root cause of all other inequalities. They also say that freedom is meaningful only to a small minority in capitalist society which owns and controls property. Great inequalities of wealth make impossible the attainment of freedom.

The removal of inequality from the human society is one of the seven revolutions of Lohia. He points out that "the poorer the country, the greater is the inequality within it." Lohia is firm in his thought that the capitalist society breeds inequality which proves antithetical to freedom. Similarly, he dislikes communist system which is based on fear; whereas, the capitalist system works under the temptation of profit. "Such systems which depend on temptation and fear for their dynamism and growth must inevitably breed inequality."

CAPITAL FORMATION

Lohia holds the view that Industrialisation is not possible without capital formation. As per his prescription, in a poor and diseased country like India, Capital could be formed only through the way of equality. "Capitalism can not perform its own functions here. Capitalism can not create capital, prosperity and thereby capital formation can come only through equality."

WORLD CIVILIZATION, WORLD PARLIAMENT, WORLD GOVERNMENT, WORLD CITIZENSHIP, AND WORLD DEVELOPMENT AUTHORITY

Lohia's thought was not confined to the national boundary. He advocated World Civilization, World Parliament, World Government, World Development Authority and World Citizenship. Lohia was opposed to 'United Nations' in its present form and was in favour of replacing it by a world parliament which will be organised on the principles of universality and equality. He was having a broad outlook and so he visulised the concept of world Civilisation, world Parliament, world Government, world Development Authority and world Citizenship. He further explains that under the atmosphere of capitalism, imperialism, colonialism and racialism, the above concepts can not be a reality. Therefore, for the realisations of world citizenship, economic inequality, political slavery and the feeling of racialism must stop without any delay. He gives the example of India which is gripped by poverty and torn by religions and castes. According to him, it seems ridiculous to make the submerged and hungry landless labourer a world citizen. Lohia shows the boldness to say that our attempt to create a new civilization through world Government must not cease. In this context, he finally concludes, "And yet this movement for world Government in conjunction with socialism may be that lever which raises the submerged millions to new hope and endeavour."

TECHNOLOGY

"The technology of Modern Europe is an imperialist technology in origin and in current substance is incapable of reproduction all over the world unless an abundance of colonies in other planets were discovered." The industrial revolution of Europe and modern technology are incapable of repetition in Asia and Africa. Too little land and too many men and too few tools are a mark of Asia, so a full application of a mass production is utterly impossible. Lohia further says that existing technology made possible by the imperialist control which European civilization exercises over the rest of the world is no longer valid. In a way, Lohia favoured the use of labour intensive technique for a country like India where there is abundance of labour and dearth of capital.

CONCLUSION

We can come to the conclusion that Dr. Lohia was an ardent supporter of Individual Freedom, Democratic Institutions and Socialism. He advocated democratic socialism. He was critical of big powers which were either following capitalism or communism. He was against direct aid of any kind from developed economies to underdeveloped economies like India because of the fact that in such aid there was a feeling of domination in the givers and a feeling of subjugation in the receivers. He recommended such aid through world Development Authority where rich nations may contribute to the poor ones. He favoured international trade but it should not be a one-way traffic rather it should be a two-way traffic. The chief contribution of Lohia lies in analysing and exposing the danger of modern capitalism and communism and putting up a proposal for a socialistic system which can ensure maximum welfare to the people through material comfort and at the same time assure freedom for the full development of individual.

References

Lohia, Ram Manohar (1963), 'Marx, Gandhi and Socialism', Hyderabad, Nav Hind Publications, p. Preface, 39.

Ibid., p. Preface XXXX.

Ibid., p. Preface XXXIII.

Ibid., p. 350.

Lohia, Ram Manohar (1963), 'Anna Sumasya', Nav Hind Prakashan, Hyderabad, p. 14.

Ibid., pp. 14-15.

Op. cit., p. 488.

Lohia, Ram Manohar (1963), 'Marx, Gandhi and Socialism', Nav Hind Publication, Hyderabad, p. 488.

Ibid., p. 483.

Harris Wofford, Jr., Lohia and America Meet Madras, Snehalata Rama Reddy, p. 81.

Lohia, Ram Manohar (1963), Marx, Gandhi and Socialism, Nav Hind Publications, Hydrabad, p. Preface XXXVII.

Ibid., Preface XXXVII.

Lohia, Ram Manohar (1966), In the article 'Equality and Prosperity' Published in *Mankind*, New Delhi, Volume X, No. 7, Dec., p. 3.

Lohia, Ram Manohar, Foreign Policy, Allahabad, P.C. Dwadash Shreni and Company Pvt. Ltd., p. 71.

Lohia, Ram Manohar (1963), 'Wheel of History', Nav Hind Prakashan, Hydrabad, p. 71.

5

Lohia's Concept of Industrialisation

SUNIL KUMAR

Village Communism based on cottage industrialisation is not a Gandhian fad, it is sound and scientific from various angles of vision. During recent times, it has won the admiration and support of several important writers. Sir William Beveridge, the well-known author of the British Social Security Plan, while discussing a similar plan for India recently remarked :

> "India's industry would probably expand, but it is important that it should be properly distributed to avoid dreadful sprawling towns that we have in this country (England) and the United States."

A noted French economist, Hyacinthe Dubreuil has shown that even the largest industrial undertakings can be organised so as to consist of a number of coordinated but self-governing groups and he has adduced reasons for supposing that such an organisation would not reduce the efficiency of the businesses concerned and might even increase. The distinguished European thinkers, Count Coudenhove Kalergi in his Totalitration Stage Against Man, has suggested the establishment of 'Agricultural Cooperatives' as a final and lasting solution of all the ills of the War Weary World.

Bombay Planners as well have not failed to take cognisance of the importance of cottage industrialism in Indian National economy.

'It is an essential part of our Plan for the recognisation of industries that adequate scope should be provided for small scale and cottage industries along with large sacle industries. This is important not merely as a means of affording employment, but also of reducing the need for capital particularly of external capital in the early stages of the Plan.

Cottage industrialism has been an eminent success in War-torn China, Nym Wales in her book, 'China Builds for Democracy', give us a vivid and fascinating account of the working of the Industrial cooperatives, or as their abbreviated form is termed 'Indusco'. By 1938 'Japanese War' machine had annihilated about 80 per cent of Chinese industries, rendering thousands of workers idle and homeless. The whole future of China hung in the balance. It was at that critical juncture of national history that a few Chinese youngmen, under the leadership of Rewi Alley, formulated a plan for 'Guerilla' industries on cooperative bases, they are now Chinese glory and wealth. They have not only served the country as impregnable lines of defence against foreign aggression, but have also sustained the vitality of the nation by providing it with all the necessary consumption goods at a time when the whole economic organisation was bombed to prices. There have emerged in China thousands of Small Cooperative Communities which are economically self-governing and self-sufficient, producing with manual labour and small machines all the necessaries of life.

It is the carefully considered opinion of Chinese industrial experts and a number of American and British observes, writes Nym Wales, that the Industrial Cooperatives can provide not only the best but the most feasible form of industry for China in the future as at present. Its potentialities are very great and mere struggle to rebuild industry on democratic basis in the middle of a battle field is an exciting one which has already captured the imagination of hundreds of observers interested in social and economic change and in the fate of China.

Writing on China's 'guerilla Industry' in the Asia and the America of May 1944, Edgar Snow expresses the same view :

> "Not only could it help to win the war in its final phase but if given a chance it could fulfil the original hope of its founders to create a happy economic foundation on which to build the future of China along democratic and peaceful lines."

The value of the Chinese 'Indusco' movement to India is very great indeed. In this connection, Nehru in course of his Foreword to Nym Wale's book makes significant observations:

> 'India like China, has enormous manpower, vast unemployment and under employment. It is no good comparing with the light little countries of Europe which gradually became industrialised with small and growing population. Any schemes which involves the wastage of our labour power or which throws people out of employment is bad. From the purely economic point of view, even apart from human aspect, it may be more profitable to use more labour power and less specialised machinery. It is better to find employment for large number of people at a low income level than to keep most of them unemployed. It is possible also that the total wealth produced by a large number of cottage industries might be greater than that of some other factories producing the same kind of goods.

As is sufficiently well-known Japan too is the home of small scale domestic industries. These dwarf units produce not only consumption goods but also machines. It is pointed out that only 34 per cent of the machinery manufactured in Japan is produced in large factories. Prof Allen in his book Japanese Industry : Its Recent Development and present condition, remarks:

"We may conclude that the predominance of the small technical units in many of Japan's industries is not an indication of the economic weakness of the country but that it represents an appropriate adaptation of industrial methods to the economic conditions existing there. In that country capital is relatively scarce and dear, while industrial labour is relatively plentiful and cheap."

The same is the case with India. This experiment may be tried with a fair chance of success which may offer solution to many problems. Thus the general trend of World economic thought is towards decentralisation. This system was in existence in India from very ancient times. Gandhiji has upheld almost the same economic plan based on village communities and rural industrialism. The Gandhian principles are the only practical and solution of various ills that harass the modern world; they point out the middle path between blood-thirsty Capitalism and freedom-thirsty Socialism.

India's 'de-industrialisation' was brought about by such people as these, and as Nehru says in his Discovery of India: 'She became a passive agent of modern industrial capitalism, suffering all its ills and with hardly any of its advantages'. Industrialisation occurred in Japan also but unlike India in Japan large industries co-existed with small industries. Therefore, there was no atmosphere thereof uncompromising struggle for survival between small and large industries and the rise of big enterprises did not cause any serious dislocation to small industries in Japan as it did in India. Neither the government nor the industrial capitalists of India made any attempt to look into Indian traditions and the socio-economic structure and they dismissed rural industries as outdated. The new rulers did not care to integrate the socio-economic structure of rural and small industries on the one hand and the technological structure of the new industries.

For this, in fact the technique of synthesis was necessary. That is, if industrialisation could have come to India in proper way, the process of synthesis of India's age-old economic industrial structure with the new industries would have been smooth and healthy, and the mill sector too could have expanded within the framework of Indian economic tradition. The consequence is that village and small industries anguished and perished due to neglect and lopisded policy, while big industries are sick and crying for subsidisation and artificial respiration. The small industreis certainly have overwhelming economic importance, but they have a related social aspect also which is highly significant. The economic point of view has to be considered as the economic set-up determines to a great extent, the social behaviour of the community and at no point of time does the economic aspect ease to have its impact on the society. A programme of Khadi and Village Industries development can be an economic solution to social ills like inequality and moral degradation. The character of production will be determined by social necessity and not by personal whims or greed.

It is clear that cottage industries should not be dubbed as 'inefficient' the village artisans have been so far obliged to use crude tools because of the apathy of the state and the vested interest. With the assistance of modern science there is absolutely no reason why cottage implements and small machines should not become models of efficiency and refined production. Efficiency is after all only a means to an end. If it leads to displacement of human labour beyond a prescribed limit and result in frictional or structural unemployment, it has to be discarded in favour of simpler and even crude machines. It is essential to distinguish between Mechanical Efficiency and Economic Efficiency, an instrument or a machine that is mechanically efficient need not necessarily be economically efficient as well. For example, huge machines and labour saving scientific devices are no doubt efficient from the mechanical and technological standpoint they are capable of producing more with less labour. But they can not be called efficient from the view point of economic welfare in general.

Gandhi differentiated between mechanical efficiency and economic efficiency and came to the conclusion that mechanical efficiency may not be compatible with economic efficiency which is a measure of welfare and social utility.

Similarly, Lohia distinguished between maximum efficiency and total efficiency. The capitalist mode of production is mad after maximum efficiency while ignoring the relevance of total efficiency which is based on the productive and gainful utilisation of enormous manpower available in India. Like Gandhi he asserts that man should be the centre of all economic activities. Potentiality of masses should not be sacrificed on the altar of capitalism based on the concept of maximum efficiency.

For a poor man the chance to work is the greatest of all needs and even poorly paid and relatively unproductive work is better than idleness. Coverage must come before perfection, to use the words of Mr. Gabriel Ardant.

> "It is important that there should be enough work for all because that is the only way to eliminate anti-productive reflexes and create a new state of mind that of a country where labour has become precious and must be put to the best possible use."

According to Schumacher, the real task may be formulated in four propositions : First, that work places have to be created in the areas where the people are living now and not primarily in metropolitan areas into which they tend to migrate.

Second, that these work places must be, on average, cheap enough so that they can be created in large numbers without this calling for an unattainable level of capital formation and imports.

Third, that the production methods employed must be relatively simple, so that the demands for high skills are minimised not only in the production process itself but also in matters of organisation, raw material supply, financing, marketing and so forth.

Fourth, the production should be mainly from local materials and mainly for local use.

These four requirements can be met only if there is a regional approach to development and, second, if there is a conscious efforts to develop and apply what might be called an 'intermediate technology'.

Professor Gadgil goes on to pled that : 'The main attention of the personnel on the applied side of National Laboratories, technical institutes and the large university departments must be concentrated on this work. The advancement technology in every field is being adequately pursued in the developed countries, the special adaptations and adjustments required in India are not likely to be given attention in any other country. They must, therefore, obtain the highest priority in our plans. Intermediate technology should become a national concern and not, as at present, a neglected field assigned to a small number of specialists, set apart'.

As Gandhi said, the poor of the world can not be helped by mass production, only by production by the masses. The system of mass production, based on sophisticated, highly capital-intensive high energy-input dependent on human labour-saving technology, presupposes that you are already rich, for a great deal of capital investment is needed to establish one single work place. The system of production by the masses mobilises the priceless resources which are possessed by all human beings, their clever brains and skillful hands, and support them with first class tools. The technology of mass production is inherently violent, ecologically damaging, self-defeating 'in terms of non-renewable' resources, and stultifying for the human person. The technology of production by the masses making use of the best of modern knowledge and experience, is conducive to decentralisation, compatible with the laws of ecology, gentle in its use of scarce resources, and designed to serve the human person instead of making him the servant of machines. I have named it intermediate technology to signify that it is vastly superior to the primitive technology of bygone ages but at the same time much simpler, cheaper, and freer than the super-technology of the rich. One can also call it self-help technology to which every body can gain admittance and which is not reserved to these to already rich and powerful.

In a way, to repeat the situation that faces India which is rich in labour but poor in material resources, poses a new economic problem and demands new technical methods for its solution. More specifically the problem is how to develop a new type of industry radically different from the present cottage and handicrafts industries as also from the present large factory industries either a type which, for the same amount of capital investment, can at the same time produce more goods per worker than the former and provide more employment than the latter.

What is required of science and technology are methods and equipment that are cheap enough, that are virtually accessible to every body and, therefore, suitable for small scale application, so that we have production by masses as against production and are compatible with man's need for creativity.

In April 1956 the Government of India laid down by way of a formal resolution, known as the Industrial Policy Resolution, that in order to realise the objective of a 'socialistic pattern of society'. It is essential to accelerate the rate of economic growth, speed up industrialisation. Particularly develop heavy and machine-making industries, expand the public sector and build up a large and growing co-operative sector. Jawaharlal Nehru made his position very clear in his speech delivered at the meeting of the AICC, held in Chandigarh on 28th September, 1959. He said :

'The primary thing about an integrated plan was production and not employment. Employment was important, but it was utterly unimportant in the context of production. It followed production and not preceded production. And production would only go up by better techniques which meant modern methods.'

It is clear if mechanised projects and industries are set-up to manufacture goods or provide services which are already being done on small and cottage scale and most of the existing industries in India fall under this category. They will merely be adding to unemployment without making an improvement in the physical productivity of the country. So that, with more and more mechanised undertakings entering the field, more and more are becoming unemployed. Thus, instead of adding to industrialisation, that is, finding employment for more and more workers in non-agricultural occupations, the modern factory, in the conditions of India has positively served to de-industrialisation of the economy. This may be the consequence of Nehru's policy of industrialisation-based on modern technology.

This view is confirmed by various studies. In 1955, 68 per cent of the industrial workers were engaged in household industries employing less than 5 workers. The census of India 1971 showed that the number of these workers came down to 6.35 million or by 30% during a course of 14 years. While it took the East India Company and the British Government full ten decades, 1757 to 1857 to decimate our domestic or village industries to the extent that according to the census of 1971, three-fourths of its artisans and cottage workers were forced to leave their traditional occupations. It took the Government of India barely 14 years, 1956 to 1970, to destroy nearly two-fifths of its surviving arts and handicrafts with the result that 3.85 million workers were thrown on the street.

A rising standard of life or material welfare as it is sometimes called is of course not an end in itself. Essentially, it is a means to a better intellectual and cultural life. A society which was to devote the bulk of its working force or its working hours to the production of the bare wherewithals of life is to that extent limited in its pursuits of higher ends. Economic development is intended to expand the community's productive power and to provide the environment in which there is scope for the expression and application of diverse faculties and urges.

These objectives were summed up in the phrase 'Socialist Pattern of Society.' Essentially, this means that the basic criterion for determining the lines of advance must not be private profit but social gain and that the pattern of development and the structure of socio-economic relations should be so planned that the result not only in appreciable increase in national income and employment but also in greater equality in income and wealth.

Among other objectives special attention was placed on rapid industrialisation with particular emphasis on development of basic and heavy industries. As a matter of fact, there was no industrial policy in pre-independence period to give a definite direction to industrial development. For the first time in 1948 Government of India announced its industrial policy which was subsequently modified and revised in 1956. It intended to give a definite direction to the industrial development.

Its impact reflected in the formulation of the Second Five Year Plan which placed greater reliance on industrialisation. The planners were unduly emboldened by the performance of the First Plan which was mainly due to favourable monsoon and congenial atmosphere. Priority was shifted from agriculture to industry in the Second and subsequent Plans. It was also due to the fact that the leaders and planners thought that once process of industrialisation was started, all other problems would be automatically solved. They considered the industrialisation and consequent installation of heavy and key industries as the panacea of all the ills and maladies from which the nation was suffering chronically. They also tried to implant the foreign model of growth based on heavy industrialisation which could not be conductive to the Indian conditions. It was, however, forgotten that no imported model or technology can deliver good which does not suit the socio-economic conditions of India. This is why subsequent plans were doomed to failure leading to alround dislocation in the economy.

Announcement of the industrial policy divided the jurisdiction of operations of public and private sectors. Some fields of industrial operation were reserved exclusively for the public sector but the Damocle's sword was kept hanging over the neck of the private sector. The threat of nationalisation after ten years as contained in the industrial policy of 1948, unnerved the private entrepreneurs, retarded capital formation in the private sector and postponed expansion and replacement of plants and equipments in the sphere of basic and heavy industries. This affected the economy adversely and subsequently government was forced by circumstances to announce in the parliament that foreign capital would not be discriminated against.

It is also a fact that public sector was thought to be the harbinger of rapid industrialisation. Theoretically this may be justified but on grounds of feasibility or practical considerations this policy proved self-defeating. It failed to achieve its purpose also because it was adopted in hot haste to prove the progressive and socialist ideas of the leaders. Having observed the effects of socialist methods, Mr. Doughlas Jay, a leading member of the British Labour Party and a close associate of Huge Gaiteskell, in his book "Socialism in the New Society," concluded that "absence of private property is also a denial of freedom." Dismissing the socialist concept of 'perfect equality' as impracticable, he pleaded for 'not equal share but fair share, not equality but social justice'.

Lohia's criticism of the strategy of Indian planning has been discussed in the previous chapter. His thinking on economic problem bears the best testimony of Gandhian economic philosophy. He tried to analyse the problem in the most unconventional manner. Unfortunately, however, his views on economic problems of India did not receive the kind of attention they deserved. This happened because most of the Indian scholars and intellectuals are supporters of *status quo* as they have been brought up and trained in western way of thinking. This explains why any scholar and ruling politician could seldom distinguish the basic difference in Indian and Western socio-politico-economic structures. His line of thinking on Indian problems greatly differed from rest of his contemporary thinkers in this country and abroad. He analyzed the problem in its totality and was perfectly justified in his approach as problem could not be divided into watertight compartment division. Economic problem cannot be properly understood in isolation from socio-political background.

Industrial policy and programme launched by the government was not compatible with Lohia's line of thinking and he was the most vehement critic of the policies of the government. He contended that as a result of faulty policy of the government, the nation could not develop.

Lohia wanted structural change in industrial system to assure better deal to the people and also for elimination of exploitation of all types whether of individuals or of particular sector. He quoted the case of price policy followed by the government via its public sector as an instrument of exploitation. Major part of sale price or any commodity consists of extravagant expenses incurred by the producers which do not constitute the cost of production in any relevant sense. For example, *streptomycin* is produced in public sector. It costs nearly 2 *annas* per ample but it is sold for 12-14 *annas*. This type of price loot is withnessed in private as well as public sector. Some people want a curb on private company, others on the government. As Lohia put it, "I like to stop the loot of all types irrespective of the sectors involved."

Lohia's support for nationalisation of certain industries and services is well known from the very beginning. While supporting the Bank Nationalisation Bill in Parliament, he made his stand crystal clear. He considered nationalisation as a means to achieve desired objectives. But some ultra-left and pseudo revolutionary people thought that if certain industries and services were nationalised, probably socialism would be achieved. But nationalisation is not socialism.

While supporting the bill for bank nationalisation Lohia repudiated the notion of the people who thought that the capitalist system would be demolished if policy of nationalisation was adopted. In certain countries capitalism has thrived despite the policy of nationalisation. However, policy of nationalisation and particularly of banks would have the effect of checking, at least to some extent, clandestine business by the industrialists and capitalists of this country. Private banks, run by the leading industrial and monopoly houses, have helped them in concealing the unearned income and black money resulting in parallel economy. But nationalisation of banks should not be confused with socialism. It would have no tangible impact in absence of wider perspective and well-defined objectives. It depends on how and for what purposes, the nationalised banks are utilised. The role and magnitude of black money has been elaborately discussed in Wanchoo Committee Report which also substantiated Lohia's contention.

On the issue of nationalisation, Lohia's views deserve to be supported by the various socialist thinkers. Social democracy supports the demand for public ownership or public control of natural resources and enterprises to the extent it is necessary to safeguard important public interest. Social democracy also seeks to stimulate private enterprises in the fields where it shows that it can combine efficiency and progressive thinking with responsibility towards the consumers, the employees and the community as a whole. Public control must be exercised over the privately owned enterprises if this should prove to be necessary in the interest of the community. Against such a background, an objective review of nationalisation, state ownership and socialist planning in our country is essential. The major objective of the planning is the employment of scarce resources to yield maximum return. The yield of the public sector is, therefore, a matter of concern since the resources employed there would have yielded better results elsewhere had the money remained with the people.

T.T. Krishnamachari, the Union Minister for Economic Affairs and Defence Production had said in February 1963 that it was better to have fewer projects which could be completed quickly than more projects which would give more political satisfaction to politicians. He deplored the predominance of political considerations which is bound to result in centralised planning.

As stated by crossland, comparative performance must be the sole test of efficiency of enterprises. If public companies can not compete on equal terms, they do not deserve to be set-up. In the name of common good, the state sector can not claim a right to go wrong, to work inefficiently or to fritter away national resources. The public and private sectors must, in the last analysis, be judged by the contribution they make in their respective spheres to the realization of the objectives of planning viz. rapid industrialisation of the country, expanding employment opportunities, raising the standard of living and bringing about a reduction in the inequalities of income and wealth.

This proves that nationalisation of industries and services should be based one economic rationality, efficiency and public interest rather than on political consideration. Lohia tried to bring about a distinction between the private and public sectors in respect of their basic foundation and motivating force. Private sector is profit-oriented and it operates on the principle of profit maximisation all over the world but it is more efficient and well managed. Public sector is more responsive to the national interest but more mismanaged. Public sector is more responsive to the national interest but more mismanaged. This is global phenomenon. In India, private and public sectors have learnt many things from each other. consequently private sector has been mismanaged and public sector irresponsive to the national requirements. Both have imbibed the demerits of each other.

Even when Lohia was supporting the bill for nationalisation, he was opposed to the management of nationalised banks directly by the government. He favoured the idea of creating some agency or corporation or some other device by which these nationalised industries were to be managed and operated. Present policy of nationalisation will not have congenial effect even in the long-run. Indian capitalists are thoroughly incompetent and incapable of expanding industries and prosperity. Industries can progress only when scope and area of public sector is expanded to the greatest possible extent.

Lohia laid down the criteria to judge the performance of the public sector. The performance of public sector and private sector should not be judged on the same criteria. Separate criteria for testing the performance of the public sector should be evolved.

(a) The first criterion is that the public enterprises should be more subservient to and conducive in the process of industrialisation than the private enterprises. The rate of growth in India is very low. Capital formation is inadequate. There is a scope for earning profit in the public sector in comparison with the private enterprises run by the public sector in comparison with the private enterprises run by the capitalists. Therefore, the surplus from the public enterprises should be harnessed for opening new industries. Thus the first and foremost test of the public enterprise is its contribution in the process of industrialisation of the economy. It should create adequate tempo and congenial atmosphere for industrial expansion in the country.

(b) The second test is to what extent the public enterprises help in achieving socialism in the country. Distribution should be more egalitarian and equalitarian. The type of gap between the labour and management or the producer and the consumer should not be in public sector which is invariably found in case of private enterprises under the capitalist. The system of distribution should encourage and facilitate the process of equality and justice.

(c) The relationship between the labour and the management should be based on democratic principle. This relationship should also prevail in the management of private enterprises. The democratic relationship between the management and labour should help the process of democratisation in general.

(d) The fourth test of the public enterprise is the furtherance of the cause of public interest. Prices of the commodity, cost of production and its availability in adequate quantity are of prime importance for the people. Things should be produced at the minimum possible cost. It should be available to the people at reasonable and just prices and also in required quantity. It should serve the basic needs of the people.

(e) The fifth test is more efficient management of enterprises. Able persons should be in-charge of public sector having sufficient consideration for the observance of the laws. He should be primarily interested in the expansion of the trade rather than pursuing his own selfish ends day out and day in.

Lohia cited the case of Rourkela which has been encouraging all sorts of inequality and disparity between different grades of employees. The operation of public enterprises in India did not create an impression that it is better than private enterprise in any respect. The operation of L.I.C. is also revealing. The difference in house rent between an officer and ordinary employee is startling and surprising. Officers get nearly Rs. 1000 per month in form of house rent of allowance and other facilities while an ordinary employee gets only Rs. 15 per month. Field workers do not get anything in term of house allowance. Whole management and organisation of public sector is based on gross disparity and inequality while the same is being persistently criticised in case of private sector industrial management.

This inequalitarian and top heavy industrial structure is responsible for lopsided industrial development and also for deprivation of the bulk of the population from the benefit of the development. Price policy followed by the public sector in India is advantageous to the private sector and detrimental to the interest of the masses. Steel which is sold in India should be cheaper. India is rich in iron ores and coal. Japan imports iron ores from India and prepares steel and that is sold in India at a cheaper rate. This situation is better suited to the interest of private sector in India. They like higher prices in the public sector to reap unearned income without being blamed for high prices.

Lohia raised the problem of corruption and wanted its eradication. As a long-term policy measure, he wanted to root out the causes of corruption, not the corrupt men. According to the old proverb, if you want to kill the devil, better to kill the mother of the devil. If circumstances leading to corruption are removed, the opportunity for corruption will be removed altoghether.

As Lohia put it, "Industrialisation is impossible so long as there is no ceiling either on consumption or on income or on expenditure. If question is asked from me regarding the nationalisation, I would have preferred nationalisation as soon as possible provided government machinery is competent and conscious of the duties entrusted to it. But at present I am of the opinion that there should be ceiling on personal consumption. Big industries should be nationalised positively and restrictions and controls be lifted from small industries. So long control is there, government officers and officials would continue to interfere in the normal working of the industries and they hamper the production rather encouraging it. They share the profit of the small industries.

It is obvious that Lohia wanted democratic decentralisation and this principle was enunciated and elaborated by him in "The Four Pillar State." He was firm in his conviction that unless all the powers and resources are decentralised, there can not be uplift of the rural masses, rather their poverty, misery and penury are bound to increase and accentuate. His assessment is amply corroborated by that statistics available in these respects:

> "If you want to be a really revolutionary, you have to be a Russian in the home and an American abroad. We should change the structure of agriculture and industry. There should be ceiling on personal consumption and curb on luxuries of the privileged class and people. We should accumulate capital for investing in farms and factories. Process of industrialisation should be accelerated."

Though the industrialisation-oriented development strategy has been adopted in the plans and sizeable portion of resources has been spent for this purpose, the performance of the industrial sector has not been upto expectations and in some cases quite disappointing. Process of industrialisation has failed to bring about any perceptible change in the structure of the economy. The share on industrial labour in the total labour force ranged from less than 3 per cent in Thailand to 16 or 17 per cent in China (Taiwan) and Philippines. The industry formed the smallest sector (in term of both measures) in the developing ECAFE countries.

If labour intensive technology prevails in this sector, the tendencies towards a widening gap between the share of industry in GDP and in total labour force may be checked. The share of industrial labour force has remained the smallest of the three sectors. If the developing ECAFE countries wish to increase the level of industrial productivity, this may be done by application of capital-intensive where necessary and more often labour-saving technology. But the share of industrial labour force will decrease further. In India peculiar situation prevails. Higher productivity is desirable but job opportunities to the people are not to be ignored. Some sort of reconciliation between these conflicting may be the only rational basis.

A combination of modern capital-intensive and labour-saving technology in substantive processes and labour-intensive and capital-saving technology in auxiliary processes may also be considered in the preparation of industrial projects in the country. Other branches of manufacturing as well as construction could be developed on the basis of labour-intensive and capital-saving technology. Share of industry may rise, therefore, owing not only to industrial expansion itself but also to the considerable decline in the share of agriculture.

India is characterised by ASI pattern of industrial structure in terms of both G.D.P. and labour force. Myrdal observes that modern industry, even if it grows at an extremely rapid rate, can not absorb more than a small fraction of the natural increment in the labour force for decades ahead.

Indian plans had multiple objectives and emphasised growth as well as social justice. But since 1954-55 the primary attention came to be devoted to growth-centred industrialisation with particular emphasis on what are known as capital goods industries. This growth process has gained momentum since the second plan and the industrial output has increased at a fairly rapid rate.

A clamour for industrialisation is noticeable in all countries of the region. Sometimes intellectual elites mean by the term underdevelopment, the low level of industrial development. The enthusiasm of the elite for industrialisation is a manifestation of their general acceptance of the goal of modernisation and the complex ideas associated with it. For instance, India's Second Five Year Plan stated bluntly that rapid industrialisation and diversification of economy is the core of development.

Given the rapid and accelerating increase in the labour force, there is no prospect that incomes and levels of living can be substantially improved or even that deterioration in standard, thus far achieved can be prevented in the long-run, unless a much larger proportion of force can be effectively utilised outside agriculture and specially in modern industry.

A rival ideology drawing its inspiration largely from traditional practices and attitudes is also strong. Now it will be desirable to assess the economic implications of this alternative doctrine and to analyse its significance for development. However, remote from the reality of the modern world, some aspects of traditional ideology may appear to contain elements of rationality.

Crafts and small-scale enterprises have deep and well-established roots in South Asia's indigenous economic environment. From a modernist's point of view, the major weakness of colonial economic policy was its failure to promote an industrial revolution for lack of which the indigenous economic pattern remained static, backward and largely untouched by stimuli for advancement. Traditionalist level quite the opposite charge against the colonial rule. In their view, colonial economic policy by promoting the sale of cheap machine manufactures upset the indigenous pattern altogether too much.

The strength of the traditionalist ideology is partly explained by the influence of Gandhi and the enthusiasm he enlisted for the revival of the villages during the struggle for liberation. Part of the explanation is also due to the fact that India's craft-men suffered harsher fate during the colonial era and the losses sustained by the village economy were off-set to a much lesser extent by compensating expansion elsewhere in the economy. Gandhi realised that their decline had helped to impoverish the village. In a revealing passage, he said, "our villages are on the verge of destruction owing to the disappearance of village industries. They can be revivified only by a revival of the village industries.

Now what are the essential elements of this traditionalist ideology? In the first place, it asserted the paramount importance of defending and protecting the village craft against further encroachment from modern industry, whether foreign or domestic, so that they might grown and develop. This in turn implied that individual villages should strive to attain greater, though, not necessarily complete self-sufficiency, as should the economy as a whole.

Nehru and other intellectuals were critical of Gandhian ideas but when they have to ask the masses to postpone improving their consumption levels, they can to some extent count on the Gandhian ideals of frugality inducing a co-operative attitude. The modern Marxist idea that wage employment implies exploitation, a nation that had considerable factual basis in Gandhi's line and is not unrealistic even now.

Much of his opposition to mechanisation generally must be attributed to his concern about the prospects for a fuller utilisation of this village labour force. He was less opposed when it could be demonstrated that mechanised techniques would not reduce job opportunities. Mechanisation is good when hands are too few for the work intended to be accomplished. It is an evil where there are more hands than required for the work as is the case in India.

Karve Committee report has also vindicated the Gandhian idea of self-employment. The principle of self-employment is at least as important to a successful democracy as that of self-government.

We assume as basic the social philosophy appropriate to Indian federal democracy progressing towards a socialistic pattern of society. In terms of economic organisation and activity we interpret this as demanding the following salient characteristics : a society composed chiefly of small decentralised units of economic activity in which the increase in scale required in any activity is brought about chiefly through mutual co-operation, horizontal and vertical, and in which centralisation and very large scale operations are resorted to only to the extent necessary to derive appropriate advantage from modern technology.

There is, realistically speaking, little hope of any large-scale industrialisation in the rural areas. The case for promoting small scale industrial enterprises in urban areas is strong. Because of their size and the stronger spread-effects, we assume, they originate, small enterprises in sufficient number can prevent the industrial growth in South Asia from being confined to a few enclaves of modern large scale enterprises as it was in the colonial time. Agriculture and household craft should also be induced to adopt modern techniques but these should be deliberately chosen to take account of the present vast under utilisation of labour and the rapid growth of the labour force. Fresh research may be needed to ascertain the most rational technology that is labour-intensive enough to employ more fully the existing and rapidly growing supply of labour.

There was an essential element of rationality in Gandhi's social and economic gospel and the programmes for promoting cottage industry as they have evolved in the post-war era, have come more and more to represent purposeful and realistic planning for development.

Gandhi's ideas of decentralisation are usually brushed aside as being irrelevant to the modern technological society. Technology is not a force of nature that man cannot control. Man can surely bend technology to his purpose. This is what Gandhi had meant when he said that he was not against the machine, but he did not want it to become the master of man. Surely the advancement of the social and physical sciences, has at least made it possible now for the society to determine its destiny.

As Gandhi's village was to be a self-governing autonomous community, he considered it necessary that it should be self-sufficient in the matter of its vital necessities. Secondly, Gandhi's village was not an exclusively agricultural community, there had to be a balance between agriculture and village industry. Had he been alive now, he might have called it an agro-industrial-community. In an unrecorded conversation with one of his co-workers, he spoke of 'urbanising' the villages and 'ruralising' the towns and cities.

The most important characteristics of non-violent method is that its means must be in harmony with its ends. If the end is a non-violent society, the means also must be non-violent, if human freedom is the end, coercive means are ruled out, if man is an end in himself, he can not be used as means, if truth is to be the basis of the new life, untruthful means are inadmissible, if the need is dispersal of power, the means can not be centralised power etc.

Thus Lohia was an ardent supporter of small-scale industries which are spread over the villages of the country and are serving the bulk of the population. Agro-industrial bases have to be broadened and spread extensively as well as intensively to provide adequate opportunity for job and income generation for the masses. This can not be done by heavy industries located in some of the centres of growth. This is also compatible with his concept of democratic decentralisation. Dispersal of small-scale industries making use of small-tool technology will be the pre-condition of economic democracy in India.

REFERENCES

Ardant Gabriel (1963), A Plan for Full Employment in the Developing Countries, *International Labour Review.*

D.R. Gadgil (1964), Appropriate Technologies for Indian Industries, SIET Institute, Hyderabad.

E.F. Schumacher (1977), Small is Beautiful, Radha Krishna, Delhi, p. 163.

E.F. Schumacher : *op. cit.*, pp. 143-44.

Economic Bulletin for Asia and the Far East, Vol XXI, No. 1/2, June-September 1970, pp. 4-24.

Economic Bulletin for Asia and the Far East, Vol. XXIII, No. 1, June 1972, p. 1.

Gandhi, M.K. (1934), Rebuilding Our Villages, *op. cit.*, p. 32, Quoted from *Harijan*, November 16.

Gandhi, M.K. (1939), Rebuilding Our Villages, Navjivan Publishing House, Hyderabad, 1952, p. 4. Quoted from Harijan, March 25.

Government of India (1955), Report of the Village and Small-scale Industries Committee, New Delhi, p. 22.

Government of India (1956), *op. cit.*, Second Five Year Plan, p. 25.

Government of India, *op. cit.*, Second Five Year Plan, 1956, pp. 21-22.

Ibid, p. 19.

Ibid, p. 233.

Ibid, p. 43

Ibid, Papers relating to the Formulation of the Second Five Year Plan, New Delhi, 1955, p. 13.

Ibid., Vol. II, pp. 11-12.

Ibid, Vol. III, p. 172.

Ibid. p. 44.

Ibid., p. 12.

Ibid., P. 1240.

Ibid., pp. 235-36.

Ibid., Vol. IV, p. 129.

Lok Sabha Mein Lohia, op. cit., Vol. 1 p. 25.

Lok Sabha Mein Lohia, op. cit., Vol. I p. 43.

Lok Sabha Mein Lohia, Vol. II, p. 13.

Myrdal, Gunnar : Asian Drama, *op. cit.*, Vol. II, p. 1210.

Myrdal, Gunnar : *Asian Drama, op. cit.*, Vol. II, p. 1239.

Myrdal, Gunnar : *Asian Drama, op. cit.*, Vol. II, pp. 1202-03.

Myrdal, Gunnar : *Asian Drama, op. cit.*, Vol. II p. 1208.

Narayan, Jaiprakash : Gandhi and the Policy of Decentralisation in "Gandhi, India and the World" Edited by Roy, Sib Narayan, Nachiketa Publications Ltd., 22, Naushir Bharucha Road, Bombay 7, p. 231.

P.N. Dhar and H.F. Lydall : The Role of Small Enterprises in Indian Economic Development, Asia Publishing House, Bombay, p. 11.

S.C. Chakravarti : Economic Development of Japan, pp. 39-40

Shraff, A.D. : "Democratic, Socialism in India," Edited by Pai, T.A., *op, cit.*

Shraff, A.D. (1967), Democratic Socialism in "Socialism in India," Edited by Pai, T.A. : Popular Prakashan, Bombay.

Shriman Narayan (1960), Principal of Gandhian Planning, Kitab Mahal, Allahabad, p. 44

Shriman Narayan : *op. cit.*, p. 47.

Shriman Narayan : *op. cit.*

Shriman Narayan, : *op. cit.*, p. 46.

6

Socialist Ideologies and Lohia's Approach of Thinking

ASHWINI KANT JHA AND BHAVNA JHA

Scientific socialist thought in India is a product of modern era. Egalitarianism, no doubt, is an ancient concept evolved in ancient religious and political literatures of India. Philosophers, poet, and religious men of hoary days stood for love, compassion, friendship, justice and brotherhood among all human beings. This has continued, with breaks here and there, till the Bhakti movement led by Sur and Tulsi, Nanak, Kabir and Chaitaṇya who raised their voice through their compositions and social behaviour in favour of equality among all mankind. But they did not know how to introduce socialism in society as a way of living. No practical formula was available with them. It indeed left for Europe to give the lead (Karl Marx, 1818-83).

Marx was a brilliant star in the European sky. His radical views attracted Indians also, though late, but assuredly. Towards the end of 19th century the most revealing classics on Indian poverty appeared which revealed the economic plight of the country and laid the basis of a new national upsurge. Dadabhai Naoroji attributed the poverty of India to drain of her wealth by Britain. His famous 'theory of drain' was the first attempt to analyse the nature of British imperialism in India. He was followed by B.G Tilak who developed this theory of drain further. His view was earlier shared by Ramesh Chandra Dutta also.

SOCIALISTS: A DISORGANISED FORCE

The socialist movement in India has a chequered but scintillating history. In the beginning the movement was deeply under the influence of orthodox Marxism, but gradually the socialist realised that it was Gandhi and the Indian National Congress that represented the fundamental urge of the nation for freedom. Those who talked of a socialist order in India without supporting the freedom struggle were, in the eyes of the socialists, hypocrites or agents of some outside organisation. On this point the socialists differed from the communists. The Communist Party of India had adopted a policy, which was not in consonance with the national spirit of India. Moreover, they failed to apply Marxism to the Indian situation, instead they wanted to induct Bolshevik thoughts in Indian affairs and this proved most tragic for them.

As years passed, the socialists gradually realised the implication of Gandhian thought but they never became perfect Gandhians as they could not be through Marxists. They realised that for the flowering of democracy in India it was the Gandhian way of life that would be more conducive to the socialist movement in India. This realisation showed the way to democratic socialism and they have stuck to the path ever since.

Freedom of the country was their immediate goal and the socialist society was their ultimate destination. Thus, nationalism and socialism were inseparable for them. The socialists, therefore, felt that the national movement would fail to evoke and enlist the interest and allegiance of the toiling millions unless it accepted the new orientation. In order to step up the pace of freedom struggle and also to strengthen it they felt it necessary to link the struggle for freedom with the struggle of peasants and workers in order to improve their lot. To this end they chanalised their energy in three main directions: (i) they penetrated into workers' organisations and gave a fillip to their movement, (ii) they steered the peasants' movement, and (iii) tried to launch a youth movement in the country. Their purpose was to eradicate all evils inherited by the Indian society either due to caste system, feudal system or religious bigotry.

The working class slowly gaining significance in the rapidly changing Indian economy and the socialists hostly pursued the communists in wooing them to their own side, since industrial workers henceforth offered a new dimension to Indian politics. The socialists kept up a secular character, and a national outlook so that they could attract more and more of the labour force. Likewise, they found that the peasantry was the mainstay of Indian's agricultural economy and they, in their turn, were the least organized politically, and were totally ignorant of the big strides the nation was talking towards attaining freedom from British rule. Both were virgin field for the socialists where they expected to raise great crops of freedom fighters and organisers of a socialist society. But as events unveiled themselves, there were too many slips between the cup and the lip. Promises were not backed by processes of fulfilment. Their diversion towards parliamentarism, their confusion regarding the ideals to be followed, their neglect of the grassroots and constructive work stood in their way of successfully organising the labour, the peasant and the youth of the country in order to achieve their dream of a free and socialist India.

The socialists of India enriched traditional social thoughts, but their endless debates over principles and programmes drained their energy disabling them to act as swiftly as the communists did or as surely as the Congress could. The question of cooperation with the government in power, or a coalition with such a government was constantly agrued upon from ethical and political angles, but ultimately this became an exercise in futility. The advent of socialist thought in India and the formation of the Congress Socialist Party raised high hopes among the intellectual politicians and the awakened people who were keenly watching the consolidation of peoples' power in Russia. There was, therefore, a hastening towards formation of a solid and strong socialist party with a broad-based constitution, after attainment of independence. Their urge to take part in election was born out of their admiration for the high ethics they created and wanted to live through them. But their poor performance at the elections brought them the awareness that to form a government high ethics was not the surest means: some sort of politicking was also required which they had certainly missed.

Failures are incentives to deeper thinking for some, while for others they are the cause of dissatisfaction and fragmentation. Between 1947 and 1955, the Congress Socialist Party split into SP and PSP. Then an occasion arose when they attempted complete merging, thus creating a platform for a synthetic socialist party. The roles of Ram Manohar Lohia and Ashok Mehta emerged as a cementing force, though unavoidably once again only temporarily.

The basic ideology of the Party is "its emphasis on freedom and equality, its ingrained opposition to authoritarianism and bureaucratism, and its consequential insistence on decentralisation of administration and economy, its policy of democratic transformation of society into a Socialist Society based upon informed participation of the people in the processes of development, its constant endeavour to foster national integration and combat fissiparous and socially disruptive forces and above all its living faith in the constructive capacities of the people which egalitarianism would evoke in abundant measure."

ELECTION MANIFESTO OF 1962

In the words of Mr. Rohit Dave the S.P. Election Manifesto of 1962 highlights three issues that need to be tackled without any delay. They are: "concentration of wealth and economic power in a few hands, the problem of unemployment and the need for keeping inflationary forces in check." However, we shall discuss in detail the economic policies of the S.P. as expressed in its Election Manifesto of 1962.

Concept of Socialism

In spite of the professions of the Congress Party that it has accepted the goal of establishing a socialist pattern of society, the working of the Congress Government, even after the adoption of this objective, shows that its conception of socialism is confined to the adoption of modern techniques of production with the smatterings of welfare programmes, whenever this could be conveniently accepted without disturbance to the present social order and to the enlargement of the public sector. The Socialist Party places its unshakable faith in the concept of socialism that challenges the present social order and accepts in its place an order based on equality of opportunity, on reduction in the disparities of incomes, on genuine participation of people in the control of social levers and on social mobility that helps every citizen in the country in the development and full utilising of all that is the most creative and enterprising within him.

Concentration of Wealth and Economic Power

The industrial development, as pursued in the decade of planning, has generally aggravated concentration of wealth and power. The top business firms have been favoured with licensees, financial aid, bank credit and assured markets. The remarkable expansion of the private sector has meant mainly strengthening the oligopolies in the country. The disparities in growth between the rich and the poor remain the outstanding characteristics of planning in agriculture as well as in industries.

These concentrations of economic power must be broken through adequate fiscal and credit policies like capital levy and through legislative and administrative measures. The credit policy would be reorientated and the licensing policy revised in favour of new enterpreneurs. Every big enterprise would have to farm out considerable work to small producers brought together in industrial estates. Industrial workers and employees would be encouraged to become shareholders. The Managing Agency system which is the chief source of interlocking directorates and concentration of economic power would be abolished. Regarding the speculative activities in urban sites it is proposed that the appreciation in values of the urban sites must be siphoned off to municipalities to enable them to provide housing and community services.

The small industries will be given special attention by providing them with economic overheads—cheap credit, technical know-how and marked intelligence. The small producers; whether by hand or machine, would be assured of market. So long as production is of the standard laid down and conforms to other conditions such as those of fair labour practices, the state would be prepared to buy any quality at a price fixed in advance. This policy will equally apply to agricultural commodities.

Another step suggested is the development of co-operative sector. If social justice is to be concretised, and if the economically weaker sections are to be helped to develop strength so as to compete on reasonable footing with the more powerful sectors, the co-operative sector will have to be given the same status and the same consideration as the public sector and the corporate sector.

Iniquitous Taxes and Accent on Inequality

The economic polices of the Government have sharpened inequalities and through price rise and iniquitous taxes have depressed the already meagre standard of the working people. Shortage of employment, of housing, of necessities of life, of educational facilities and medical aid coarsen men's lives and embitter mutual relations. The Five-Year Plans, despite heavy burdens on the people and erosion of levels of living of the working people have meagre achievements to show. The Government pursues increase in aggregate wealth, yet improvement in living standards remains a tragic casualty. Aggregate wealth can enhance the power of a country, not the welfare of the people. "The sacrifice of welfare, however, has proved wanton because the nation's strength has not grown much. In the decade of planning, national income has grown just by 3.5 per cent per year. As the Plans become bigger and 'bolder', the gains become smaller: per capita income grew by 2 per cent in the First Plan, by 1.5 per cent in the second! The bigness and boldness of the Plans perhaps lie in the burdens heaped on the people, in the widening of economic disparities."

In the myriad villages of India the changes have been generally disadvantageous to the poorer section of the people. Land reforms riddled with loop-holes have brought little justice to the villages. Ambiguous in enactment, they have been extensively evasive in implementation. The benefits of the development programme have gone to the richer elements in the villages. The programmes of aid, with their predilection for status and property stake, have weighted in favour of the rich; administration's delays and complexities likewise favour the privileged.

Equality, Security and Participation

The S.P believes that in India the urge for freedom expresses itself in the fight for equality. This fight is directed against class distinction of all kinds, whether they relate to economic position, social status or cultural advantages. They Partly abhors differences in income caused by social or economic power, and accepts only those differentials, which are due to differences in skill, responsibility, initiative and output. Such differential could not justify the ratio between the minimum and maximum income which is wider that 1: 10

The Party will, therefore, endeavour to bring income disparities within this limit. Reducing disparities in urban incomes, through price policies and administrative credit and fiscal measures is the crying need of the hour. It is equally important to safeguard the consumption level of the poor by abolishing all excise duties and sales-tax from articles of food and coarse cloth.

In spite of all the talk of equality, women in India continue to suffer under a variety of taboos and social inequalities. The evil of dowry still persists. Therfore, measures are needed to remove the present disabilities. The Party will provide free education at all stages for women. In the Gram Panchayats and Municipalities substantial number of jobs would be reserved for women. There are also several other fields like education where preference in employment can profitably be given to them.

Freedom is rooted in security. Freedom gains in meaning and asserts itself only when economic and social security are assured. The S.P. programme strives to provide security to India's anxious millions socialist.

Democratic socialism's test lies in the security it offers to the citizens. While comprehensive social security may not be possible here and now, the assurance of work to all and the universal right to receive education would mean substantial advance. To them will be added modest old-age pension. To augment savings and relieve farmer's anxiety, crop and cattle insurance will be progressively extended. Through wise fiscal and monetary policies, price fluctuations would be vigorously restrained and tax burdens sought to be related to actual increase in incomes realised.

Freedom grows through participation; that is the surest way to arrest abuse of power, counter encroachment against individual rights, whether they be committed by public bodies, private employers, organisations or individuals. Such a sense of belonging has to be imparted to every citizen through not only self-governing institutions but also providing him a voice in the decisions in economic life which determine the direction of production and the pattern of distribution of the national product. The S.P. aims to humanise the state and the economy, not statise man.

Planning by People

The Socialist Party believes that economic planning needs as much attention and emphasis at the base as it is wont to receive at the apex. Democratically organised district administration has to be the principal unit of economic planning. Under its direction integrated land reforms would be implemented as a time bound programme. It would be closely connected with development plans so that land reforms and reorganisation proceed hand in hand. Credit and technical assistance would move closely together. Credit will be governed by needs as well as by the expanding capacity to use, not by status and property as is the case today. The landless poors are to be assured prompt and effective implementation of the Minimum Wages Act and efforts will be made to improve their economic condition through employment in projects of economic development. Tillers of the soil will be recognised as owners of the land and those unjustly evicted will be restored of their lands.

Employment for All

The district development programme would embrace village plans whose main purpose would be the full use of labour, land and water resources. The S.P.'s firm conviction is that work is the fundamental right of man, it is the supreme badge of citizenship. The district plans will offer opportunities of gainful employment to every person. Through co-ordinated work projects, untapped resources and idle hands will be brought together in fruitful co-operation. The Government's principal responsibility is to foster and facilitate these production programmes. However, the promise of work for all can be implemented only in a phased manner. A beginning will be made in selected areas where weaker section of society like scheduled castes predominates.

By providing the needed inducements and incentives the holders of dwarf holding will precede polling of land. On reclaimed lands and such surplus land as becomes available the landless will find work and home and land

Through rural development projects, rural housing will be improved. Villages will not only be rebuilt, with varied community facilities, but urgent attention will be paid to housing the landless and the socially depressed. These development activities will fully exploit local resources, reconstruct economic and social life on the basis of full employment. It will be the responsibility of planning not just to assure full employment but also help, through diffusion of skills and provision of improved tools and credit, to raise the technical level of production. The administrative and economic organ of the development and change will be the Panchayat and co-operative working as a unit entity.

Industrial Policy

Industrial policy as pursued in the decade of planning has generally aggravated concentration of wealth and power. The sheltered markets and easy profits have allowed considerable under utilisation of plants. The new industries have often grown at the expense of traditional producers. Modernist development and debris of artisan production exist side by side. The public enterprises show poor efficiency, their rate of profit remains fractional, their management is top-heavy and the administrative structure throttles initiative and team-work.

The S.P.'s endeavour would be to correct and drastically alter the contours of industrial development. It would revise the licensing policy, reorient the credit policies in favour of new entrepreneurs. In capital-hungry India a careful watch must be kept on unused plant capacity and policies elaborated including appropriate labour policies to maximise plant use. Industrial workers and employers would be encouraged and helped to become share-holders. With the strengthening of trade union co-determination by capital and labour would characterise management. By organising machine and tool banks and co-ordinating them with credit institutions traditional artisans, with restraining when necessary, would be enabled to participate in the march of progress. Constant efforts would be made to develop small yet economic units of production as even to-day it is possible to set-up industries as complex as fertilisers or cement. Small units would mean not only better distribution of industries but firm check on accumulation of wealth and power.

The S.P. not merely favours dispersal of industries but believes it to be imperative to involve the rural people in the process of industrialisation. The processing industries and many of the consumer goods industries as also light engineering industries that will serve the need of rural people and agricultural development, including irrigation, would be offered to district councils and they would be helped technically and financially, to own and operate them. The District Councils may in their turn entrust the task to lower units like the Block Panchayats or Group of Panchayats. The intertwining of agricultural and industrial development is essential for a democratic social growth.

Price Policy

On the price policy emphasis is laid on increasing supply through the utilisation of unused capacity, and the development of the co-operatives and small-scale sector. Certain strategic sectors would be earmarked exclusively for State Trading Corporations. A sector will be defined where the state could intervene to correct inbalances in the markets of articles of common consumption as well as of articles of industrial raw materials as and when a critical situation develops in any one of these markets. Effective regulation of credit structure, licensing and fiscal policies will be used to regulate the rest of the trade sectors.

Trade Unions

The industrial expansion requires a change in the status and outlook of the workers. The wage and salary earners and Government employees have the right to free association in trade unions. National industrial unions whose membership would be obligatory but whose internal democracy would be legally safeguarded would enable the workers to collectively bargain, organise social security, receive technical and general education and participate in the planning of production. Happy industrial and employer-employee relation can be established by devising quick, inexpensive, impartial and permanent negotiation and arbitration machinery by establishing inviolable codes of conduct, designed to protect the weak against the strong, and by building up social and moral pressures against the misuse of strength.

Investment in Man

Important as investment through labour is to economic development, even more valuable is investment in human being to social change. The party would make secondary education progressively free and compulsory. The talented pupils through sustained scholarships would be helped to receive the education for which they are qualified. Education needs to be reformed to two directions. Technical bias has to be increasingly imparted and teaching reoriented to subserve national outlook and integration.

Scheduled castes and scheduled tribes which have not been much benefited by the Five Year Plans will be given due attention. These are some of the programmes which the S.P. had in mind for the economic progress of the country.

Among the socialist thinkers Lohia was brilliant but others were not less than any body. Brilliance kept them separated from each other. Though, Lohia had given his own thinking on every matters.

"Ever since I started thinking, I have been a philosophical liberal", said Lohia. His philosophical bent of mind was nurtured in the German environment where he went for higher studies. In Germany, he came in contact with followers of Hegelian and Marxian schools of thought. His knowledge of German language helped him to go deep into the Hegelian and Marxian ideas.

Lohia was a profound nationalist. Naturally, like other socialist leaders of his time he felt that the burning question was to free his country from the yoke of foreign domination. He became a prominent leader of the Congress Socialist Party and propagated his socialist ideas through the party platform and the party organ 'The Congress Socialist'.

In his presidential address at the special convention of Socialist Party in 1952 at Pancmarhi, he pleaded for the need of assimilation of Gandhian ideas in socialist thought. He advocated the significance of a decentralised economy and cottage industries. Like Gandhi, he was against big machines and pleaded for incorporation of small machines because of their requirement of less capital and maximum utilisation of labour power in the country.

Expressing full agreement with the Gandhian method of struggle he said: "Whatever may have been inadequacies of Gandhism as a governmental doctrine of doing good, it was unmatched in all history as a people's doctrine of resisting evil. Civil disobedience both as individual's habit and collective resolve is armed reason, and anything else is either weak reason or unreasonable strength. Such civil disobedience is Gandhi's direct gift to mankind.[4]

As a socialist intelectual, Lohia examined the main postulates of Marxian doctrine but he was not a blind follower. Pointing out the inadequacy of Marx's theory of capitalist development, Lohia said: "Marx's capitalism was that of a self-moving West European circle, no doubt causing great repercussions in the outside world. But the principle and laws of its own movement were exclusively internal.

This was an unreal picture, according to Lohia. He was of the opinion that in free Western countries the law of capitalist development operated differently from that in the subject and colonial countries. He observed: "In its place must arise a picture of two circles representing the free capitalist structures with their dynamics in the contradiction between capitalist profits and mechanised labour, the outer circle representing the colonial economy of the rest of the world with its dynamics between imperial exploitation and colonial labour; the rim of the inner circle possessing an enormously porous capacity to suck into itself the dynamic of the outer. This is the only way in which we can join up the capital-labour dynamics with the empire colony dynamics and arrive at a consistent understanding of the development of capitalism.

To Lohia capitalism as well as communism were inadequate in the context of prevailing problems of the world. Both were closed systems. Capitalism to him was a doctrine of the individual and free enterprise that led to ever-changing application of science to industry and agriculture. And communism was a doctrine of social ownership and of release of means of production from the shackles of private sector. Rejecting both the systems he started: "The accusations against each other of capitalism and communism, of the US and USSR, mount, but they are unable to slay the twin demons of poverty and war and what they say or do only serve to heighten their demoniac quality. They have enveloped the world with fear and hate. Man is no longer at peace with himself. He must move away from existing civilization in both its aspects of capitalism and communism. Their kindred qualities and drives have made them both equally irrelevant to the venture into a new civilization.

Lohia, therfore, felt that the socialist movement in India must develop its own ideology of socialism in the light of its special circumstances. In the presidential address at Pachmarhi special convention he stated: 'As long as the doctrinal foundation of socialism is not secured, the Socialist Party will continue to be torn between the Congress Party, which will often appear as the instrument of democracy and national stability, and the Communist Party, which will as often appear to be a party of change...The Socialist Party must be willing to take risks, to see in itself the expression both of national unity and of change, and to act irrespective of immediate and apparent consequences'.

Lohia was of the opinion that while it was essential to give a firm foundation to the doctrine of socialism, it was equally important to discover appropriate forms of action through which the doctrine could be realised. He lamented at the mentality of the socialists in the country to lay too much emphasis on electioneering activity as well as insurrectionary activity. He stated: "No greater disaster could befall socialism than if the historical peculiarities of its career in Europe were sought to be universalised and reproduced in the other two-third of the world. Socialism in Europe has been gradual, constitutional and distributive. Socialism henceforth, and in the rest of the world, must be drastic, unconstitutional, when necessary, and lay the accent on production."

Lohia held the view that in history there always had been a tussle between class and caste. Heb observed: "All human history hitherto has been an internal oscillation between class and caste and an internal shift of prosperity and power from one region to another. This external shift and internal oscillation are related to one another."

Lohia believed in decentralisation. He conceived the idea of a four-pillar state, which distributes sovereignty at all the four levels of the village, the district, the province and the centre. He pleaded for abolition of the office of district magistrate as first step towards decentralisation.

Police power was to be vested in the district, village or city panchayats and they were also to be in charge of the welfare function.

Lohia was opposed to the gross inequalities prevailing in society. To eradicate this evil, he pleaded for social ownership of property. He allowed private property only to the extent that a family could itself manage without the help of hired labour. He noted: "Inequality is of seven types—inequality between male and female, rich and poor, inequality of caste, inequality of colour, inequality in armaments, inequality due to the crossing of limitation, improper relationship between the individual and society or state or government."

He stood for abolition of all types of inequality. He pleaded for special opportunities for backward classes. Lohia rejected the Marxian view of equality of opportunity because according to him Marx had knowledge of only class not of caste.

It is, therefore, a sad epitaph that the party which started its career with high hopes and peoples' esteem, which pledged itself to democratic socialism and fought in front lines for national freedom, along with the Congress, could hardly redeem the promises made in its manifestos. Great political figures like Nehru, Bose, Acharya Narendra Deva, Kripalani, Jayaprakash, Lohia, Mehta and S.M. Joshi shone brilliantly for a while and then went their own way without securing the fresh air of altruism, equality and social justice. They did not need a vision but concrete directive principles, a watchfulness which every player of a political chess-board is required to maintain. India's greatest intellectuals leaned towards socialism, but none could discover the right means to establish what they considered far sweeter than freedom itself. Destiny may throw up such a genius in the political field, for; nothing short of socialism is the destination of India's political march.

References

Lohia, Ram Monohar, *Marx, Gandhi and Socialism,* Preface, p. 17.

Ibid., p. 16.

Ibid., p. 17.

Ibid., p. 357.

Ibid., p. 209.

Lohia, R.M., *Wheel of History,* p. 40.

Ibid.

Lohia, R.M., *Will to Power and Other Writings,* p. 132.

Lohia, R.M., *Samajvadi Andolan Ka Itihas* (Hindi), p. 111.

Ibid., p. 120.

Rohit Dave, The S.P. Manifesto in 1962, *General Election in India* (1962), (Ed) Poplai, S.L.

Resolution of the National Executive of the S.P., September 1956, in *All India Election Guide* (1956), p. 60.

Socialist Party Election Manifesto, October 1961 in 1962, *General Election In India* (1962), p. 86.

7

Lohia's Vision for India's Economic Development

BIRENDRA KUMAR JHA AND SHAMBHU SAH

Rammanhor Lohia began to be styled as a great freedom fighter, outstanding statesman, true socialist leader and veteran Parliamentarian but a very important aspect of his personality went untouched and it was his role as an economic thinker. As a profounder of an economic ideology he has no less prominent than he was in other various capacities and his economic vision earns a place for him among the body of economists. Lohia who was "Kaleidoscopic in his vision, free and frank in his dealings and crystal clear in his thought" (R.B. Singh, 1986, p. xii), never believed in imported ideas, models of thought and strategies.

The economic ideas of Rammanohar Lohia did not grow in vacuum. Actually, these ideas resulted from the age and environment in which he lived and worked. He being a true patriot was never satisfied with the attainment of more political Independence but he always kept on thinking upon the Indian economic maladies and prescribing recipes to them. His politics was a preface to his economics that he wanted to be for India.

There are the seven Revolutions, as he called them in which humanity was engaged in the middle of the 20th century, were : (i) for enquality between man and woman, (ii) against political, economic and spiritual inequality-based on skin colour, (iii) against inequality of backward and high groups or castes based on long tradition and for giving special opportunities to the backward, (iv) against foreign enslavement and for freedom and world's democratic rule, (v) for economic equality and planned production and against the existence of and attachment for private capital, (vi) against unjust encroachments on private life and for democratic methods, and (vii) against weapons and in favour of satyagraha. He weaved his thoughts and programmes around these above-mentioned struggles or revolutions "that earned him the opprobrium from the upholders of the old order which these struggles sought to overturn" (G. Fernandes, 1986, p. vi). His concepts of small tool technology, world government, four pillar state, land army, principle of preferential treatment, abolition of caste and class, uniform education through the medium of mother tongue are the landmarks in the field of new ideas and innovating thinking justifying the remark that his foresight into events always put him in a situation of being at least twenty years ahead of his time. Once he himself declared, "people will listen to me perhaps, after I am dead. But will certainly listen to me" and time has come when people are listening to him because the borrowed model for economic development of India has proved misfit in Indian context and the prevailing scenario in the country has compelled policy-makers and planners to think over an appropriate model or economic strategy which can succeed in solving our basic economic problems.

Lohia was such a libertarian who remained always ready to fight for justice and prosperity of all mankind, especially for the retarded people and the main targets of his offensive were exploitative political structure, disparate and inequities economic system as well as archaic social practices and structure. His ideas and actions crossed the barriers of geographical boundaries and he dreamt of the world government where all people of the world would enjoy the fruits of the development. In his economic thinking he came out with a new will and approach as might be linked with world justice and welfare.

WORRISOME FEATURES OF INDIAN ECONOMY AND LOHIA

In an article entitled 'Indian Economy in Figures' Lohia like Dadabhai Naoroji held the British government responsible for the poverty of India. In his word, "The greatest single factor that has caused the poverty of India is British's rule over India. The relationship between Britain and India is that of the exploiter and the exploited. Britain draws out of India profits in three major ways: as dividends and her investments, as salaries and pensions and as benefits out of foreign trade between a manufacturing country and raw-producing country. The poverty of India is vast and for its removal not only the imperialist system must be destroyed but the entire population should be engaged in a mighty and cooperative economic endeavor." (Lohia, Jan. 18, 1940). Thus, India suffered tremendously under the colonial rule and its huge resources were drained out under various heads resulting in the pauperization of the masses. He was so much engrossed with the idea of removal of poverty from India in particular and the world in general that he felt desirable for Indian government to persuade the leaders of the U.S.A. and the U.S.S.R. to hold a summit discussion to find out ways and means for this purpose. Depicting the picture of poverty he pointed out that "An abysmal poverty prevails in this two-thirds of the world. It appears as though capitalism had made a compact with imperialism that almost all its progress would be located in the master lands, while nearly all the misery would be inflicted on the colonial countries." (Marx, Gandhi and Socialism, p. 99). He held the twin demons of imperialism and corruption responsible for gripping the economy of India and to him the present planning in India was not less responsible. It is the defective planning which is held responsible for attaining the European standards by five to ten lakhs of the population in each five year plan while the rest keep on wallowing in abject squalor and so he was in favour of socialist concept of planning which will aim not at the spectacular progress of the few but the progress, however slow, of whole population. Such a planning must begin with a process of simultaneous leveling down of the peaks of wealth and prosperity and leveling up of the deep depressions of poverty. When the whole population of the country has been brought within a reasonable range of inequality, the fruits of planning and enterprise will be available not to a few but to all. He was critical of the strategy of economic planning in India and to him it proved to be a wishful thinking due to wrong strategy and advocated for having suitable strategy formulated consistent with the socio-economic conditions of the country and capable of achieving highest possible rate of growth along with other sincere objectives like reduction in inequality, creation of more employment opportunities and removal of poverty.

Of course, the problem of economic inequality in India pained Lohia much more. To him "Indian ranges of inequality are high like her mountains and her canyons, unparalleled in the world" (Lohia, Rs 25000 a Day, p. 113) in the sense the land paid about Re 1 on agricultural labourer whereas Rs. 25000 a day was spent on the Prime Minister. He further added, "Regional inequality in production is the world's most dangerous and obstinate disease. An hour of labour in the United states produces three times as much as in Europe and fifteen to twenty times as much in Asia and Africa" (Lohia, Fragments of a World Mind, p. 2). He opined that "all men must not be equal within a nation but also among the nations" (Marx, Gandhi Socialism, p. 463) and to him both national and international inequalities are related with each other and hence affect each other and so he went to the extent of saying that so far inequality among the nations is not removed, inequality within a nation cannot be completely eliminated. And for expansion of world trade and economy this great rock needs to be removed for which the theory of International trade based on the geographical division of labour must be re-stated because this theory appeared to be faulty in Lohia's vision as it is based on the belief that through International trade all the nations of the world shall be benefited, and there shall be regional division of labour. He in a seminar at Athens in Oct. 1961 stated, "But the fate of that theory shows that no matter what Universal terms it has, there lies behind them some kinds of a national interest and Mr. Keynes, therefore had to formulate a theory that brought in a clause, relating to full employment. Britain could not compete with America and, therefore a theory of full employment had to be put in." (Lohia, 1969, p. 5). He visualized no use of full employment providing to those depressed economies where ten to fifteen hours of strenuous labour produced as much wealth as an hour of human labour of the developed economies in exchange of goods with the latter and so for having a universal valid theory of world trade all these concepts of international division of labour full employment and national production need to be brought together. "There is need not alone to secure full employment but also such employment as produces comparatively equal wealth in all the regions of the world." (Wheel of History, p. 81) and to him the only way to overcome. The ushering of a new civilization and a new technology for which "smelt unit technique can be a better road to engineering to achieve new formation of capital on a world scale." (Fragments of a World Mind, p. 8). In the Indian scenario for reducing the prevailing inequalities he advocated for ending the era of extravagance, wasteful expenditure, production oriented economy and confiscation of property acquired by graft and corruption. He was in favour of imposition of citing on all the incomes so that the maximum might not be more than ten times to minimum, post-monument of the modernization of consumption till such time as the means of production had been thoroughly rennovated and rationalized on the basis of big machines where necessary and small unit technology where possible. In his opinion regarding ceiling on income and expenditure lies in his worlds, "This programme of drastic cut on expenditure and on amenities is probably the most radical economic measure that has ever been conceived any where in the world." (Lohia, 1967, p. 11). He had calculated in his time that could would save between 1000 to 1500 crores of repees if all expenditure above Rs. 1500 per family was banned by law thus he was in favour to strike at the root of all the luxurious and superfluous expenditure. For postponing modernization of consumption he wanted the stoppage of production of such things for a definite period about 20 years.

The strategy of development adopted in India which achieved neither the targeted rate of growth nor promoted the cause of social justice and equality, also pained Lohia. Due to misconceived and misconstrued notion of economic development neither industry nor agriculture could be developed property and we remained far behind other developing countries of Asia and Africa and disparities increased constant. He was critical of the strategy of development based on western model which misfitted in the Indian scenario on accounts of various limitations and his view strategy of economic planning was the main reason for failure of plans leading to misery, unemployment and greater disparities of wealth and income and ultimately to the dislocation of plan itself. In his opinion capitalism, socialism and communism being born in European environment cannot be universally valid doctrine and he found that "they are valid only for certain period of human experience and they are valid in connection with certain accidents of history." (Lohia, 1964). To him both capitalist, i.e. and communist path of development are misfit in Indian case and he was in favour of such path of development which could prove as a brake on conspicuous consumption, luxury-oriented production and exploitative price policy. He detested the centralization, violence and suppression of the mind implicit in the communist system. He was dedicated to the ideals of social and ecomomic equality and a firm opponent of the pretension of the state to control every aspect of national life although he was appreciative of what the communist societies did to ensure the minimum consumption needs and social security guarantees for the common people. He advocated the replacement of capitalism by socialism because "capitalism brought great progress to the European part of the mankind in the past but it is on the point of ceasing to do so today. To the rest of mankind it never brought any progress" (Marx, Gandhi and Socialism, p. 106) as it is mainly based on profit motive.

LOHIA AND INDIA'S ECONOMIC DEVELOPMENT

The development strategies outlined in different five year plans remained failure in fulfilling the objectives incorporated in Indian constitution and could not get rid of the different problems such as poverty, unemployment, stagnation, inequality etc. that have been more or less the legacy of the British Raj tasking its achievement on three tests, i.e. (a) growth achieved in comparison with its past, (b) our progress in comparison with our neighbour and other countries, and (c) the expectations and aspirations of people. Lohia found that the other countries were marching ahead with a terrible speed while India was simply creeping. Lohia came to the conclusion that "even if it is conceded that we have made nominal progress in comparison with the past, the rate of growth in comparison with the neighbour and other countries is very low. If we take our expectation an aspiration into consideration, we have moved in a backward direction during the last 15 years and our hopes and aspirations have met all round frustration." (R.B. Singh, 1986). He would not have been impressed by the official reviews of our economic and social development carried out at varying intervals. Comparison of the achievement with that of China where almost similar situation prevailed, revealed the fact that India had a comfortable lead over China in 1950 but in the 30 years since China had forged ahead in many respects and India's early lead has disappeared for which responsible factor in Lohia's vision was the plan which was formulated and its objectives were laid down without going deeper into the crux of the problem, hence priorities were also not in consonance with the national interest resulting in all the objectives to be of the theoretical importance rather than for practical purpose. Is it not true that agriculture, the most important sector of the Indian economy, could not get proper priority and required allocation? No doubt, the planning process of economic development was found the only alternative for the developing countries like India as free economy system for economic development proved inadequate for such countries due to unfettered competition between developed and developing countries in which the former where in a advantageous position, but even planned process of development depending upon the requirement of particular nation and the stage of development. India was right enough in adopting planning process for economic development but something wrong in giving priorities was committed by our planners in this process resulting in failure in achieving targeted outcomes. Priorities needed to be determined in consonance with the national interest and Ultimate objective and finally available resource should be allocated in accordance with the well-defined priorities in order to ensure the achievement of the objectives of economic planning. Removal of poverty, tackling the problem of unemployment as well as underemployment, reduction in inequality, etc. were listed as the foremost goals along with several other objectives but the performance in this concern in the past unmasked the reality and left the scope for thinkers like Lohia to point out shortcomings in the strategy of development adopted in the country. It is needless to say that in any country investment pattern appears to be the best mirror for reflecting the priorities of plan as well as the strategy, which guide the plan. Agriculture which got relatively fair allocation in the first plan, was relegated to the background in the subsequent industrialization-oriented plans and even small scale industries and agro-industries particularly which needed to be encouraged and promoted in rural regions for lessening the population pressure on agriculture, failed to attract the proper attention of our planners and remained devoid of due share in allocation of fund. And the total result was nothing but damaging. Lohia was critical of the price policy of the government as exploitative and discriminatory resulting in further price hike and strengthening black money in the economy rather than anti-inflationary. He had cited an example of the Price loot, which "is equally applicable in public and private sectors. Some people want to impose curbs on private company while others on the public sectors. I want to stop the loot of all types irrespective of the sectors or parties involved." He visualized the price loot in the way. "For any commodity produced in the factory, the price consists of 40% of the average cost, 30% government tax, 20% profit and 10%

extravagant expenditure incurred by the management for maintaining liaison with the Ministers and bureaucrats." (Quoted by R.B. Singh, 1986). Lohia was also critical of consumption and production policy of the government and held this policy responsible for the economy growing sick day by day despite successive five-year plans. He was of the opinion that production should be based on indigenous resources and small technology evolved as well as invented indigenously to suit the Indian condition. He was against the modernization or Europeanisation of consumption, which has been rapidly followed, in India even actual modernization of the production system. He opposed the idea of mixed economy adopted in India and wanted immediate and complete socialization of all the industries. To him, the co-existence of public and private sectors in our caste-ridden society has brought corruption and is responsible for on unholy alliance between the capitalist and the bureaucracy. To him both public as well as private sectors are inefficient and greedy. In the Lok Sabha, Aug. 23, 1963 he said, "Every where the private sector is more conscious of profit earning but manages better. The public sector has greater consciousness of duty but suffers from a certain amount of mismanagement. This is all over the world. In India both sectors have learnt the vices of each other." (Lohia, 1963). To him, "Indian Planning has greatly suffered because of enormous expenses on modernizing of consumption while all savings should have been used on instrumentals for building the means of production" (Lohia, 1962) and defective which has chosen to adopt the course of increasing inequality constantly, although the reduction in inequalities of income and wealth and a more distribution of economics remained objectives of most of the successive plans. According to him "50 lakhs of people who have imitated his way of life and have done incalculable loss to the nation. 50 Lakhs privileged people have grabbed Rs 50000 million out of Rs. 150000 million of national income and only Rs. 100000 million are left for 43.5 crores of people" (Lohia, 1963) and in his opinion this has hampered the process of capital for motion. He found that the triangle consisting of the politicians, the bureaucrats and the businessmen numbering about 60 lakhs was looting the country and so the end of this corrupt triangle was highly desirable in his vision. Lohia was of the opinion, that if any economy is to be reformed, there should be no corruption. In his vision, Indian economy is not expanding as it is based on the motive of grab—what you can and increase one's own share. In such an economy "everyone is busy in increasing his own share, because he thinks that the total cannot be increased." (Lohia, 1967).

Lohia was a socialist who discarded both capitalism and communism because of the compulsive pressures of social-economic conditions prevailing in the country, which were characteristically different from the problems of the countries of the third world as well as those of the European American nations, but above all he was one of the best pioneers of Gandhian tradition and throughout his life, he was an out and out Gandhian. And so he was a critic of India's strategy of development based on the pattern of the western countries. He being a firm supporter of the symbolic relationship between man, society and nature disliked modern technology, large-scale production and indiscriminate industrialization based on capital intensity and imported technology without considering the absorptive capacity of the economy and adaptability of the people. Of course, during the early days of freedom it was misconceived that when industrialization is achieved, all the problems will be solved with this magic. Like Gandhi, Lohia asserted that man should be the center of all economic activities and potentiality of masses should not be sacrificed on the altar of capitalism based on the concept of maximum efficiency instead of total efficiency. Of course, "It is important that there should be enough work for all because that is the only way to eliminate anti-productive reflexes and create a new state of mind that a country where labour has become precious and must be put to the best possible use" (Gabriel Ardent, 1963). Indeed, for a poor man the chance to work is the greatest of all needs and Lohia found that there was no possibility for all the poor to be employed in the present India's strategy of development. He saw no possibility to industrialize India on the pattern of the western countries because it would require about 2000 billion rupees of capital investment to industrialize India on the modes of America or Russia and even then this development could be achieved only at the cost of untold suffering for the great majority of people while he estimated that India was hardly capable of making more than Rs. 150 per worker capital investment. And so as an alternative to the large-scale industrialization he was an ardent supporter of smell scale industries and proposed a programme of economic decentralization, demoralization and the small unit machine. He said, "the mind must no longer be clogged by antiquated notions of large scale industry or of cottage industry. A rigorous search must be made to see how far power, whether in the form of oil or electricity or coal, can be used for the propelling of machines that donot need heavy capitalization" (Lohia, 1956, p. 391). Indeed, industrialization by means of the small-unit machine will have a number of advantages. Such a machine would be comprehensive manageable and full of economic efficiency and at the same time, suitable due to investment scarcity in the underdeveloped countries like India, providing more jobs and hence solving the problem of unemployment, an embodiment of the general principle of decentralization and avoiding the shiffing of working population to urban areas. In his Presidential address at Panchmarhi, he pleaded the case of small unit machine in these words, "This machine will not only solve the economic problem of the underdeveloped world, and it will also enable a new exploration and achievement of the general aims of society." (Marx, Gandhi and Socialism, p. 326) but it does not mean that he totally rejected the idea of large-scale industries and he was in favour of retaining those where these were must. He held a clear-cut concept in this concern. When he said, "we donot want the large scale machines of America or Russia nor the desiccated tools of ancient India, neither the automatic loom nor the *charkha*, but the small machine unit run by power. We donot want the ghost of Mahatma Gandhi but his Principles." (Will to Power, p. 198)

Lohia agreed with Mahatma Gandhi who said, "From the very beginning it has been my firm conviction that agriculture provides the only unfailing and perennial support to the people of this country." (Gandhi: Village Swaraj, p. 92) and was shocked to find the Indian peasantry in a deplorable condition where poverty had stayed, improvements had stopped, farmers were ejected and where artificiality had been created due to delay in abolishing wicked laws about ownership. He pointed out the fact that in India where an agricultural worked around 1.5 acres of land, any scheme to rationalize it on the basis of the communist or the capitalist variety would be an utter failure and he advocated for considering the agricultural problem of India from the angle of its depressed personnels like agricultural labourers, share-croppers and old tillers of uneconomic holdings for which his suggestions were to improve agricultural wage, to fix the share-croppers share at the minimum of 2/3rd of the produce and to abolish rent on uneconomic holdings. He gave due emphasis on the provision of better irrigations roads and manure as well as efficient organization of tools for improvements in agriculture. In his opinion inequality of wealth and income was mainly due to disparate possession of means of production and incidence of abysmal poverty was the main feature of the rural economy resulting from inequitable distribution of land holding which was the source of livelihood for 70 per cent of the total population.

Lohia had framed an alternative strategy of economic development which must necessarily be based on certain objectives like highest possible rate of growth, comparable status with developed and developing countries, egalitarian structure, regional parities, self-sufficiency, full employment and decentralized system. The strategy of economic development must be capable of assuring highest possible rate of growth but this must be consistent with certain values, which must not be sacrificed at any cost. For achieving these objectives Lohia was a critic of Indian Planners thought that external assistance was very much needed for the economic development of India and suggested for planned and productive utilization of India's own resources because "foreign aid, as it is presently administered, tends to corrupt the giver as well the taker" (Marx, Gandhi and Socialism, p. 466). For raising capital Lohia's suggestions were for abolition of Privy Purses and special Privileges, stoppage of production of articles for modernization of consumption, ceiling on income and expenditure, transfer of government servants to productive work, nationalization of big industries, taxation abolition of special public schools and voluntary labour of an hour to nation.

CONCLUSION

Rammanohar Lohia projected himself as a socialist in true sense and above all a nationalist in his thought and action. His ideas, his approach to different issues, his suggestions for solving the prevailing problems, his way of analysis of problems all are enough to reveal his Gandhian outlook in most cases. He was supporter of evolving own pattern of development instead of western pattern in consonance with the socio-economic conditions prevalent in India. He championed the cause for equality not only for justice but also for greater efficiency and promoting economic development. His suggestion was to concentrate on research for evolving appropriate technology suited to the socio-economic conditions of the country instead of relying on imported ideas and technology. He advocated the use of small-scale low capital technology not merely to conserve capital and prevent unemployment but also to avoid the concentration of economic power and growth of unmanageable megalopolis and discarded the Indian government preference for capital-intensive technology under the plea of having a very high rate of growth.

References

Gabriel Ardant (1963), A Plan for full Employment in the Developing countries, *International Labour Review*.

Lohia (1956), *Mankind*, Nov., p. 391.

—— (1962), *Mankind*, March, p. 31.

—— (1963), *Lok Sabha*, Aug., p. 23.

—— (1967), *Mankind*, July, p. 27.

—— (1967), *Mankind*, Aug., p. 11.

Lohia (1968), Speech in the University in U.S.A., May 11, 1964, *Mankind,* March-April 1968, p. 6.

—— (1969), *Mankind,* June 1969, p. 5.

Lohia, Marx, Gandhi and Socialism.

—— Fragments of World Mind.

—— Wheel of History.

Singh, Ram Binod (1986), India's Economic Development and Lohia's Thought, Pratipaksh Prakashan, Delhi.

8

Economic Ideas of Dr. Ram Manohar Lohia

BHARAT BHUSHAN

In the 2nd half of the 19th Century as the outcome of the economic policies, educational system and political system of the British Government giving change to social economic life system gave birth to a new thought. Since there are the policies and economic thought that emerged were the result of protest of the British Empire in India.

Really Dr. Lohia was a political thinker, but being influenced by the ills and evils of the British Government, he has given new economic ideas keeping in view the Indian society and economy. Really the economic ideas of Dr. Lohia were influenced by the following factors/matters concerning the British Government:

GROWING POVERTY

The British Government adopted such a policy deliberately which eliminated the Indian rural self-reliant economy. He set up such an educational policy which produced a new class of clerks so that the Britishers may rule over the country without any hindrance. The educated Indians were not assigned key-posts in the Government departments. During the 150 years rule of the British Government the aim of the commercial policy of the Government was to serve the interest of Great Britain ignoring the needs and requirements of the Indian people. The result of this discriminatory policies of the British Govt. was the shattering of the industries of Mumbai. A long with the rapid progress of the British Empire India was forced to brave bankruptcy. 1/4th accumulated income of India was spent on domestic expenditure of Great Britain. In addition to it, millions of rupees was sent to England as an individual deposit. During 1900-1901 its total amount was Rs. 175 Lacs. At that very time the per capita income of India was only 2 pounds whereas in another British colonies it was 48 pounds. During the British Empire India was the only country where poverty was at its climax. On account of the adoption of the free trade policies of the British Government the foreign goods flowed in the country and the domestic industries vanished or declined. The establishment of Railways in India paved the way for the flow of foreign goods in India. As a result India became poorer and poorer.

THE RISE OF INDIAN NATIONALISM

As a result of growing poverty and extension of the British education, the people of the country began to think that the economic and political systems of the country were completely defective. It led to the national awareness among the people of the country. That is why the Indian National Congress came into existence. The Indian Leaders gave a clarion call that so long as the British Rule in India is not brought to an end, India could not get rid of its poverty and mis-management of the British Rule. Thus the foundation of the freedom movement was laid downs. During this period, the Indian Leaders among whom Dr. Lohia was prominent, gave thought which were not completely economic by nature but was political–economic. In this way, the economic ideas of Dr. Lohia were influenced mainly by Indian National Movement.

MISCELLANEOUS CAUSES

Due to the contact with the Western Countries, the pacle of economic ideas of our country grew. Dr. Lohia drew inspirations from Western thoughts on freedom, equality and brotherhood and was fully convinced that getting rid of the British Rule was essential for the development of mental power and fulfilment of economic and political objectives. The work of Dr. Lohia was not confined to the development of economics but tried to resolve the problems/bottlenecks that come in the way of well functioning of Indian Economy.

The economic thought of Dr. Ram Manohar Lohia seems to be influenced by the above mentioned problems with which the Indian people were struggling. Dr. Lohia occupies great importance among the socialist economic thinkers since December 1955, Dr. Lohia edited 'Mankind' magazine from Hyderabad and tried successfully to bring his socialist economic ideas before the people of India through this mouth piece.

Dr. Lohia was leader against caste system and this was the reason that Dr. Lohia called upon the people to break the barrier of caste and creed first and foremost. He thought that prevailing caste system in our society adversely affects our economic development. We are witnesses to the fact that the caste politics and castcism has eaten into the vitals of economy of our state during the last over and half decade.

Dr. Lohia had clear view that the increase in price of goods and commodities had adverse effect on the economic condition of the poor people of the country. This was the reason that Dr. Lohia gave the slogan in the parliament of India 'Control Price Measures', 'dam bandho'. The Finance Minister of India, Dr. P. Chidambram proposed many remedial to control prices of goods and take inflationary measures bearing in mind the above idea of Dr. Lohia.

Dr. Lohia tried to a great extent for the unification of India and Pakistan because he was of the clear view that the division of India and Pakistan would badly affect the economics of both the countries. We experience this ills and evils in India in the case of jute mills. 60% jute mills are located in India whereas 60% areas of jute production went to

Pakistan. Thus the jute mills in India have grave problem of raw materials. Owing to the partition of the country tension is mounting from time to time increasing the expenditure on internal and external security of the country.

Dr. Lohia was an adorer of equality. This was the reason that Dr. Lohia locked in horn with Late Pt. Jawahar Lal Nehru Government. Dr. Lohia carried a debate in Indian Parliament on 'teen ane v/s chaudah ane' in the regime of Nehru Government. He shook the nation saying that in our country there were 20 crore peoples who were forced to lead their family life on 3 ane per day on the one hand and on the other hand the income of Birla was in crores a day and Rs. 25,000 was spent per day on the maintenance of Prime Minister of the pauper country like India.

Dr. Lohia demanded public debate on plantoon policy and said clearly that the time has come that plantoon/forces be not trained on the pattern of Send Herts and Dehradoon training. Regiments be not called by caste names and the recruitment of forces, payment policy and system of training must be democratized. In consequences, we can say that the basis of Lohia policy was that in India big traders, bureaucrats and politicians-trio were ruling over the country who were arch rivals of mother tongue and owners of more than 80% wealth/property of our nation. He also made clear that the limit of the country was decreasing on the one hand and on the other hand the poor and poverty are increasing like a giant. Dr. Lohia was aware of the poverty of our country and always tried for eradication of poverty.

Dr. Lohia also expressed his clear view on the revenue of the land. Advocating equality on this count, Dr. Lohia said that thousand years old revenue system on land must be replaced with such a revenue policy in which the poor should be exempted from paying land revenue and instead it need to be levied more on the rich and land lords. He classified agriculture into two parts; profitable agriculture and unprofitable agriculture. He was dead against levying rent/ revenue on unprofitable agricultural land.

Dr. Lohia held that any independent country had independent economic policy lent when a country is slave; the economy of the country is run by the policy of the ruler of the country ruled. This is why Dr. Lohia opposed tooth and nail that the English should not rule over India.

In his analysis Dr. Lohia said that the philosophy of history can look for the order and the time of change from caste to class and from class to caste. How the prevailing caste system in India was formed is a subject of guessed in itself. In reality, it evolved such a system which brought inactiveness in our society. Both the things are wonderful. The caste formation on social level or external down-fall go hand in hand whatever be the gap between the period. In this regard, Dr. Lohia was the first economic thinker who not only changed the directions of Indian social thinkers but also gave new thought and new direction.

As Dr. Lohia was in the good know of the Indian social problems as well as powerful orator, that is why his economic thinking indicates the solution of the social problems. With the reference of Dr. Lohia as a social economic thinker Khuma Kher said clearly in the German Parliament in 1946:

"There is a man on Indian soil who saw God in the bread of daridra narayan (the poor)."

When Dr. Lohia was asked in Betul whether he was a Gandhian, he replied, "I am neither fully Gandhian nor fully Marxist. Nor am I fully anti-Gandhi, nor fully anti-Marx. Whatever is good in Gandhism or Marxism, I would like to draw out of it and this difference provides a solid lease for Indian socialist economic thinkers." At some other place Dr. Lohia said, "first of all the western countries ruled over the world with this intention that they used capitalist for this objective and now, they are using Marxism for getting their goal." Really, this was the contribution of Dr. Lohia. He had a style of stating. What he wanted to say is that in the 19th century, Marx tried to place some solutions regarding the then Western European social conditions. Their world was industrially developed, but afflicted world from the social injustice, exploitation and enmity. His aim was not to search new technology of production but only to search new process of distribution or production. This is another unfortunate thing that Marxism got prominent first of all in a country exploited by the Tsars and in agricultural country like Russia and again in Governors of Suami and high Royal family of China and the people exploited by extremists of Japan and another agricultural countries. This is because Karl Marx centered his philosophy around industrial mechanism and capitalist countries whereas the peasants looked such backward that were anti-revolution by nature. That is why Marx considered their elimination from the country to be proper solution to the problem.

In this way Krotiya's above remark about Lohia is up to the mark that he was neither Gandhian nor Marxist. Really, Lohia took out good thing of the two. This is the reason that he is impressed to some extent by both.

When Dr. Lohia considers rationalism as a base for socialistic economic thinking, the question arises whether rationalism is only a geographical necessity or a concept beyond geography according to the concept of Rechard Park, Lewis Mawford and Oram.

The greatest contribution of Dr. Lohia is his suggestion that we should try to go ahead keeping in view the reality of our Indian society. This is why Dr. Lohia expressed his view that class struggle and caste struggle would go together in India. In his view, class is indicator of dynamic society where caste is the indicator of static/stagnant inept social system. He clearly thought that India had been slave for the last 25 years because there was in place as rigid caste system. Dr. Lohia was of the firm view that there is only one caste of all the people that is mankind.

In deed, Dr. Lohia was such a socialist economic thinker in which the good of both Gandhism and Marxism is embodied. Dr. Lohia considered slavery and poverty obstacles/bottlenecks in the way of economic development of a country. Along with it he defined class and caste in a good way and he wished that caste should be abolished and there would be only one caste that is mankind. For this he struggled till his life. Even in parliament he fought for the poor and the downtrodden in the voice of the poor. In a great extent he contributed and played a pivotal role in the formation of economic policies of the government.

To sum up, we can say that really Dr. Lohia was a political thinker but what he realized in his practical life, he dared to place before the country his economic and social thinking. If the way shown by Lohia is embraced even today, definitely the progress of society as well as the whole economy is possible. In this way, we can say that the economic ideas of Dr. Lohia is more important and appreciative and the society will benefit from it.

9

Content of Lohia's Economic Thought

Abhas Saurabh and Bharti Kumari

INTRODUCTION

In the evolution of the socialist movement and elaboration of the socialist thought in India, Dr. Ram Manohar Lohia occupied significant place. His socialism was fundamentally different from most of the socialist thinkers in India, who advocate either the western or the Russian models of socialism before cold war to be adopted for India. His socialism was a product of the Indian soil. He borrowed freely from the western as well as the Russian models of socialism and coated his new brand according to the Indian way of life, traditions, and habits of the people. He relieved socialism from much of its obsolete technical jugglery, discarded Hegelian dialectical materialism, set aside Marxian materialistic interpretation of history, and even avoided Lenin's theory of the class-war. Although these concepts had their utility for him, he considered that Indian masses needed a simple and an understandable form of socialism. He knew that the socialism of text-books was beyond the comprehension of the common man in India, as he is shrouded in superstitions and obsolete customs, poverty and ignorance. He, therefore, constructed his socialistic mansion in a rather simple form, avoiding nooks and corners, porches and pillars, windows and balconies, and the complicated Hegelian or Marxian architecture. As such, Lohian socialism was so simple that even an illiterate labourer, or a traditional farmer or a petty shop-keeper or an ignorant mill-worker could understand its broadly visible dimensions without any mental strain or puzzling quarries or endless controversies that usually surround socialism. Actually, an everlasting contribution that Dr. Lohia made in the field of conternporary Indian socio-economic profiles.

LOHIA: A MAN OF VISION

Ram Manohar Lohia (1910-1967) was a man of vision and also a noted parliamentarian of rare ability. He was an agitator par excellence and a leader of the socialist movement in India. He was brutally frank, forthright and fearless. Indomitable courage and doubtless optimism in the face of grim and dire odds were the essence of his character.

He willed and worked for power no doubt, but power for the people, for the oppressed, for the downtrodden, for the lowliest and the lost. His love for the poor and weak was only next to that of Mahatma Gandhi. He rebelled against everthing that sought to encroach upon the freedom of individual. Freedom, he used to say, was not merely the end of slavery but essentially of the slavish mentality, and of the craze to imitate the west blindly.

Though an advocate of agitational politics, Lohia was a votary of non-violence and a respecter of principles. Gandhi had once called him a socialist with pronounced leanings towards non-violence. Trying to remove the concept against him as preaching violence. Trying to remove the concept against him as preaching violence, he declared. "Ours is a new principle which goes to the new world where no one kills another or sucks another, and for a new world we are willing to give our own blood. The Ganges will flow with blood but it shall flow with Indian blood. We ask not a drop of the enemy's blood in return for what we have suffered." It is thus clear that his agitational politics was tempered by compassion and his hatred for injustice by sympathy for the sufferer.

Like Gandhi, Lohia had the capacity to reuse and dramatize public opinion. His famous slogan of 'Do or Die' on Congress Radio, 1942, had a great emotional and imaginative appeal. In 1967, he created the climate of non-congressism and promised to bring radical changes in first six month of non-Congress ministries. Although the promise proved to be fantastic, it, nevertheless, heightened the emotional appeal of his leadership.

DEVELOPMENT OF LOHIA'S SOCIALISM

His abiding faith in the dignity of the individual provided him with the necessary fervour to fight against those ideas and institutions which tended to separate man from man, and as such in his early days he was much closer to the beliefs of those whom Marx called the utopian socialistist rather than to doctrines of the West European socialist thinkers.

Later his close association with Gandhi and his study of the socialist theories of Marx, Engles, Buber, Bernstein, Rosa Luxemburg and others in Europe as well as his observation of the real condition of the people in India led him to develop some sort of concrete ideas on the subject.

(a) Marx's Theory of Evolution of Capitalism Faculty

The Marxian theory of capitalist development has another contradiction between the exchange value and the use value of labour, and the surplus value thus generated. According to Marx, labour is the sole creator of value of the four factors of production—land, labour, capital and organisation. These three are sterile or constant and labour alone is variable. It is capable of reproducing a surplus over and above its equivalent. Labour produces two values: one which the laborer himself gets in the form of his wages and the other which the employer gets as a share in the total produce. The labourer does not get all that the produces, and the margin between the result of labour and payment for it is ordinary, called Marxist doctrine as 'Surplus Value'. Lohia commented that surplus value can not be calculated nor can it be understood on the Marxian basis of differences between labour's requirement and its produce. Surplus value, wherever it appears and to the extent that it does so, is the difference between the actual earnings of labour and the per worker world production of the time. Hence in the words of Lohia, "we will have to consider a new the law of surplus value, the contractions of capitalism, and the law regarding revolution and therefore our entire strategy and tactics will also have to be revised because the strategy and tactics of Marxism are the inevitable outcome of this law of capitalist development."

(b) Gandhian Commitments of Lohia's Views: Decentralisation of Power

Lohia envisages a simple society where power is decentralised, and which is free from the blemish of what Lewis Mumford calls Giantism. He recommends a four-pillared structure of the state based on self-rule from the bottom and without the over-riding authority of an all-powerful centre. He also pleads for the establishment of a World Parliament without which equality among nations and equality among men world never be feasible. Thus, Lohia has systematized Gandhi's idea of village self-rule and Panchayati Raj like Gandhi, he is convinced that so long as the masses do not involve themselves in the process of changing the political administrative, economic, educational and cultural modes and institutions socialism world remain an empty slogan a myth and a sterile dream.

Lohia is a Gandhian of the revisionist type. He calls himself a heretic-Gandhian. He accepts the technique of struggle and philosophical framework of Gandhism, but its approach to socio-economic problems, specially its theory of trusteeship, is not acceptable to him. Gandhism always thinks in terms of personal salvation and wants to improve the individual internally, morally and spiritually, and thereby to change the external environment. Socialism, on the other hand, seeks to improve the external environment to enable the individual to improve himself. Lohia stands in between the two. He says that Gandhi has tended to over-emphasize the individual and under-emphasize the environment, whereas socialism has tended to over-emphasize the environment and under-emphasize the individual. Thus we see that Lohia's objectives are Marxian but his approach is Gandhian. To him, the fundamental formulations of Marx are incomplete, and, standing by itself, Gandhism too does not seem to be of much use to the world. He has therefore, arrived at a conclusion that instead of seeking to elaborate a new doctrine of Gandhism, if some of the ideas from Gandhi's life and action are woven into a consistent cloth of socialism a new civilization may emerge and mankind may hope for an age of peace and decency.

CONTENTS OF ECONOMIC APPROACH

Economic Aims and its Contents

Lohia borrowed his economic aims from communism and non-economic and general aims from capitalist democracy. The mass production, the establishment of social ownership over means of production and some kinds of a planned economy are the acknowledged economic aims and methods of communism. Lohia attempts to explore the economic and general aims of society and to integrate them into a harmony, with a view to creating a new philosophy of socialism capable of becoming a powerful force of social change in the world. He recognized it as a new socialism, which comprehends the following fundamental principles:

(i) Maximum attainable equality,
(ii) Social ownership,
(iii) Small-unit technology,
(iv) Four-pillar state,
(v) A decent standard of living, and
(vi) The World Parliament of Government.

Lohia regards equality "as high an aim of life as truth or beauty." He maintains that if there is no equality among the individuals and also among the nations, justice, human dignity, morality, brotherhood, freedom and universal welfare cannot flourish in society. He propounded, Sapta Kranti model for his economic ideas, they are:

(i) Equality between man and woman;
(ii) The abolition of inequalities based on colour;
(iii) Elimination of inequalities of birth and caste;
(iv) National freedom an ending of foreigh influences;
(v) Economic equality through increase in production;
(vi) Protecting the privacy of individual life from all collective encroachments, and
(vii) Limitation on armaments

Thus we find that, though there are many common elements, there is considerable differences in composition and emphasis which make Lohia's concept of socialism entirely different and novel. The three ingredients of his socialism, maximum attainable equality, four-pillar stated and decent standard of living, are absolutely original. His emphasis on small-unit technology and on 'SATYAGRAHA' as the only rightful weapon to fight against injustice, gives a new colour and form to his economic socialism.

Agrarian Revolution

According to Lohia, the backwardness of Indian agriculture in terms of production, size of holdings and dependence of too many people on it, is, therefore, the first basic economic problem which must be tackled if Indian economy is to be accelerated. He propounded his scheme of the agrarian revolution in India which contained the following items:

(i) Reclamation of waste land;
(ii) Equitable distribution of land;
(iii) Abolition of Land revenue;
(iv) Bhoosena or 'Food Army'; and
(v) Emphasis on small and medium schemes of irrigation.

RESTRICTIONS ON EXPENDITURE AND CONSUMPTION

Socialists in India claim that by nationalizing all principal industries and trade, by imposing ceilings on economic holdings, and through a progressive taxation policy the existing gap between the rich and the poor can be narrowed. Lohia does not deny the utility of such measures but to make these measures effective and real, he presents his policy of immediate restrictions on expenditure and consumption in India.

Lohia strongly holds the view that the lowest and highest income or expenditure in this country must keep within the limits of 1 to 10 and no unreasonable allowances or provisions should be allowed to defeat this policy of achieving maximum equitable attainable economic needs in the present context.

THE SOCIO-ECONOMIC APPROXIMATION OF MASSES

The struggle against inequality in India has another dimension. The fight for political and economic equality must also extend to the social realm. The class struggle against feudal capitalist exploitation can only succeed if it is coupled with the struggle for social equality. Lohia claims to achieve social equality through following actions:

(i) Preferential opportunities to Dalits, tribals, backward sections of the India society;
(ii) Alindus-Muslim;
(iii) Removal of English;
(iv) Free, compulsory and uniform education; and
(v) Free, Compulsory and Uniform Education.

Lohia was of the view that nation must take up the task of spreading literacy and importing efficient education to the whole population as its first and foremost duty. He believes that "the education upto the Middle standard should be free and compulsory and that educational facilities should be provided free or cheap at higher stages, particularly to the Scheduled Castes, Tribes and other poorer sections of the society. The medium of instruction should be the mother tongue, upto the first degree level. There should be a uniform pay-scale for all teachers and uniform standard of books for all students. Children of Bhangi, Brahmin, Kurmi, Kisan, Prime Minister and President should go to the same school and get the same education. This, according to Lohia, "is the first necessary reform for India without which nothing can be done."

Further, Lohia in favour of bringing all primary schools under the direct control of municipalities and district boards. According to him, 20 per cent of the state's revenues and 10 percent of central revenues should be ear-marked for education and the Government should see that these amounts are usefully and property spent."

THE 'THIRD CAMP' IN WORLD POLITICS

Lohia was not in favour of the policy of "non-alignment with great power groups" established by the first Prime Minister of India, Jawaharlal Nehru for having a just and equitable socio-economic order in India. According to Lohia, there were many serious shortcomings in Nehrus Policy of non-alignment, so he presented his policy of the 'Third Camp' at the Nasik Conference of Socialist Party in 1948.

Introducing the resolution on International situation at the conference, he said, 'the need of today is a call for the third camp to have uniform policy for economic development of the country'. Lohia stressed the need for a construction of economic approach to world economy. "The third camp must not be an umpire to control over means of the factors of production but a participation in the international factors of production." It must endeavor to literate the human being from the exploitation of the octopus grip of the two camps at that time, and extend its support to socialist movements all the world over and to all other popular economic movements which are striving to combat hunger and poverty with the weapons of socialist-based economic policies.

LOHIA'S PROGRAMME *VIS-A-VIS* THE PROGRAMME OF HIS CONTEMPORARY SOCIALISTS

If we compare Lohia's programme of India's reconstruction with that of his economic ideas we find that his approach to India's economic problem is concerned with three important schools of the Indian socialists :

In his first schools of socialist, on significant progress in India can be made unless the state or the community controls the means of production and distribution and that is possible only when the dominant class of tomorrow, viz. the proletariat, gets an edge over the dominant class of today, namely, the capitalists.

The second school of socialists favours the Gandhian approach of the change of heart. This school believes that if the stronger sections are convinced that an unpardonable inequality has been perpetrated and they were the sinful recipients of the unlawful gains, a major battle is won. It is then possible for the community to insist that the strong should hold all the advantages social, political and economic in trust for the unprivileged and solely for their good. The weaker sections on their part should be taught to realize what is legitimately due to him.

The third school of socialism in India holds the view that while the expansion of the public sector in India should be carried out at the maximum speed possible. The realities of the Indian situation should also be recognized. Our administration is not capable of running big public projects efficiently the only class that does some effective saving and turns it into industrial investment is the capitalist class, this class alone possesses the requisite entrepreneurial ability and without its active cooperation rapid industrialization is not possible. Therefore, as a measure of temporary expediency, the capitalist class should not only be permitted to exist but should also be allowed to grow, if need be, so as to serve the basic purpose of the Indian economic development today, which is increasing production so as to increase the share of each factor of production. This school, therefore, advocates planned economic development and mixed economy in which the private sector is allowed to function and to earn profit under overall state regulation and control.

Dr. Lohia does not belong to any of these schools of thought. His objections to their approaches are based on the thesis that they ignore the essential needs of the vast army of artisans in India working with primitive technology and supplying the needs of the local population. He advocated that "The essential thing to note is that capitalist as well communist rationalization makes use of identical technology and that it is totally useless for Asia in view of its too few forces of production. Socialists of Asia must themselves understand and make it clear to the people of Asia that communism cannot give bread even after it destroys freedom."

Dr. Lohia's approach involves a change in the attitude. It is based on voluntary efforts of our masses, on one hand, and on state control (to the extent it does not encroach upon the privacy of the individual) on the other. It is rooted in his general approach of equity between groups of people and also between regions. His insistence on ceilings on income and expenditure, on the sacredness of physical work, on lowering the margin between the highest and the lowest is largely due to his anxiety to see that the principles of equity and equality are really operative in our economy.

Lohia was finally pessimistic about the gradual upliftment of the status of the unprivileged. If the unprivileged cannot be immediately lifted to the affluence of the privileged let the privileged be deprived of a few of their privileges so that the community can be more homogeneous. Similarly, he wants immediate closure of public schools and immediate removal of English. He comments as English will go only at a stroke and never gradually other Indian socialists donot subscribe to this view. They are in favours of a gradual transformation of the Indian economy.

CONCLUSION

As a socialist theoretician, Lohia was the most orthodox. On the one hand, he broadly accepted the Maxist prognosis of capitalism and regarded Marx as basically a democrat but on the other hand, he refuted that Marx did not think about the economically backward countries because his theories are not applicable to the developing world. He maintained that socialism could acquire that integral character and dynamism only by absorbing the three fundamental ingredients of the Gandhian Philosophy, viz. purity of means, satyagraha, and the devolution of *political and economic power.*

Lohia rejects all doctrines of restricted capitalism and mixed economy. In socialism, there must be the socialization of all means of production, which hire labour. Mass production technology should be replaced by the small-unit technology, because large scale industries lead to economic centralization and unemployment. The basic economic problem in India is agrarian reconstruction for which Lohia recommends five important measures, namely, reclamation of wasteland, equitable distribution of cultivable land, abolition of land revenue bringing the new land under cultivation and minor irrigation projects. Lohia does not want to depend on foreign arid for economic development. He asks to impose restrictions on our expenditure and articles of consumption, as one of the measures of capital formation and to shun sloth and somnolence for our rapid progress. Though, Lohia's programme of India's reconstruction has great potentialities, it is not the answer to all problems that torment country. There is no doubt, Lohia's programme would set India on the road to socialism where there will be maximum attainable equality and greater prosperity.

Reference

Arora, V.K. Basu, Rammanohar Lohia and Socialism in India, Deep & Deep, New Delhi, p. 27.

Karanth, K.S. (1905), 'Memories of Dr. Lohia', *Mankind*, pp. 9-16.

Kelkar, Indumati (1963), Lohia Siddhant and Karma, *Navahind*, Hyderabad, pp. 30-4.

Lohia (1963), "Marx, Gandhi and Socialism", *Navhind*, Hyderabad.

Puri, Rajendra (1967), *Weekend Review*, October, pp. 13-14.

Singh, R.B. (1986), *India's Economic Development and Lohia's Thought*, Pratipaksh Prakashan, Delhi.

Singh, R.B. (2003), Poverty and Sustainable Development: Global Perspective, *IEA 86th Conference Volume*, pp. 301-19.

Yadav, Devendra Pd., Lohia ek Samajik Andolan, Annual Report of Ministry of Agriculture, pp. 77-81.

10

Economic Ideas of Dr. Ram Manohar Lohia

SARITA KUMARI

Dr. Ram Manohar Lohia was a notable stalward in the stream of Gandhian thought. During brief period of 14 years of post-colonial India, he played very significant role in all spheres of National Political Activities. He was identified as firebrand Gandhian Socialist. Dr Lohia had been at authoritative commands of several national and international issues of Public importance. He was not a serious politician only but a political thinker too. He was fiercely abhorant to the vast gap prevalent between sayings and deeds of politician of the day. His works and thoughts covered vast spectrum of topics like castism in India, gender, racial and ethnic discrimination, communal disharmony, poverty, economic deprivation, etc. and most part of his thoughts came in through his lectures. Only a few books have come which had been written as such. "Marx, Gandhi and Socialism" is one of them in which his writings have been collected. Some chapters of this book relate to his comments and thinking on economic theories. Among them "Economics after Marx" is the master piece which, despite having been written in 1943, is still very relevant.

In his wonderful "Economics after Marx" he has opined that neither Marx nor Gandhi was complete. He declared that he was neither anti-Marx nor pro-Marx and that equally applied to his attitude towards Mahatma Gandhi. He said, "No man's thought should be made the centre of political action. It should help but not control. Acceptance and rejection are varying form of blind worship. I believe that it is silly to be Gandhian or Marxist and it is equally so to be anti-Gandhian or anti-Marxist. They are priceless treasure to learn from Gandhi as from Marx, but the learning can only be done when the frame of reference does not derive from an age or a person.

With this outlook Dr. Lohia identified the shortcomings of Marxism. It was the common man around which all his economic thought revolved. Dr. Lohia propounded his own economic theory which is best suited to the Third World countries and specially India. He asked why it was so that whenever India arose, it squandered to world profusely and did not take from it but during its abysmal fall it forgot all its past glory. While studying in Germany he asked these questions to the Marxists but they had no satisfactory answer to these questions. Why all the scientific inventions and accumulation of capital occurred in Europe and not in Asia? Why soul of Europe was awakened and not that of Asia? After very deep research he reconstructed his own theory of Capitalist Development. He found that Marx's initial fallacy was to have examined capitalism in the abstract, to have wrenched it outside of its Imperialist context. He arrived on the conclusion that Marxism is quite accurate in its finding on capital accumulation, correct from one angle on question of industrial crises, of monopoly and socialisation of labour, but fatuallly wrong in the spheres of accumulating proverty, casual class struggle and world revolution.

Dr. Lohia propounded that "Socialism must forever shatter this unreal Marxist picture. In its place must arise a picture of two circles, one placed inside the other, the inner circle representing the free capitalist structures with their dynamic in the contradiction between capitalist profits and mechanised labour, the other circle representing the colonial economy of the rest of the world with its dynamics between imperial exploitation and colonial labour, the rim of the inner circle possessing an enormously porous capacity to suck into itself the dynamic of the outer. This is the only way in which we can join up the capital–labour dynamic with the empire-colony dynamic and arrive at a consistent understanding of the development of capitalism."

And noted "Some persons will here remark that the two dynamics are present in Marxist studies of capitalism. Nobody question that the issue is whether the two dynamics are so interconnected and the basic laws of this interconnection so discovered as to give a consistent understanding of the world. It is this interconnection that socialism must study. For a type of intellect which can only be satisfied by crude evaluations, let it be said here that of all other Europeans, Karl Marx is the greatest economist of European history. But we must not be satisfied with that, for we need the economics of world history.

He declared that what we have hitherto had as the science of economics are nothing else but the rules of accountancy, industrial management, trade and banking. The science of economics is yet to mature. This is further illustrated by the pitiful use that economics makes of statistics.

According to Dr. Lohia, University economics has tried to understand the distribution of wealth among various countries of the world and is preserving this understanding with the help of a few concepts. He examined the major concepts like

(I) NECESSARY REQUIREMENT OF LABOUR

The requirements of labour are supposed to vary from country to country. Colder climates like those of England and Germany are believed to necessitate richer food, better housing, more clothing, and so forth, than tropical climates like those of Africa and India. As a result of these higher calories of food and so forth, labour in colder climates is also believed to be more productive. Thus the teaching has sprung up of the greater productivity. Thus, the teaching has sprung up of the greater productivity and also the greater requirements of labour in colder climates.

Quite obviously, therefore, there are no such things as the necessary requirements of labour; there are only such requirements as varying political fortunes have bestowed upon this country or that. The Indian peasant who is today supposed naturally to sleep in the open and work may as naturally be supposed, in a different political climate, to require for his labour a pukka house lighted and ventilated by electricity. This brings us to the question of what labour produces.

(II) PRODUCTIVITY OF LABOUR

The teaching that credited labour in colder countries with a higher productivity by virtue of the climate itself is so patently untrue that is has almost been given up. It is now clothed in different garments. Such concepts as the lack of proper food or of training and skill are introduced to explain the low produce of colonial labour. Indian economies and businessman make free of these concepts.

Despite the concept of ill-fed and ill-skilled labour as an explanation of the low produce in our industry Indian workers use as much, if not more, muscle-power and skill as labour elsewhere. Is it then their own incompetence which Indian capitalists seek to transfer to our labour?

(III) CAPITALIST ENTERPRISE

Capacity to mix in the most profitable proportion the three factors of production, land, labour and capital and the readiness to take risks or to break our into unexplored regions of technique and industry are regarded as a part of the entrepreneur's skill in text book economies. The Indian capitalist is as skillful in the selection of sites for his industries and in marketing as the European; if anything, he is even more skilled in the manipulation of labour. This teaching of entrepreneur's skill, whatever may be its role in the internal economy of a country, has absolutely no meaning when applied to distinguish one important country from another. This explains why the Indian capiculation, is wholly crippled when it comes to breaking out into new techniques and industry. On industry risks he is as dishonorable as the tortoise, probably because he knows that the moment he takes our his head he will be decapitated. It is to this dishonour of a colonial economic structure and not to the supposed lower yield or lower needs of our labour, nor even to entrepreneur's skill, that our low economic productivity should be traced.

(IV) NATIONAL RESOURCES

Attempt is often made to refer to a country's natural resources to explain and justify what in university economics is known as the geographical division of labour. This does not, however, mean that there are no such things as differing natural resources. It is to these resources that the United States owes, in part, its preponderant position in the world; with 6 per cent of the world's population, it control nearly 25 per cent of the world's resources. Here again one has to be very careful. The factor of scientific inventiveness can almost equalise differing natural resources. The present estimate of a country's resources power, and so forth, which have already have required acquired key importance. But one can depend on science to produce petrol out of coal, and sugar out of wood, and if these ersatz industries may with some reason be regarded as a waste in the perspective of world economy, there are remarkable new inventions in fields such as plastics or electronics which open out the prospect of wholly new industries. Firmly entrenched vested interests of iron and steel in the already industrialised countries may kindly it impossible for the plastics industry to grow, whereas another country with less resources in iron may develop this new industry with great profit to itself. Scientific inventiveness can thus add to the great variety of key natural resources and equalise the differences among various countries. No doubt applied science will have to be more alert and alive and diversified as between one country and another than it has been so far; it must not blindly follow already explored lines. In this way differences in natural resources can be equalised and a country poor on the present showing may even aspire to gain a lead, however short lived, over others. In order that we can have a really beneficial world trade and obtain a true teaching of the geographical division of labour, science must have unfettered scope in various parts of the world and also make intelligent, human use of its possibilities. Until this is done text book teaching on natural resources must be viewed with suspicion, and be looked upon as a justification of the existing geographical divison of labour, that is, of imperial structures on the one hand and colonial structures on the other.

We have found that the concepts of the necessary requirement of labour, of the productivity of labour, of capitalist skill, and of natural resources when used to distinguish one country from another, are either meaningless or harmful to proper understanding. To understand world economy, as it is and as it has traveled through the past two centuries, we need such concepts as the politically effective requirements of labour, the productivity of the total economic structure, the imperial-colonial division of labour.

And then he defined surplus value. According to this definition, labour, whether of peasant or the factory worker, creates surplus value to the extent that its earnings fall below the average per worker world production of its time. He established that surplus value, which makes up the entire profit and high earnings of the capitalist system is derived mainly from colonial farms, fields and mines.

Dr. Lohia was with the Gandhian idea of small unit machine that arose out of a specific need of the Indian situation, actually that of all coloured with retarded peoples. Among retarded peoples, the relationship of available manpower and possible investments is almost inversely different from that among Euro-American peoples. While there is profusion of man-power in one, in the other, investments are profuse. Investments are scare among the retarded peoples. In order to employ available manpower with as much rationally as possible, a mode of machine was thought out, which would be born out of such savings as were possible. Upto this point, the reasoning seems strictly logical.

Extensions of this reasoning were made. What was born out of the inadequacies of retarded situation appeared also to correspond to the more ultimate human requirements. The monster machine is both incomprehensible and unmanageable. The common man is unable to understand it. He manipulates it almost as its object. And yet he is supposed to control and direct it as a constituent unit in the sovereignty of the people. The incomprehensible machine becomes also the unmanageable machine and therefore violates the idea of government by the people. In contract, the small-unit machine is by definition more comprehensible and manageable.

CONCLUSION

Dr. Lohia identified the melody of *Price-loot* and mind or skill imperialism pollutes relationships between countries of primary produces and those of manufactures and modern skills. A worse pollution is in evidence within peoples, particularly such as are exceedingly poor. The poorer the country, the greater is the inequality within it. Some measure of inequality is indeed endemic to all peoples. The total national produce of a country is nowhere evenly divided among its population nor is properly equally owned. In his tireless endeavour to fulfil his dreams he ceaselessly fought day and night but before he could finally formulate findings of his research in its completion the cruel hand of death snatched him from us.

References

Marx, Gandhi and Socialism by Ram Manohar Lohia.
Dr. Lohia, Ek Jivani by O.P. Deepak and Arvind Mohan.
Biography of Dr. Lohia by Indumati Kelkar.
Dr. Lohia, Ek Jivani by Onkar Sarad.

11

Economic Ideas of Ram Manohar Lohia

HARI NARAYAN PD. SINGH AND BINOD PRASAD

INTRODUCTION

Ram Manohar Lohia was born on March 23, 1910 at Akbarpur in Faizabad District (U.P) in a Marwari (vaish) family, Which acquired the surname of Lohia for its dealings in the business of *Loha* (Hardware) for many generations. He lost his mother when he was hardly three years old. His father, Hira Lal Lohia was a true symbol of patriotism and throughout his life, he was greatly instrumental in generating the spirit of Indian nationalism in the mind of his son. He was sent to Berlins for higher education. During his stay there was greatly influenced by the Philosophy of Marx and Engle's.

Ram Manohar Lohia left us on Oct. 12, 1967. Lohia left behind him no property, no family, but only his ideas to be followed. He said, "I have nothing of my own except the fact that the poor and common people of India believe that perhaps I belong to them."

Lohia Jee wrote about the emergence of new economic

trends in the world. "The history of capitalist development is in the history of increasing poverty of colonial masses and their reduction into starving and landless labour . . . unless prevailing economic trends are reversed and that does not seem very likely, the increasing poverty of colonial masses will be greatest single factor to words the undoing of the west European Economy."

After several years he gave recent to his feelings about the doctrine of Socialism. Which was creed of his long drawn political carrier. Extracts from the presidential address of Rammanohar Lohia to the special convention of Socialist Party held in May 1952. Lohia attempts to give doctrinal foundation for Socialism independent of its bases in Communism and capitalist democracy, with special reference to the conditions in the economically under-developed areas of the world—an attempts worthy of closer study by students of political thought.

ECONOMIC THOUGHTS OF RAM MANOHAR LOHIA

Ram Manohar Lohia's economic thought come out with a new zeal and spirit as might be linked with world Justice and Welfare. It is rooted his brief that 'all men must not be equal within a nation but also among the nations'. Lohia visualised the economic inequality prevalent both within a national and among nations. Both national and international inequalities are related with each other and hence affect each other. So far inequality among the nations is not removed, inequalities within a nation can not be completely eliminated. Lohia Jee said, "Regional inequality in production in the world's most dangerous and obstinate disease. An hour of labour in the united state produces three times as much in Europe and fifteen to twenty times as much in Asia and Africa."

With these many worlds of economics, one world of politics cannot be possible. World trade and economy cannot expand until this great rock is removed. The desire of wealthy Nations to give and of the retarted Nations to take technical assistance will not solve the problem. It is a one-way traffic and is erroneous in conception and harmful in consequences. In place of one way programme, Lohia pleaded for a two-way traffic.

For ending the regional inequality the theory of international trade must be re-stated. Adam Smith was the first in the modern times to formulate such theory and based it on the geographical division of labour. Lohia considers such a theory to be faulty as is based on the belief that through international trade all the nations of the world shall be benefited, and there shall be regional division of labour. Lohia in a seminar at Athens in October 1961 stated: "But the fate of the theory shows that no matter what universal terms it has, there lies behind them some kind of National interest and Mr. Keynes, therefore had to formulate a theory that brought in a clause, relating full employment. Britain could not complete with America and, therefore, a theory of full employment had to be put in." In an article Indian Economy in figures and Indian agriculture in figures, Lohia said, "the greatest single factor that has caused the poverty of India is Britain's rule over India. The relationship between Britain and India is that of the exploiter and exploited, Britain draws out of India profits in three major ways : as dividends and her investments; as salaries and pensions and as benefits out of a foreign trade between a manufacturing country and a raw producing country. The poverty of India is vast and for its removal not only the imperialist system must be destroyed but the entire population should engage in a mighty and co-operative economic endeavour."

Lohia found British economics thought 'not creative, not historical, not even logically simple, but perhaps negatively helpful'. Lohia has also stood as a critic of Marxian Laws of capitalist development which state that socialism is an inevitable outcome of highly capitalised economics and all that is to be done is to evolve a ruthless will. On the other hand, to Lohia, 'socialism requires a great new effort at renewed understanding of capitalism as much as it requires an efforts of will. To believe that the task of understanding was completed by Marx is the greatest Communist error.'

Lohia said Marxism is not applicable to India. In a country like India with the very special characteristics which one not found in all other Asian countries. We can not think of any policy of direct application of Marxism. We can indeed say that the same is true with Keyne's economic thinking but the differences is that Keyne's ideas have not spread among the people in India as that of the ideas of Marx.

Similarly, Capitalism, Socialism and Communism beings born in Europe can not be universally valid doctrine. Lohia said: "they are valid only for certain period of human experience and they are valid in connection with certain accidents of history."

THEORY OF CAPITALIST DEVELOPMENT

The fascination of marxism does not lie in its ultimate aim but in its analysis of Capitalism and the analysis gives birth to the ultimate aim. To Lohia, 'the essential core of Marxist doctrine is the analysis of capitalist development, and will the element force of this sociological law of capitalism ties up the ultimate picture of society which Marx and Engel's drew. Lohia realised that Marx didn't give a consistent theory of capitalism development. His initial fallacy was to have examined capitalism in the abstracts, and to have wrenched it outside of its imperialist context. He painted the picture of capitalism only on the basis of west Europe entity.

Lohia remarked, "Marx's capitalism was that of a self-moving west European circle, no doubt causing great repercussions in the outside world, but the principle and laws of its own movement were exclusively internal. Marxism of this day remains stuck in this picture, no doubt formulating laws about these outside repercussions, but wholly unable to state the basic interacting principle of the two, internal and external, movements of capital."

Lohia gave his own theory in capitalist development. Lohia, in his speech in Hyderabed in Aug. 1952 rightly asserted : "Marx was of course much aware of the fact that these capitalist economies of west Europe had drawn a great deal of profit from Asia and other countries of the world. This awareness is to be seen in many utterances of Marx. But it acts as an addendum to his main doctrine. It does not act as an integral part of his doctrine but somewhat like the tail of an animal."

Describing capitalist development of two circles in which the internal west European circle draws its dynamic from the external world. Lohia came to the conclusion that capitalism 'as a historical entity has produced a greater contradiction between increasing force of production in the western European capitalist economy and decreasing force of production in the rest of the world'.

Another defect in the Marxist doctrine of capitalist development is that in it 'riches and poverty should go along side in a single region or county, fabulous riches and abysmal poverty should exit side by side.' But according to the law of capitalist development 'The richer a country has become under the capitalist civilization, the narrower is its scope of inequality, the poorer a country has become the wider is its scope of inequality.'

Hence the socialists must try to shatter the established nation and frame out new laws of capitalist development and surplus value. As this law of capitalist development has been proved wrong, and as there is possibility of the capitalist chain snapping not in the area were the force of production have been stunted and dwarfed, an entirely new thinking becomes necessary.

THEORY OF SURPLUS VALUE

Lohia explained the theory of surplus value in context of the joint capitalist—imperialist development. To him, 'capitalism like any other sociological Phenomenon, is not just an abstract entity.' It is an historical phenomenon: it has to be understood in all its historical aspects.

Marx Theory of Surplus Value is based on the theory of that 'labour is the sole creator of value.' Marx says that human labour has two values, one which the labourer himself gets in the form of his wages and other, which employer gets as a share in total produce. But to Lohia, all this needs to restate in the light of both labour's value and use value.

While explaining his theory Lohia has pointed out that labour under capitalism has two forms—'imperial and colonial'—and there is a cast difference in their values. The source of the surplus value, we must keep in our mind the distinction between imperial and colonial labour and their wages. Lohia defined surplus value as follows : "Labour, whether of the peasant or the factory worker creates surplus value to the extent that its earning fall below the average per worker world production of its times."

IDEAS OF CAPITALIST ECONOMY

Lohia, who advocated the replacement of capitalism by socialism in under developed countries, criticised capitalist economy. He defined capitalism 'as a doctrine of the individual and of free enterprise that leads to ever changing application of science to industry and agriculture. In its economic aims, it seeks mass production and low costs and profit to owners. In its general aims, it seeks democracy and morality through adjustment of diverse interests and peace through balance of power. But this capitalist economy has only been beneficial. According to Lohia capitalism in underdeveloped countries can not even carry out its own function of raising capital. In the white countries, capital, population, technology have all grown together. So that there has been no insurmountable imbalance. In Asia and other similar areas, populations have grown, white capital and technology have lagged far behind so that socialism alone can now master the problems it has based on profit motive and there is no scope of profit in the underdeveloped countries.

Lohia said 'such a capitalism can no longer be pruned or amended, it must be uprooted and there is not much time to lose.'

IDEAS OF COMMUNIST ECONOMY

Lohia also made a several attack on communist economy which could not provide prosperity to the underdeveloped countries. Lohia said, 'communism is a doctrine of social ownership and of release of means of production from their relations of private property. It foresees a stateless society, but for it, it believes in a centralised party and a centralised state. Lohia pointed out : 'To communism, the morality of stateless society is in no contradiction with the immorality of a dictatorial party and state, for it has achieved such a complete integration of economic and general aims that the latter inevitably flow from the former.'

Hence the whole Communist doctrine and its general theory of human civilisation are proving faulty, for the capitalist relations of productions are snapping where the forces of production are least developed in the area of high density and low technology.

The greatest fault of Communism is that it only wants to smash the capitalist relations of productions, but inherits from capitalism its technique of production. The another defect of Communist Party is that it believes that general aims of the society do flow out of economics aims. But the communists do not show any new way to rationalise the underdeveloped economy.

DEFECTS OF THE PRESENT INDIAN ECONOMY

Lohia criticised the Indian economic system which without keeping in view Indian particular conditions of high population and poor equipment. He found that twin demons of imperialism and capitalism gripped the economy of India. In the Lok Sabha, Lohia said : "Indian capitalism is not modern it is feudal. The Indian capitalists earn so enormous profit that I wander how there can be such profit of 25 or 30 per cent." In Indian economy Lohia found that the triangle, consisting of politician, the bureaucrats and business man numbering about sixty lakhs was looting the country. Lohia pleaded for an end of this corrupt triangle. It is true that all the world over business and bureaucracy work together. But India due to caste bifurcation, some special caste supply the politicians, the bureaucrats and the businessmen. Lohia said, in India business and politics are in hard and glove. They are the part of the same family. One part deals with business, the others with politics. To end this corruption provision should be made that persons holding high posts in politics should refrain from entering their relatives in high posts through back doors.

Another defect of Indian economy is that in India both the public and private sectors are equally inefficient and greedy. Lohia said : "Everywhere the private sector is more conscious of profit earning but manages better. The public sector has greater consciousness of duty but suffers from a certain amount of mismanagement. This is all over the World. In India both sectors have learnt the vices of each other, the public sector has become greedy. While private sector has learnt mismanagement.

Lohia is also criticised of present planning in India. Indian planning has greatly suffered because of enormous expenses on modernising of consumption while all saving should have been used on instrument for building the means of production. Due to the defective of planning in each Five Years Plan period five to ten lakhs of the population attain the European standards, on the other hand, Lohia, while describing socialist concept of planning said, "the S.P. stand for a planning which will aim not at the spectacular progress however slow of the whole population. Such a planning must begin with a process of simultaneous leveling sown of the peak of wealth and prosperity and leveling up of the deep depressions of poverty. When the whole population of the country has been brought within a reasonable range of inequality, the fruits of planning and enterprise will be available not to a few but to all."

Lohia said, Indian economy is not expanding as it is based on the motive of 'grab-what-you-can' and increase 'one's-own-share'.

IDEAS OF SMALL-UNIT MACHINE

Lohia's view of idea of small-unit machine has arisen out of specific need of the Indian situation, where the relationship of available manpower and possible investment is almost inversely different from that among the Euro-American peoples. While in India there is a scarcity of investment and profusion of manpower.

Lohia, clarifying his conception an interview at Athen's in Oct. 1961. He argued : "By small-unit-machine I don't means cottage industries that may be put to work by electricity and light. I would like to have a small unit machine which is propelled with some kind of power-electricity atomic power or hydrogen power, which is this megaton power, whatever you call it. So the thing which I have in mind is more modern that the current practices."

Lohia totally rejected the idea of large-scale industries. He wanted, that the Bureau of scientific management should entrusted with the job of inventing for us precisely these small-unit-machines.

Ownership of the small unit machines should also be decentralised. While the large-scale industries like Iron and Steel, Railway, etc. Should be nationals, the ownership of small-unit-Machine should go to district and village government as well as to the produces and peasants' co-operative.

PRICE POLICY

The control over price fluctuation is a decisive factor for regulating the economy of a country. Abnormal rise and fall in the prices cause hardship both to the producers and the consumers. Hence, Lohia wanted to keep the price fluctuation within limits. According to Lohia 'prices and wages are two bullocks of a cart'. If one goes fast and other doesn't keep pace with his partner, that cart is bound to break down.

Lohia, some suggestion for controlling the prices fluctuations as followed :

(a) The sale price of essential manufactured commodities should under no circumstance exceed one and a half times their cost of production which means that the tax and profit must be kept within limits. For example, if 60 *Paisa* is the cost of production, the sale prices should be 90 *Paisa* including all taxes and profit.

(b) Fluctuations in the prices of grains should not exceed between two harvests.

(c) A relationship of justice and parity must exist between the agricultural and the industrial prices and farmers must get prices that cover their cost and minimum standard.

Parity Between Agricultural and Industrial Prices

Lohia said, the principle of parity between the agricultural and industrial prices does justice to all the sections of the population and ensures production and well-being. In many countries, bureau functions whose main job is to work out cost of production, price index and profit rates between agriculture and industry. These bureaus arrive at a legitimate norm and when prices fluctuate from this norm, steps are taken to restore the balance.

Nationalisation of Big Industries

Lohia wanted immediate nationalisation of foreign companies. These foreign companies earn huge profits and take back their capital in two or three years. He also wanted that the government should Nationalise all mass producing property, native and foreign.

AGRICULTURAL POLICY

Lohia emphasised the interest of farmers in fixing the prices of agriculture produces rather than the interest of those agencies which involved in marketing of those products. He wanted intensive farming so that there could be more production on a small piece of land. He wanted co-operative relation between mill-owners and farmers. He stressed upon increasing productivity through co-operative efforts, non-intervention of bureaucarts and active participation of farmers in the management of agriculture and development of new systems of production.

To conclude, it can be said that Ram Manohar Lohia has a great vision of revolutionary struggle against exploitation and wished to establish the economy based on equality. I would like to conclude the paper with the words of Lohia, "I want to transform the economic struggle into freedom struggle. I want social, economic and political revolution which can't come the other way." If his ideas would have been implemented then the face of India might have changed having her head high.

References

Alexander Gray (1963), "The Socialist Traditions", London, p. 462.

Chandradeo Prasad, 'Political Ideas of Dr. Ram Manohar Lohia.' Janki Prakashan, Ashok Rajpath, Chauhatta, Patna – 4 [Published, 1989], p. 135.

Danial Thorner (1956), "The Agrarian Prospect in India", pp. 78-79.

Gandhi, M.K. *Harijan,* July 26, p. 238.

Kirplani, J.B. (1965), "Gandhi and Lohia", *Janta,* Dec. 12.

Limaye, Madhu (1958), "Problem of Socialist Unity of India", *Mankind,* Oct.

Lohia, Ram Manohar, "Fragments of a World Mind", Allahabad n.d., p. 3.

Lohia, Ram Mahohar (1963), 'Wheel of History', Hyderabad, Nav Hind Prakashan, pp. 2-3.

Lohia, Ram Manohar (1963), "Marx, Gandhi and Socialism", Hyderabad, Nav Hind Publication, pp. 74-75, 131-32.

Lok Sabha, Debates, Vol. 26, p. 2418.

Lok Sabha, Aug. 23, 1963.

Lok Sabha Speech, Feb. 25, 1964.

Narayan Jaiprakash (1954), "Socialism, Sarvodaya and Democracy", Bombay, Asia Publishing House, p. 235.

N.C. Mehrotra (1978), 'Lohia—A Study', Published by Atma Ram & Sons, Kashmeri Gate, Delhi, p. 167.

Wofford, Jr., Harries (1969), "Gandhi, Socialism and the Third Camp", *Mankind,* June-July.

12

Economic Ideas of Dr. Ram Manohar Lohia

BANARSI YADAV

Dr. Ram Manohar Lohia was a thinker, a unique leader and a rebel. He played an important part in the making of modern India. But Lohia was not an ivory tower philosopher or an academic system builder in the tradition of Kant, Hegel or Comte. He was essentially a man of action. Lohia says that an individual is both an end and a means. An individual is the product of enviornment. He is an end in himself. He is the maker of his distiny. He is free to be a aware of himself. As an end he is the unfolder of love unto all. It means that his love becomes universal. He sees one in all. But after being conscious of himself, he cannot remain a silent spectator. He cannot tolerate the miseries of the masses. He revolts against all sorts of tyranny. As a means he tries to mould the environment. Therefore, he is an end for the purpose of his awareness and a means for awareness of his relationships the purpose. According to Lohia, "The individual is both an end and a means, as an end, he is the unfolder of love unto all, as a means, he is the tool of revolutionary anger against tyranny." So Lohia's conception of the individual as an end as well as a means is different from the Gandhian thinking which regards the individual as an end and not as a means.

Lohia was a disciple of Gandhi and drew inspiration from him. He firmly believed in Gandhian tenets but at the same time he was a born rebel and iconoclast always ready to demolish what did not stand the test of the ideas, democratic norm and human values.

Lohia was not a professional economist. He was a political thinker as well as activist who confronted all the problems of socio-economic and political system of the country. He was a firm supporter of the symbotic relationship between man, society and nature which has been disturbed by modern technology, large-scale production and indiscriminate industrialization based on capital intensity and imported technology without considering the absorptive capacity of the economy and adaptability of the people.

Lohia looked at the problems of reconstructions and revolution in the context of India. He took into account the peculiarities of the Indian situation, namely:

1. predominance of custom and tradition,
2. widespread illiteracy and lack of education,
3. the vestiges of the feudal order and the prejudices and irrationalities associated with it,
4. the vastness of India's population,
5. the rural inhabitation of the great bulk of the population,
6. the tendency of the people to rely on fate or force external, political or divine,
7. caste ridden structure of the Indian society,
8. relegation of a vast number of the population to the status of servility and dependence,
9. backwardness of the vast sections of society including the female folk, and
10. interlinking between social backwardness and economic poverty. Or between caste and poverty.

In view of all these facts Lohia held the socialist challenge in India was more serious than it had been in Europe. Apart from that, the vastness of India's population made the question of technology or developmental strategy very important. In India there was lack of capital and technical skill, but there was too much to be employed in the terms of production. Here hands were too many and capital was scarce. This meant that India could not follow, benefit, the development strategy of Europe or Russia. In this context Gandhian ideas, supported by Nurksean techniques, would have been more appropriate and better suited to the Indian conditions. In view of the Socio-economic conditions prevailing in the country, Lohia advocated adoption of small tool technology and also suggested for evolving appropriate technology for the third world. Those technology is fit for India which did not require too much of capital and which allowed and encouraged a labour intensive approach to development.

In fact, among the socialists and leftists of India it was Lohia who alone came under the greatest influence of Gandhi's ideas regarding revolution and development. He not only appreciated Gandhi's view of the unity of means and ends, but also his stress on peaceful struggle and his advocacy of a small machine technology on the basis of which decentralized production could be carried on in countless villages and job opportunities could be provided to the vast masses.

Lohia holds that the kind of technology that has been adopted in the west, the technology geared to heavy and capitalist production and intended for trade and commerce and therefore, of the exploitation of the underdeveloped peoples of the world is unsuitable for the needs and conditions of the Afro-Asian countries. The capitalist mode of production developed as it has been in the west thus, cannot be beneficially employed for the purposes of socialist reconstruction.

Gandhi and Lohia reject the western capitalist model of production and development and both advocate small machine technology in view of the peculiarities of India's problems and as consistent with the demands of justice and equality. But while the Gandhian choice for the simple and small machine is promoted by his great concern for the ideals of truth and non violence, that of Lohia is inspired by his passion for socialism or his concern for equality and justice. Gandhi's approach is spiritual and philosophical. Lohia's is empirical, socialistic and scientific.

According to Lohia, the problem of industrialisation is different for the retarded people. No industrial policy was formulated in pre-independence period and even post-independence industrial-policies were also not in consonance with the existing conditions of the country and they failed to serve the purpose.

For economic development and poverty eradication programmes question of resource constraints are frequently raised. In order to raise capital in India, Lohia came out with a number of suggestions. The following suggestions are in addition to Food Army and Small-Unit Industrialisation:

1. Abolition of privy purses and special privileges.
2. Stoppage of production of articles for modernisation of consumption.
3. Abolition of special public school.
4. Ceiling on income and expenditure.
5. Transfer of government servants to productive work.
6. Nationalisation of big industries.
7. Taxation.
8. Voluntary labour (an hour to the nation).

These are various conditions which must be fulfilled before and developed in the course of industrialisation. More directly agricultural production should be sufficiently abundant to feed and nourish the whole population and provide for the nation a surplus for export. There is the need for the prior development of a powerful agricultural base to provide the means of industrialisation. Otherwise, we would be faced with alternative of being subjected either to an imperialist power or selling of the natural resources of the nation through the over-exploitation of mineral wealth.

Industrialisation on a mass scale, as Gandhi points out, would necessarily lead to passive or active exploitation of the villages, as the problems of competition and marketing come in. While Gandhi is driven to advocate a decentralized order by his faith in ideals of truth and non-violence. Lohia stands for a decentralized order in order realise the goal of democracy and socialism which he upholds as his paramount political ideals.

Lohia's choice for decentralisation is evident in his theory of the four-pillar state. Lohia's concept of four pillar state is based on democracy and socialism. The four-pillar states means The Village, The District, The Province and The State.

Lohia regarded redistribution of land not alone as an act of social justice, but primarily as a measure to increase production through voluntary development. Lohia categorically observed that the socialist plan of Indian Agriculture will consist of: (a) improvement in existing cultivation, and (b) extension of new farming. Extension of new cultivation will be undertaken either through a department or an autonomous organization. Lohia's view of agricultural development and rural uplift is in consonance with Gandhian ideas and particularly suited to Indian conditions. Lohia was supporter of the idea of co-operative farming to increase the production of agricultural sector and also for better and fuller utilisation of the agricultural tools and implements available to the farmers.

Lohia wanted that the agricultural problem of India must be considered from the angle of its depressed personnel. They were: (a) Agricultural labourers, (b) Sharecroppers, and (c) Old tillers of economic holdings. For them, Lohia also suggested such programme as: (i) improving agricultural wage, (ii) legal and actual fixation of the sharecroppers' share at the minimum of 2/3rd of the produce, and (iii) abolition of rent on uneconomic holdings.

As a first step towards land reform, Lohia wanted a drastic change in agrarian land ownership. Even a few days before independence. Lohia suggested that the declaration of independence should at the time be accompanied with the issue by the government of a proclamation abolishing landlordism. Unless this is done the man in the street would not feel that India is entering the temple of freedom.

Lohia suggested to prepare special seven year plan for irrigation of agricultural land and advised the government to invite America and Russia, the so-called friends of India, to help the government in preparing this plan and in executing it sincerely. He also suggested that provision for irrigational facilities free of cost to every inch of cultivable land.

In the view of Lohia Industry and agriculture taken together must be capable of absorbing the entire working force and for this purpose a proper balance between the two sectors must be brought about on the basis of appropriate technology. Regarding the techniques, it is to be admitted that labour is abundant and it can be organised for higher level of participation, duration and efficiency while capital is scarce. Lohia was opposed to indiscriminate industrialisation based on capital-intensive technology at the cost of the pauperisation of the villages and rural population.

India is not only underdeveloped in respect of economic parameter but also in social, cultural and other respect. The problem of economic backwardness is a complex one and it can be solved only when all these economic and non-economic factors are taken into consideration.

Lohia raised the problem of caste, language, educational system, etc. as essential factors of economic development. For changing the socio economic structure, it is essential to change the outlook of the people.

According to Lohia, caste has caused shrinkage of abilities and opportunities and as a result, ninety percent of the population has become mentally paralysed and atropied. He held that the caste system and the hierarchical-order based on birth were the single most important factor for the decline of this great nation and its repeated subjection to external aggression and foreign rule. He launched a "destroy caste" movement. In a traditionally unequal society, he said, equality cannot be established by merely providing equal opportunities to all.

Lohia was critical of the education policy of the government. He launched movement for "Angreji Hatao" and advocated that education should be imparted through mother tongue. Lohia wanted to replace English by the Indian languages because thereby the door to equality or equal opportunities would be opened to all.

Lohia shows serious concern with the problem of social

justice. Lohia's conviction is that without social revolution, mere economic transformation will not fulfil in India.

In this way, we can say that Lohia's formulation stems from what he has called the principle of equal irrelevance. According to this, capitalism and communism, being system of political and economic centralisation are not relevant to the Asian problem of progress with large populations and low capital equipment. Lohia has therefore, endeavoured a new approach by assimilation of Gandhian principle of immediacy into the triple tasks of industrialisation, people's revolution and decentralisation of power.

References

Almust, Ajay Singh (1998), Lohia: The Rebel Gandhian, Mittal Publications, New Delhi.

Arumugam, M. (1979), Socialist Thought In India: The Contribution of Ram Monohar Lohia, Sterling Publishers Pvt. Ltd., New Delhi.

Bhatnagar, Rajendra Mohan (1978), Dr. Ram Monohar Lohia: Bharat Ke Gaurav, Kitab Ghar, Delhi.

Madhu Limaye (2000), Galaxy of the Indian Socialist Leaders, B.R. Publishing Corporation (A Division of BRPC (India) Ltd.), Delhi.

Prasad, Chandradeo (1989), Political Ideas of Dr. Ram Manohar Lohia, Janki Prakashan, Patna, New Delhi.

Singh, Dr. R.B. (1989), India's Economic Development and Lohia's Thought, Pratipaksh Prakashan, 0-31, A-3, Dilshad Garden, Shahdra, Delhi.

Sharma, Dr. Yatindra Nath, Dr. Lohia (1979), Arth Darshan, Chitra Prakashan, Kanpur.

Thakur, Krishna Nandan, Dr. Ram Manohar Lohia Ke Arthik, Rajnitik Evam Samajik Vichar, S. Chand & Co. Ltd., Ram Nagar, New Delhi.

13

Dr. Lohia's Non-Marxist Socialist Path of Development

SHRMISHTHA PRITI AND INDURANI KESHARWANI

Dr. Ram Manohar Lohia (1910-67) was the most original Indian socialist thinker of mid-twentieth century. He was not an economic thinker in strict sense of the term. Neither he prescribed a model of economic development. He was a political thinker. Before Dr. Lohia, there was nothing like Indian Socialism. Indian socialists were either Marxists or believer in the ideology of western social democracy or Utopian Socialism or Fabian Socialism. The entire credit goes to Dr. Lohia who dedicated his life in shaping Indian form of Socialism from panchmarhi conference till the last breath of his life. The essence of socialist struggles in general and in India in particular are following seven Revolutions:

1. For equality between Man and woman.
2. Against political, economic and spiritual inequality based on skin and colour.
3. Against ineqality of backward and high groups or castes based on long tradition, and for giving special oppurtunities to the backward;

4. Against foreign enslavement and for freedom and world democratic rule.
5. For economic equality and planned production and against the existence of and attachment for private capital.
6. Against unjust encroachments on private life and for democratic methods.
7. Against weapons and for Satyagraha.

It is around these struggles or revolutions that Lohia weaved his thoughts and programmes, constantly spearheading movements that earned him the opprobrium from the upholders of the old order which these struggles sought to over turn. While studying at Berlin, Dr. Lohia realised the irrelevance of the internationalism of labour movement as envisaged by Karl Marx and the second world war created ideological convulsions that drove the worker more and more into their own-national cocoons. This futility of ideological dogmas made him an iconoclast and a thinker who sought to interlink precept with practice both at personal and political level. It was also he reason that the thought both capitalism and communism irrelevant for the establishment of socialist society in the Third Word. Lohia asserted that "communism inherited from capitalism is technique of production and only sought to smash the capitalist relation of production." But socialist system for third world has to develop its own technique of production. He advocated for intermediate technology relevant for non-Marxist path of socialist society.

The another salient feature of Lohia's concept of non-Marxist socialist path of development is his accent on production. Whereas all brands of western socialism including Scientific socialism of Karl Marx laid emphasis an distributive justice. Here he came nearer to Gandhism and developed his concept of decentralisation in a superb theoratical framework in his four-pillar system popularly called "Chaukhambha Raj." He also took from Gandhijee individual and mass civil disobedience against in all forms and for the creation of a new order of course he did not rule out pontaneous violence at a certain stage of an intense struggle by the people. However, he believed in peaceful struggle to change political and economic order to establish a socialist society.

In Dr. Lohia's model of development along with economic variables social paradigms also were combined in innate may and not mechanically. Here comes his original analysis of Caste *Vs.* Class. He held the view that static class is caste and dynamic caste is class. Caste denotes lack of immobilism and class stands for mobility. The wheel of history is full of examples of transference of class into caste and caste into class. The five thousand years of immobility in the Hindu Society has deprived the eighty percent of population from the full growth of their personality. Therefore, he advocated for special opportunities or preferential treatment of the socially deprived sections of humanity. He gave real meaning to the concept of equally but was vehemently criticised both by traditionalists and Marxists who believed in class and not in caste.

Dr. Lohia was a socialist in true sense of the term, in thought as well as in practice. For this he had to suffer a lot. Mahbub-ul-Haq following remarks apply to him, "I have always believed that those who make a virtue out of institutional confirmity and loyalty serve their institutions far more poorly than those who are willing to express their dissent and pay the necessary price. He was a freedom fighter. So, he was out and out against British rule. Once he said, "the greatest single factor that has caused the poverty of India is Britain's rule over India."

Dr. Lohia was in favour of possible equality and not absolute equality. While describing Socialist concept of planning once he said, "The S.P. Stands for a planning which will aim not at the spectacular progress of the few but the progress, however slow, of whole population. Such a planning must begin with a process of simultaneous levelling down of the peaks of wealth and prosperity and levelling-up of the deep depressions of poverty. When the whole population of the country has been brought within a reasonable range of inequality, the fruits of planning and enterprise will be available not to a few but to all. His reasonable range of inequality was 1:10. He was highly critical of western model and strategy of planning and held responsible for the growing unemployment, disparity and concentration of wealth in a few hands. His alternative strategy of planning was consistent with socio-economic conditions of India laying emphasis upon highest possible rate of growth, regional parities, self-sufficienty decentralised system and with appropriate technology where there is profusion of manpower and scarcity of capital. As an alternative to large scale technique Dr. Lohia proposed :

> "The mind must no longer be clogged by antiquated nations of large-scale industry or of cottage industry. A rigorous search must be made to see how far power whether in the form of oil or electricity or coal, can be used for the propelling of machines that do not need heavy capitalisation. Lohia also suggested structural changes in the industrial system capable of eliminating exploitation of all types and balance between agricultural and industrial prices. Price should not be more than 20 per cent of cost of production. Lohia's concept of food Army; an hour valuntary labour to nation and his views on agricultural development and rural uplift in is consonant with Gandhian idea's and suited to Indian Conditions.

In nutshell, Lohia believed that only four-pillar State, a decentralised social order and small-unit machine industrialisation can solve the problems of the retarded world when the twin objectives of prosperity and equality will be achieved. Symbolic relationship between man and society on the one hand and nature on the other will be restored which is necessary for harmony and cohesion in socio-economic system. He defined economic development in terms of prosperity and equality and asserted that equality without prosperity is meaningless and prosperity without equality is impossible in the Third World countries. Lohia believed in the proper balance between general aims, i.e. democracy, truthfulness, good conduct, peace of the heart and of the world, general state of culture with economic objectives; with ultimate objective of World parliament or government.

Dr. Lohia rejected Marxian analysis that imperialism is the highest stage of capitalism and held that both are twins. Marx is of opinion that capitalism digs its own grave on account of its inner contradictions. According to Lohia any civilisation not based on total efficiency is bound to crumble down in the long-run. To achieve total efficiency Dr. Lohia wanted to establish an egalitarian social system where all the people, irrespective of their caste, colour and sex would have an equal opportunity to develop their personality to the fullest possible extent.

Lohia raised the problem of Caste, language, educational system and religion as essential factors of economic development as against Marx who dwelt upon only economic factors, for changing the socio-economic structure, it is essential to change the outlook of the people. Attitudinal factors are important ingredients of development. Modernisation of people's outlook is a condition precedent to the modernisation of economic system.

It short, both Marx and Lohia thought of the emancipation of manking from poverty and exploitation but Marx wrote in the context of socio-economic canditions of western world while Lohia dealt with the problems of Third World with special reference to India where Marxian prescription does not apply, Marxian analysis was materialistic while Lohia combined materialism with spiritualism. To Marx the development of society was dialectic but to Lohia it was circular. Marx analysed the industrial society while Lohia concentrated on agrarian society. Marxian tool was class analysis to establish classless society while Lohia's total was caste analysis to establish casteless and classless society. Marxian assumption was internationalism of labour but Lohia analysed in national moorings except, the vision of world government. Marx believed in violent methods of class struggle but Dr. Lohia was essentially a votaries of non-violence, and peaceful means of struggle except possibility of sporadic brust of violence during struggle. Marx supported capitalist technique of productive while Dr. Lohia propounded the concept of Intermediate technology. To Marx only economic factors decided the destiny of society but Lohia included many social factors, other non-economic factors in the analysis of movement of Society. In fact; Dr. Lohia was the true and only original socialist thinker of Third World particularly in Indian context.

Lohia left the world 40 years ago and during the interval many disciples of Dr. Lohia got the opportunity to rule the country both at State and National level but sooner they came to power, they forgot the ideals for which Dr. Lohia stood. Their short sighted, selfish and corrupt practices for self-agrandisement have blurred the sharpness of Lohia's ideology. Dr. Lohia called himself 'Kujat Gandhiwadi' and in the same fashion thousands of Kujat Lohiawadi spread throughout India still uphold the values and ideals for which Dr. Lohia stood. Except some modifications on account of changing situation, Dr. Lohia's non-Marxist socialist path of development is relevant in the era of liberalisation and globalisation also. The porphecy of Dr. Lohia is true that "people donot listen to me but they will perhaps listen to me after my death." The relevancy of Dr. Lohia's ideas cannot be denied even today and perhaps for many more years to come.

References

T.P. Singh, (1991), Bhartiya Samajwad : Bhoot, Wartman Aur Bhavishya; Naya Sangharsh, February.

Dr. R.M. Lohia, Seven Revolutions; Navahind Prakashan, Hyderabad.

George Fernandes, Foreward of India's Ecomomic Development and Lohia's Thought, by Dr. R.K. Singh, p. vi.

Ibid. : pp. vi and vii.

Dr. R.M. Lohia, (1963), Marx, Gandhi and Socialism; Navahind Publications, Hyderabad, p. 203.

Ibid. : p. 216.

Dr. R.M. Lohia, Four-Pillar State.

Dr. R.M. Lohia, A Broachure, Navahind Publication; Hyderabad.

Dr. R.M. Lohia, Wheels of History, Navahind Publications, Hyderabad.

Dr. R.M. Lohia, Jati Pratha, Navahind Publication, Hyderabad.

Mohbubul Haque, Poverty Curtain.

Dr. R.M. Lohia (1940), Indian Economy in Figures; *The National Herald*, January 18.

Dr. R.M. Lohia, Quoted in India's Economic Development and Lohia's Thought by Dr. R.B. Singh.

Dr. R.M. Lohia, *Mankind*, May, 1957, p. 363.

Dr. R.M. Lohia, Fragments of World Hind, Navahind Publication, Hyderabad, p. 2.

Dr. R.M. Lohia, Marx, Gandhi and Socialism.

Dr. R.M. Lohia, Wheels of History.

14

Economic Ideas of Dr. Ram Manohar Lohia: Relevance for Indian Economy

Shambhu Deo Mishra and M. Masood Alam

The Economic ideas of Dr. Ram Manohar Lohia are most relevant for the present socio-economic conditions of India as well as of Bihar. In the words of Mahatma Gandhi *Lohia is a top-class scholar, civilised gentleman, has liberal ideology and high moral character.* In a meeting of the Congress Working Committee Gandhi said, *I cannot sit quiet as long as Dr. Ram Manohar Lohia is in prison. I do not yet know a person braver and simpler than him. He never propagated violence. Whatever he has done has increased his esteem and his honour.*

Dr. Lohia was a great propounder of economic development. He encouraged public involvement in post-freedom reconstruction. He pressed people to construct canals, wells and roads voluntarily in their neighborhood. He volunteered himself to build a dam on river Paniyari which is standing till this day and is called "Lohia Sagar Dam." Lohia said *satyagraha without constructive work is like a sentence without a verb.* He felt that public work would bring unity and a sense of awareness in the community. He also was instrumental in having 60 per cent of the seats in the legislature reserved for minorities, lower classes, and women. As a democracy, the Parliament of India was obliged to listen to citizens' complaints. Lohia helped create a day called "Janavani Day" on which people from around the nation would come and present their grievances to members of Parliament. The tradition continues even today. When he arrived in Parliament in 1963, the country had a one-party government through three general elections. Lohia shook things up. He had written a pamphlet, "25000 Rupees a Day", the amount spent on Prime Minister Jawaharlal Nehru, an obscene sum in a country where the vast majority lived on 3 annas (less than one-quarter of a rupee) a day. Nehru demurred, saying that India's Planning Commission statistics showed that the daily average income was more like 15 annas (a little under a rupee) per day. Lohia demanded that this was an important issue, one that cried out for a special debate. The controversy, still remembered in India as the "Teen Anna Pandrah Anna (3 annas—15 annas)" controversy. Member after member gave up his time to Lohia as he built his case, demolishing the Planning Commission statistics as fanciful. Not that the Commission was attempting to mislead, but the reality was that a small number of rich people were pulling up the average to present a wholly unrealistic picture. At that time, Lohia's figure was true for over 70 per cent of the population. Unlike the Marxist theories which became fashionable in the third world in the 50's and 60's, Lohia recognised that caste, more than class, was the huge stumbling block to India's progress. It was Lohia's thesis that India had suffered reverses throughout her history because people had viewed themselves as members of a caste rather than citizens of a country. Caste, as Lohia put it, was congealed class. Class was mobile caste. As such, the country was deprived of fresh ideas, because of the narrowness and stultification of thought at the top, which was comprised mainly of the upper castes, Brahmins and *Baniyas*, and tight compartmentalisation even there, the former dominant in the intellectual arena and the latter in the business. A proponent of affirmative action, he compared it to turning the earth to foster a better crop, urging the upper castes, as he put it, "to voluntarily serve as the soil for lower castes to flourish and grow", so that the country would profit from a broader spectrum of talent and ideas.

In Lohia's words, "Caste restricts opportunity. Restricted opportunity constricts ability. Constricted ability further restricts opportunity. Where caste prevails, opportunity and ability are restricted to ever-narrowing circles of the people." In his own party, the Samyukta (United) Socialist Party, Lohia promoted lower caste candidates both by giving electoral tickets and high party positions. Though he talked about caste incessantly, he was not a casteist — his aim was to make sure people voted for the Socialist Party candidate, no matter what his or her caste. His point was that in order to make the country strong, everyone needed to have a stake in it. To eliminate caste, his aphoristic prescription was, "Roti and Beti", that is, people would have to break caste barriers to eat together (Roti) and be willing to give their girls in marriage to boys from other castes (Beti).

Lohia was early to recognise that Marxism and Capitalism were similar in that both were proponents of the Big Machine. It was his belief that Big Industry was no solution for the third world (he even warned Americans, back in 1951, about their lives being taken over by big corporations). He called Marxism the "last weapon of Europe against Asia." Propounding the "Principle of Equal Irrelevance", he rejected both Marxism and Capitalism, which were often presented as the only alternatives for third world nations. Nehru too had a similar view, at least insofar as he observed to Andre Malraux that his challenge was to "build a just society by just means." Lohia had a strong preference for appropriate technology, which would reduce drudgery but not put the common man at the mercy of far away forces. As early as 1951, he foresaw a time of the 'monotonic mind', with nothing much to do because the problems of living had been all addressed by technology. Aside from the procedural revolution of non-violent civil disobedience, bridging the rich-poor divide, the elimination of caste and the revolution against incursions of the big-machine, other revolutions in Lohia's list included tackling Man-Woman inequality, banishing inequality based on color, and that of preserving individual privacy against encroachment of the collective.

Many of Lohia's revolutions have advanced in India, some with greater degrees of success than others. In some instances the revolutions have led to perverse results which he would have found distasteful. However, Lohia was not one to shy away from either controversy or struggle. Lohia believed that a party grew by taking up causes. He was a strong believer in popular action. In India's parliamentary system, where elections could be called even before the term was over, he once said that "Live communities don't wait for five years (the term of the parliament)", meaning that a government which misruled should be thrown out by the people. He carried out this idea by moving the first no-confidence motion against the Nehru government, which had by then been in office for 16 years.

Lohia is often called a maverick socialist, a cliched but nevertheless apt description. He gave that impression not to be controversial, but because he was always evolving his thoughts, and like his mentor, Gandhi, did not hesitate to speak the truth as he saw it. He often surprised both supporters and opponents. He astounded everyone by calling for India to produce the bomb, after the Chinese aggression of 1962. He was anti-English, saying that the British ruled India with bullet and language (bandhook ki goli aur angrezi ki boli). Full of unforgettable phrases which would characterise a point of view, he captured who was a member of India's ruling class in with near-mathematical precision that have not been bettered in three decades—"high-caste, wealth, and knowledge of English are the three requisites, with anyone possessing two of these belonging to the ruling class." The definition still holds.

Lohia wanted to abolish private schools and establish upgraded municipal (government) schools which would give equal academic opportunity to students of all casts. This he hoped would help eradicate the divisions created by the caste system. At the Socialist Party's Annual Convention, Lohia set up a plan to decentralise the government's power so that the general public would have more power in Indian politics. He also formed Hind Kisan Panchayat to resolve farmers' everyday problems. Lohia was a socialist and wanted to unite all the socialists in the world to form a potent platform. He was the General Secretary of Praja Socialist Party. He established the World Development Council and eventually the World Government to maintain peace in the world.

In find Dr. Lohia imparted to socialism an earnestness and dynamism much needed in the context of the problems of reconstruction and development along the lines of the values of creativity, justice, equality and freedom—the values which he called eternal in significance. He emancipated socialism from the anaemic schism of European socialism and projected it as an independent and full-fledged system of social transformation in its various aspects—political, economic, cultural and spiritual. He advanced socialism as a revolutionary yet democratic ideology with the dimensions that are variegated but well concatenated. In developing socialism as a complete and coherent philosophy and ideology of social reconstruction, Lohia adopted numerous insights of Gandhi in order to ensure that socialism could deliver not only the immediate but also the permanent goods of life and at the same time save humanity from the evils that bedevilled the realisation of its values of justice, freedom and dignity of man and equality and real democracy at the hands of Europe, the then Soviet Union and the United States. It was on the basis of the Gandhian insight of Satyagraha that he forged his weapon of struggle in keeping with the spirit of democracy and reverence for the forms of life, including particularly the human. Again, it was the Gandhian idea of importance of the small machine technology which showed him the path of solving India's problems of employment while, at the same time, avoiding the pitfalls associated with the heavy industrialism of the west.

In Gandhi's emphasis on decentralisation and people's participation, Lohia found the key to making socialism democratic and democracy socialist. Unless resource is had to these twin avenues, the people cannot avoid the evils of Capitalism with its possessiveness and Communism with its tendency to stamp out diversity and suppress creativity with its proneness to regimentation.

References

Ideas and Society (2004), India Between the Sixteenth and Eighteenth Centuries, Eugenia Vanina. Reprint. New Delhi, Oxford University Press.

Ideas on Socialism and Social Justice : A Study of Jawaharlal Nehru, Rammanohar Lohia and Asoke Mehta, Santanu Bagchi. New Delhi, Kanishka, 2002, x, pp. 224.

Identity, Consciousness and the Past (1997), Forging of Caste and Community in India and Sri Lanka : Edited by H.L. Seneviratne, pp. 207.

Ideologies and Social Work (2002), Historical and Contemporary Analyses by Murli Desai. New Delhi, Rawat Pub., pp. 235.

Ideology and Political Theory (2003), A Study with Special Reference to the Disintegration of the Soviet Union by Kundan Kumar. New Delhi, Discovery, xxviii, pp. 260.

I.K. Gujral (1997), New Hope of India by S. Vandana, pp. 298.

Lohia (1998), The Rebel Gandhian : Ajay Singh 'Almust', pp. 256.

The Idea of Delhi, Edited by Romi Khosla, Mumbai, Marg, 2005, pp. 132.

The Idea of Rajasthan, Edited by Karine Schomer, 1994, 2 Vols, Vol. I, pp. 419, Vol. II, 319.

The Ideal of India : Secular Democracy with Development by Ranjit Sau. Kolkata, K.P. Bagchi, 2001, xiv, pp. 176.

15

Governance, Democracy and Development in Bihar

CHANDRIKA PRASAD

INTRODUCTION

Politics and economics are without doubt the two main disciplines that determine policy choice in any country. Democracy came in power with French Revolution and rapid economic development started in Industrial Revolution of England. Political compulsions have, in the past, been the main drivers of economic reforms in India and China. Although Governance, Democracy and Development is difference in tone and content. Both are related to each other. Development as the process of enhancing people's capabilities for improving quality of life. Human development is defined as a process of enlarging people's choice to lead a long and healthy life, to acquire knowledge and be educated, and to have access to resources needed for decent level of living.

A striking feature of most of the recent writing, cutting across different disciplines, is the universal administration for India's democracy combined with dis-satisfaction with its actual functioning and its failure to deliver sufficient benefits to the people. Another common theme is the recognition of its vast economic potential along with frustration with the slow pace of reforms in the governance and administrative structure. At the beginning of the twenty-first century. India's relation as a democracy and as an emerging global economic power is at its peak. On the other hand, not so long ago, in 1991, India went through one of its worst economic crisis. While on the surface economists, political leaders and administrators are working together in a more fundamental sense, the reality is vastly different. Poorer social groups appear to have a limited capacity to present a reform agenda that addresses issues of basic rights and ensures livelihoods.

STUDY PLACE BIHAR

Bihar was the part of Bengal Province which was upgraded a separate province on the 12th December, 1910 and Orissa was separated in 1936. Again on November 15, 2000 a new state Jharkhand separated. There are Himalayan Hills and Nepal in the North and Jharkhand in the South. Utter Pradesh in the West and West Bengal in the east. It is purely an agricultural state. The population of Bihar is 8.29 crores.

There is no universal reason why Punjab is rich and Bihar is poor. Bihar is the most sufferer state in India. Regional disparities continue to hunt the policy-makers. At a certain times, the issue has become explosive warranting immediate attention from the policy-makers. The investment pattern like governments, financial institutions and Foreign Direct Investment has been found to be perpetuating regional disparities. This has influenced and been influenced by the level of infrastructure development across the state. Bihar has lowest level of infrastructure facilities as compared to those available in rich state. There should be considerable investment in infrastructure development.

WHY DOES GOVERNANCE AND ECONOMY LAG BEHIND OTHER STATES?

As Bihar is one of the least developed states of India,

the state Government has had a weak resource-base. There is huge migration of farm labourers from Bihar to other developed states. The absence of a good and efficient government is a great of stable to economic progress. As a matter of fact, Bihar has been branded by most outsiders as "a state of non-governance", which in turn is closed related to caste, a vicious circle that has nurtured feudalism and hampered social and economic progress. The political instability of the state in the immediate past was a build-up from those social tensions. But even during the period the government enjoyed stability the state did of travel much further on the road to economic progress due to a weak political will to take decisive and firm action. Casteism is one of the most formidable obstacles to the social and economic progress of the state. The growth of a new outlook on life and work has been slower in Bihar because of the age old hold of the feudal and semi-feudal mentality. Female education self-help groups and co-operative movements too have progressed less, in consequence thereof, of late, the villages in Bihar have become the scene of plunder, kidnaping, killing and loot. Extreme poverty of Bihar retards its economic growth, and its retarded economic growth reinforces its poverty. The behaviour of government plays an important role in stimulating or discouraging economic activity.

Some components of human development indicators for health and education continue to lag behind the improvement in income and India's rank in terms of Human Development Index (HDI) and Gender Development Index (GDI) continue to be low compared to even some countries of our region. India ranked 127 in HDI for 2002 and 103 in GDI in which Bihar is in the lowest rank. High regional disparity in HDI across the states has also been a source of concern. The colonical effect was also important. The British administration had been about two hundred years while there was one hundred years that administration in Punjab. But, after independence, the government should improve the various problems which was not done. Land improvement is the most burning problems before the Bihar government. Even today, about 60 per cent M.L.As. or M.L.Cs. are in the grip of feudal or semi-feudal nature of the society. The existing bureaucratic organisation have developmed for the maintenance of law and order, collection of revenue is inadequate for carrying out the tasks of development change. There is necessity of restructuring the bureaucratic organisation on one hand a radical change in the orientation, attitude and behaviour pattern of the bureaucrats on the other hand for the transformation of rural society steeped in ignorance and lacking in resources. A majority of administrations are developmentalists, but the level of their commitment in mode missing value is low.

Development and administration are closely related. Development and mass common welfare have remained basic objectives of the welfare government. The planning, schemes, projects, etc. of a government to change the socio-economic face of a society or to constitute and egalitarian society cannot be implemented until administrative branch of the government is efficient enough. No developmental scheme can be implemented fully and efficiently without strong, smart, honest and active administrators. If administrators are corrupt and inactive or non-interested in the welfare scheme, nothing remarkably can be achieved. Moreover, corruption in administration is like a paralysis. Much depends upon the will and interest of the administrators who are made responsible for implementing development schemes, people's participation in administration is also a valid point. Today when government is committed to change the socio-economic face of the people and rural areas, it has become much more important to allow the people to participate in development administration.

NEED TO IMPROVEMENT

Good governance and strong political will power are the main solution of Bihar. China is marching ahead with over 10 per cent gross domestic product (GDP) growth rates over the last two decades. China has followed a conventional path is transiting from an agricultural economy to a robust industrial economy. India's GDP growth is 6 per cent over the last decade. Bihar's GDP growth is from 1 to 27 and which is the lowest. At present, the Bihar government has announced the strictly implementation of good governance for development which his reasonable and useful. His main objectives is to bring up the good governance.

To discipline the Government servants upon whose shoulders the responsibility to implement the policies lies, there is an urgent need to take strict disciplinary action against those who are found indulged in corruption or whose who are shirking from the responsibility. It is observed that the bureaucratic pattern of Bihar is still based on the line established by the British whose only aim was to maintain law and order, and collect revenues. Bureaucrats should be compiled to change their old concept of thinking. They should realise that they are servants of the people not the masters. To corrupt authorities must be given hard punishment including discharge from their services. It would be better if some special courts are constituted with the power to award summary decision to deal with such corrupt administrators of Government Services.

To make the society free from criminals, kidnappers, the anti-social elements like smugglers, hoarders, black marketers, etc., suitable laws with severe penalty must be passed. No mercy should be shown to these elements because they are the real enemy of the people.

It is fact that the Government has failed to arrest tax evasion and unearth blackmoney. The public works have been badly affected due to stagnation of money. Hence all the possible efforts should be applied in this regard.

The unemployment is mounting over. They have last their faith in the principles of social justice incorporated in the constitution. They have lost their faith in the ways and means adopted by the Government to remove poverty and reduce economic inequality.

Problems of land reform is very important. Political and caste consideration have motivated official in their anti-land reform attitudes. Consolidation of holding is firstly necessary. Lack of political will is responsible. So, political will should be created. For this landless, small and marginal farmers representatives should be given representation in local panchayat bodies and Ministries so, it has been recognised to constitute a vital element both in terms of the anti-poverty strategy and for modernisation and increased productivity in agriculture.

Bihar was one of the first states to take-up the co-operative movement but today due to large scale corruption and bungling the whole thing is virtually in shamble. Loan recovery has been disappointing. Most defaulters come from amongst the rural rich rather than from the poorer sections. Another important area, where all citizens can play a role, is to ensure that the movement towards universal literacy is accelerated. There is already a strong statewide consensus on this score. However, the progress in reaching this goal has been slower than planned. All local institutions including Panchayats have to assume greater responsibilities in this area. Literacy among all those who are entitled to vote and select their representatives in local bodies, legislatures and parliament would ensure that political leaders are accountable for delivering what they promise to the people in their manifestors or their joint Common Minimum Programme.

However, as we have seen, the democratic governance has not yet been able to eliminate the worst form of poverty. Despite some of its limitations, Bihari is feeling enjoy in constitutional democracy, with a free press, independent judiciary, freedom of speech, freedom to join political parties and free elections in which millions of voters cast their vote and choose their government. An important task for the future is to further enhance the freedom that we already have, and to remove some of the limitations of the political system so that a reformist and distributive economic agenda become a reality.

References

Bimal Jalan (2006), The Future of India, Penguin Books, New Delhi.

K.N. Prasad (1983), Problem of Indian Economic Development, Sterling Publishers Private Ltd., New Delhi.

Ram Sakal Singh (2006), Rural Poverty, Anmol Publications Pvt. Ltd., New Delhi, First Published.

Eco. & Pol. Weekly, Vol. XLI, No. 30, July 29-August 4, 2006, p. 3321.

Eco. & Pol. Weekly, Vol. XL No. 10, March 5-11, 2005, p. 934.

Economic Survey, Govt. of India, 2004-05.

16

Economic Philosophy of Lohia

Ravi Shankar Bhakta and Bijay Kumar Prasad

In fact economic Philosophy of Lohia came out with a new will and approach at might be linked with word Justice and Welfare. Lohia visulised the economic inequality. Both national and international inequalities are related with each other and hence affect each other. So far inequality among the nations is not removed, inequality within a nation cannot be completely eliminated. But efforts to stay both the monsters of poverty and inequality should continue and one should not be postponed for the sake of the other.

ECONOMIC PHILOSOPHY OF LOHIA

Lohia wanted to end the era of extravagance, wasteful expenditure, production-oriented economy and confiscation of property acquired by graft and corruption. He opposed the idea of mixed economy. On the other hand, he wanted immediate and complete socialisation of all the industries, both Indian and foreign; ceiling on all the incomes, official and non-official, so that the maximum might not be more than ten times to minimum; postponement of the modernization of consumption till such time as the means of production had been thoroughly renovated and retionalised on the basis of big machines where necessary and small-unit technology where possible. To Lohia, the co-existence of public and private sectors in our caste-ridden society has brought corruption and is responsible for an unholy alliance between the capitalist and the bureaucracy.

LOHIA VIEW ON CAPITALIST DEVELOPMENT

The fascination of Marxism does not lie in its ultimate aim, but in its analysis of capitalism and the analysis gives birth to the ultimate aim. To Lohia, "the essential core of Marxist doctrine is the analysis of capitalist development." And 'with the elemental force of this sociological law of capitalism ties up the ultimate picture of society which Marx and Engels drew'. Lohia realised the Marx did not give a consistent theory of capitalist development. "His initial fallacy was to have examined capitalism in the abstract, and to have wranched it outside of its imperialist contest. He painted the picture of capitalism only on the basis of west Europe entity, with the later additions of America and Japan to its fold, with him the capitalist dynamic is placed within its internal structure, 'in the contradiction between the value and use-value of labour-power, between the working class and the capitalist class of the selfsame structure'. Lohia remarked:

> "Marx's capitalism was that of a self-moving west European circle, no doubt causing great repercussions in the outside world, but the principle and laws of its own movement were exclusively internal. Marxism to this day remains stuck in this picture, no doubt formulating laws about these outside repercussions, but wholly unable to state the basic interacting principle of the two, internal and external, movements of capital."

In order to shatter this unreat Marxist picture, Lohia gave his own theory of capitalist development. To Lohia, capitalism did indeed arise in West Europe, grew in West Europe, and attained its full maturity there, but even while it grew, it took a lot of dynamic out of the territories which came under its imperialist control, but which were not part of West Europe. In order, therefore, to understand capitalist economy as consisting not alone of an internal circle represented by the West Europan economy but of two circles, an internal West European circle and an external world circle, from which the internal West European circle draws its dynamic, its surplus value, its exploitation, its sucking and so on, Lohia in his speck in Hyderabad in August 1952, rightly asserted:

> "Marx was of course very much aware of the fact that these capitalist economics of West Europe had drawn a great deal of profit from Asia and other countries of the world. This awareness is to be seen in many utterances of Marx. But it acts as an addendum to his main doctrine. It does not act as an integral part of his doctrine but somewhat like the tail of an animal" which the internal West European circle draws its dynamic from the external world, Lohia came to the conclusion that capitalism as a historical entity has produced a greatest contradiction between increasing forces of production in the West European capitalist economy and decreasing forces of production in the rest of the world."

Due to such a capitalist development in the past 300 years, the people of Asia have been reduced to the status of 'half-horse and half man'. Forces of production have tended to decrease in two-thirds of the world, including Asia, population has tended to increase, and, therefore, living standards have to go down. Depicting the picture of poverty in two-thirds of the World. Lohia said: "An abysmal poverty prevails in this two-thirds of the World. It appears as though capitalism had made a compact with imperialism that almost all its progress would be located in the master lands, while nearly all the misery would be inflicted on the colonial countries. Lohia also included Russia as a member of the European family."

Another defect in the Marxist doctine of capitalist development is that in it 'riches and poverty' should go along side in a single region or country, fabulous riches and abysmal poverty should exist side by side. But according to the law of capitalist development the richer a country has become under the capitalist civilisation, the narrower is its scope of inequality; the poorer a country has become the wider is its scope of inequality. Lohia pointed out: "There is far greater inequality in India and such like countries than there is in America and England or else where."

Hence, the socialists must try to shatter the established notion and frame out new laws of capitalist development and surplus value. As this law of capitalist development has been proved wrong, and as there is possibility of the capitalist chain snapping not in the area where the forces of production have been stunted and dwarfed, an entirely new thinking becomes necessary.

LOHIA VIEW ON SURPLUS VALUE

Lohia explained the theory of surplus value in context of the joint capitalist-imperialist development. To him, capitalism, like any other sociological phenomenon is not just an abstract entity. It is an historical phenomenon, it has to be understood in all its historical aspects.

In brief, Marx theory of surplus values is based on the theory that 'labour is the sole creator of value'. Marx says that human labour, unlike other commodity, has two values. It has a use value and an exchange value. In other words, human labour has two values, one which the labourer himself gets in the from of his wages and the other which the employer gets as a share in total produce. These two are different. The labourer does not get all that he produces, and therefore, there is a Margin between the result of labour and the payment for it, that which is paid out to the labourer himself and which the capitalist or employer receives for himself, the wages and the profits, and the Marx in what is ordinarily called in Marxist doctrine, surplus value. But to Lohia, all this needs to be restated in the light of both labour's value and use values.

Lohia observed Marx's weakness in treating labour as an ideal abstract entity. It is based on the doctrine that capitalism is only a West-European entity. It has neglected the historical phenomenon and it should be understood in its historical aspects. In the historical career of capitalism during the past 300 or 400 years it is essentially a phenomenon which has involved such a traffic as from India, China, Malaya and Burma to England, France, Germany and like countries.

While explaining his theory Lohia has pointed out that labour under capitalism has two forms—'imperial and colonial'—and there is a vast difference in their values. For the proper understanding of the sources of the surplus value, we must keep in our mind the distinction between imperial and colonial labour and their wages.

Historical development has proved that a colonial labourer can work even on a very meager wage. Thus, we find two distinct wages of labour—those effective in the imperial countries and those effective in the colonies. 'This distrinction between imperial labour and colonial labour and their respective wages is of utmost importance for a proper understanding of the source of surplus labour." Similarly, the concept of use-labour, i.e., produce of labour should be considered in contest of the joint capitalist imperialist development. The current high produce of labour of many generations of the labourers of the colonies.

Some economists, including the Communists, praise the high productivity of labour in Western countries and try to explain it on a number of grounds, viz., necessary requirements of labour, productivity of labour, capitalist, enterprise and natural resources. But Lohia does not agree with such propositions. To him, the people should keep this formula in their mind 'that labour's use of muscle power and skill is the same all over the World, and granted equal conditions of techniques would yield equal produce'. Yet the high produce of imperial labour is due to the many generations of imperial-colonial division of labour in the World. Lohia said:

> "Behind this fantastic exchange lies the history of layer upon layer of saved labour from generations of tillers and miners of India, China, Java, Malaya, Africa, South America and other lands, which has continually been

> converted into the gigantic machine of England, Germany and Japan." To Lohia, 'One might almost say that the ghosts of hundreds of millions of colonial toilers are invisibly moving the machines in imperial factories. The highly elaborate machinery, and its continuing improvement in capitalist countries are due, in large part to the surplus value, created on colonial firms and mines'.

Hence, if capitalism has extracted surplus value from its home labourers by paying them less than what they produce, upon this extraction it has continually acted the far greater surplus value derived from colonial toilers. Now it is difficult to calculate how much the rich persons and the vast middle classes of England and Germany, receive surplus value from the home labour from colonial labour and in what ration. In order to get of his labyrinth, Lohia advised: "We must for ever abandon the habit of examining a country's economic structure as a self-moving entity, we must, therefore, abandon the Marxist understanding of capitalism as a self–moving West European entity. Capitalism from its origin to its recent, most development has moved mainly on the imperial dynamic." The only way to understand it is to group at the same time the internal and the external dynamics of capitalism. So, we have to evolve a new theory which does not consider the isolated produce of labour within a single economic structure, but as a world total production averagely distributed over its working population.

Thus, surplus value cannot be calculated, nor understood on the basis of difference between labour's requirements and its produce as expounded by the Communists. It is the difference between the actual earnings of labour and the per-worker World production of the time. To Lohia, surplus value is mainly derived from the colonial forms, fields and mines.

Lohia defined surplus values as follows:

> "Labour, whether of the peasant or the factory worker, creates surplus value to the extent that its earnings fall below the average per worker world production of its time."

III. LOHIA VIEW ON PRICE POLICY

The control over price fluctuation is a decisive factor for regulating the economy of a country. Abnormal rise and fall in the prices cause hardship both to the producers and the consumers. Hence, Lohia wants to keep the price fluctuation within limits. According to Lohia, 'prices and wages are two bullocks of a cart. If one goes fast and the other does not keep pace with his partner, that cart is bound to break down'. In a press conference at Calcutta on March 24, 1961, Lohia pointed out:

"In a civilised society, incomes and prices must keep in step, but in India, prices gallop at horse speed, while incomes lag behind at donkey pace. Pay Commissions and interim relief for Government servants and others are just no solutions at all. What is needed is a Permanent Prices Commission for the orphaned, consumers of the country, which means the entire population, bar the top million." For controlling the price fluctuations, Lohia wanted certain directive principles to be followed:

1. The sale price of essential manufactured commodities should under no circumstances exceed one and a half times their cost of production, which means that the taxes and profit must be kept within limits. For example, if 60 paisa is the cost of production, the sale price should be 90 paisa including all and profit.
2. Fluctuations in the prices of foodgrains should not exceed an anna a seer or 16 per cent between two harvests.
3. A relationship of justice and party must exist between the agricultural and the industrial prices and farmers must get prices that cover their cost and a minimum standard.

By advocating the fluctuations of prices within certain limits, Lohia wanted to save both the consumers and the agricultural producers from the clutches of profit-makers, hoarders, etc. Lohia pointed out: "We are all consumers and in our capacity consumers we are thoroughly unprotected, because there is nothing to protect us against the exploitation of high prices."

The farmer is not benefited from increased prices of food stuff, because the prices at the time of harvest is low. The petty shop-keeper of retailer is also not benefited from these high prices, for he cannot and does not buy cheap and hold large stocks and sell them dearer. To Lohia the tendency of selling the essential commodities of every day use at many time of its actual cost of production is nothing but the sucking of the blood of the poor masses.

It is due to sequandermania of the Government on useless modernisation of top-level consumption and its anti-national planning.

But the implementation of such a price policy required revolutionary changes in the social and economic sphere. It would be a severe blow to the taxation policy, profiteering and the interest of the big landlords. For it, a ceiling on a income will have to be imposed; the tax structure to be overhauled, and a change in the industrial management to be brought about, Lohia said. "To attain this price structure is definitely not easy. Either a modest calling on all personal expenditure inclusive of allowances must be imposed or all large industries must be nationalised or preferably both the solutions must be practiced simultanelusly."

Lohia wanted a struggle for the implementation of people's price policy. To him such small struggles of securing D.A. would not bring emancipation to the workers. That was the reason why in 1957 Lohia suggested the setting up of a Price Commission instead of a Pay Commission to check the rising of prices.

Reference

Dutt, R. Palme (1955), *India Today and Tomorrow*, People's Publishing House, Delhi

James, W.H. Morris (1954), The Government and Politics in India, London.

Kelkar (1963), Indumati, Lohia—Sidhant Aur Karm (Hindi), Navhind Prakashan, Hyderabad.

Kriplani, J.B. (1961), Gandhian Thought, Orient Longmans, Calcutta.

Mashruwale (1951), K.G. Gandhi an Vicher Dohan (Hindi), Sasta Sahitya Mandal, Fifth Edition.

Narayan, J.P. (1946), Towards Struggle, Bombay, 1946.

Santhanam, K. (1961), Satyagraha and the State, Asia Publishing House, Bombay.

Shah, Jagdish (1956), Socialist Paralysed, Amritsar.

Tendulkar, D.G. Mahatma, Vol. VII and VIII, Govt. of India, Ministry of Information and Broadcasting. The Publication Division, New Delhi.

Kriplani, J.B (1965), 'Gandhi and Lohia', *Janta*, Dec. 12.

Index